Aesthetic Citizenship

performance works

SERIES EDITORS
Patrick Anderson and Nicholas Ridout

This series publishes books in theater and performance studies, focused in particular on the material conditions in which performance acts are staged, and to which performance itself might contribute. We define "performance" in the broadest sense, including traditional theatrical productions and performance art, but also cultural ritual, political demonstration, social practice, and other forms of interpersonal, social, and political interaction which may fruitfully be understood in terms of performance.

Aesthetic Citizenship

Immigration and Theater in Twenty-First-Century Paris

✦

Emine Fişek

NORTHWESTERN UNIVERSITY PRESS
EVANSTON, ILLINOIS

Northwestern University Press
www.nupress.northwestern.edu

Printed in the United States of America

10 9 8 7 6 5 4 3 2 1

Library of Congress Cataloging-in-Publication Data

Names: Fişek, Emine, author.
Title: Aesthetic citizenship : immigration and theater in twenty-first-century Paris / Emine Fişek.
Description: Evanston, Illinois : Northwestern University Press, 2017. | Series: Performance works
Identifiers: LCCN 2017017806 | ISBN 9780810135673 (cloth : alk. paper) | ISBN 9780810135666 (pbk. : alk. paper) | ISBN 9780810135680 (e-book)
Subjects: LCSH: Theater—Political aspects—France—Paris—History—21st century. | Theater and society—France—Paris. | Immigrants—France—Paris—Social conditions—21st century. | Paris (France)—Emigration and immigration. | Immigrants in literature.
Classification: LCC PN2636.P3 F55 2017 H| DDC 792.09443610905—dc23
LC record available at https://lccn.loc.gov/2017017806

Sevgili Anneme ve Babama . . .

CONTENTS

ACKNOWLEDGMENTS

If no book is an island, entire of itself, this book is, quite literally, a piece of more than one continent. I began this project in Berkeley, California, and concluded it in Istanbul. The journey in between those two very different cities was sustained by a series of social, intellectual, and financial structures for which I continue to be grateful on a daily basis. First and foremost, I would like to thank the theater artists and social and humanitarian aid workers in Paris and beyond who made time for me, allowed me into their homes, work spaces, and city haunts, read my long and confusing forms, and answered my questions. These individuals not only responded to my questions with hospitality, they did so despite the fact that sometimes they could not quite place me in the world. The experience of migration, with all of its attendant vulnerabilities, had either touched some of these lives or existed at the perimeters of the lives of others. Over the course of writing this book, I concluded that it would be best to maintain anonymity, but my debt remains and it is to them that I owe the utmost gratitude. Making one exception, I would like to extend a special thank-you to Salikha Amara and Philippe Tancelin. Although I have since shared my writing with them, I have not adequately expressed how encouraging our conversations were. Thank you, again.

The seeds of this research were sown at Swarthmore College, where Ursula Neuerburg-Denzer patiently brought out the actor in me, and Allen Kuharski taught me how to be a scholar. Allen's introduction to French theater and the passion with which he framed the questions of theater history were central to my decision to pursue graduate study. I thank him for his ongoing mentorship and for inviting me, years after my departure, to revisit his phenomenal theater history seminar as a colleague. Most of all, my gratitude goes to Swarthmore for giving me my anchors: Poulami Roychowdhury, Elizabeth Nolte, Elçin Akçura, and Güneş Bender's lives have crisscrossed mine in academia and beyond, and I am thankful for their long-standing, nurturing friendship.

My greatest debt is to Shannon Jackson, who oversaw this project's initial conception, and whose own exemplary scholarship continues to reveal its wisdom in layers that unfold over time. I am grateful for Shannon's trust as well as her invaluable feedback at every step of this project. Saba Mahmood, Shannon Steen, and Soraya Tlatlı were spirited, thoughtful mentors who showed tremendous patience as this project fluctuated between versions both legible and illegible. I thank them for always listening with care and responding with passion. Saba kindly read drafts long after I had left Berkeley, and I thank her for her encouragement and for posing the critical questions that now permeate chapter 2. At the University of California at Berkeley, I learned from every occasion that my path crossed those of Brandi Wilkins Catanese and Catherine Cole. Brandi and Marty Berman deserve special thanks for discovering and mentoring the teacher in me, as does Mary Ajideh, for confronting the bureaucratic hurdles of international student life with joy. The program in Women, Gender and Sexuality led me to Juana María Rodríguez, whose generous feedback remains with me and is embedded throughout this book.

California was an island peopled with the best of friends and colleagues, and my heartfelt thanks go to my cohort members in performance studies, Joy Crosby Palacios, Khai Thu Nguyen, and Kelly Rafferty; and Michelle Baron, Nina Billone, Kate Kokontis, and my intellectual younger brother, Marc Boucai. The members of my California family, Shasha Geng, Nellie Tong, Alex Young, Caren Ballestamon, Celine Piser, Christine Hancock, Helaine Blumenthal, Gabriel Hetland, Zeynep Gürsel, Ojig Yeretsian, and the dear members of Opening the Mountain filled the Bay Area backdrop with sweet memories and landmarks. Back then and ever since, the awe-inspiring Melike Acar, Nilgün Bayraktar, and Ayşe Ercümen have made my numerous transatlantic confusions and disorientations make sense. And Ardan Araç now stands guard over my previous home, where I know I can always find her. It gives me great pleasure to thank them, one and all.

My time at Johns Hopkins University proved indispensable to my ability to slow down and look at the larger picture. In the Department of German and Romance Languages and Literatures, I am grateful for the generosity of Jacques Neefs, Wilda Anderson, and Elena Russo. Above all, I am thankful for the mentoring and friendship of Gabrielle Spiegel. Gaby's energy, her intellect, and her unparalleled ability to care for others continue to inspire me to be a better colleague, mentor, and friend. I thank Tobias Wofford, Urmila Nair, and Rani Neutill; the members of the Mellon Seminar on Concepts of Diaspora, especially Yi-Ping Ong and Anne Eakin Moss; and last but not least, the wonderful Andreea Marculescu, for filling my days in Baltimore with laughter and friendship.

I grew up in the orbit of Boğaziçi University, yet it is the Department of Western Languages and Literatures there that made it my home. The indomitable Cevza Sevgen ushered me in, and Aslı Tekinay's caring leadership has taught me the value of institutional memory, departmental camaraderie, and grace under pressure. I am thankful for the friendship of my wonderful departmental colleagues, Aylin Alkaç, Işıl Baş, Naz Bulamur, Eda Dedebaş Dündar, Özlem Görey, Ethan Guagliardo, Jameson Kısmet-Bell, Louis Mazzari, Hande Tekdemir, and Cihan Yurdaün. Özlem Öğüt, Didar Akar, and Matthew Gumpert deserve special mention for welcoming me in to their sunny, laughter-filled office and Başak Demirhan and Kim Fortuny for welcoming me into their lives. Above all, I am grateful to my larger Boğaziçi community, dispersed across the university, for making my workplace a place of friendship and sustenance. Finally, in Istanbul, it is a great pleasure to thank my oldest friends for sharing the path.

While many read and commented on my work over the course of this journey, there were a number of contexts where my thinking grew in leaps and bounds. Zeynep Gürsel, Faruk Birtek, and Arzu Öztürkmen's unguarded reactions to my ideas proved transformative at key moments and I am grateful for their ongoing encouragement. In Paris, my path crossed those of Olivier Neveux and Michel Feher only briefly, but their research suggestions ultimately proved indispensable. Susanne Unger's intellectual companionship and friendship have enriched my thinking and my life, in both academia and beyond. A special thanks goes to Charlotte McIvor, who has made some of my most cherished learning experiences possible, from Berkeley to Galway. I am indebted to conversations with Mark Ingram, who read and commented extensively on chapter 4, and whose generous suggestions were pivotal to solidifying my argument. Andrew Sofer and Margaret Litvin offered key advice during the process of preparing this book and I thank them both. Finally, I am grateful to the two anonymous reviewers for Northwestern University Press for the enthusiasm and generosity with which they offered feedback.

The initial research and writing for this project was made possible by the Dean's Normative Time Fellowship, the Chancellor's Dissertation-Year Fellowship, and a Center for the Study of Race and Gender Graduate Grant at the University of California-Berkeley as well as a Dissertation Research Award from the American Society for Theater Research. Later research was made possible by a Mellon Postdoctoral Fellowship in the Humanities at Johns Hopkins University, and the final stages of the writing process were supported by the Scientific Research Projects (BAP) Division of Boğaziçi University. The funding and equipment that I received via BAP #10160 were indispensable to the conclusion of this book.

Finally, many thanks to Patrick Anderson and Nicholas Ridout for including this book under the "Performance Works" series. I would also like to thank Michael Levine, Gianna Francesca Mosser, Nathan MacBrien, J. D. Wilson, and Marianne Jankowski at Northwestern University Press for their patience and generosity, and Osman Serhat Karaman at the Sakıp Sabancı Museum for helping me track down Abidin Dino's illustration. Portions of chapter 1 first appeared in "Animating Immigration: Labor Movements, Cultural Policy and Activist Theatre in 1970s France," *Theatre Journal* 64, no. 1 (March 2012): 41–59, and I am grateful to the Johns Hopkins University Press for allowing me permission to reprint that material here.

In closing, I thank Ziya Umut Türem and Mehmet Fişek for our intertwined lives, and my beloved parents, Güler Okman Fişek and Mustafa Hamit Fişek, for my own. I am in awe of their life's work and it is to them that this book is dedicated.

Aesthetic Citizenship

INTRODUCTION

This is a book about theater, but I cannot resist beginning with an excerpt from a film: Abdellatif Kechiche's *L'Esquive* (2004; *Games of Love and Chance*).[1] Midway through this brilliant work, the audience is confronted with a painfully embarrassing scene. The film's teenage protagonist Krimo, short for Abdelkrim, is standing in front of his skeptical classmates dressed in the colorfully geometric costume of Arlequin, the comic servant figure that has permeated Western theater since the Middle Ages. The scene is drawn from the eighteenth-century French playwright Pierre Marivaux's *Le Jeu de l'amour et du hasard* (*The Game of Love and Chance*), in which the servants Arlequin and Lisette switch places with their respective masters, so that the betrothed aristocrats can, unbeknownst to each other, study each other's personalities. Krimo's task is thus doubly difficult, as he is to deliver a role that is itself a disguised identity. The young actor falters. His only motivation for appearing in the scene is the proximity it offers to Lydia, his lively love interest and the actress cast in the role of his onstage partner, Lisette. As Krimo scans the floor of the classroom, glances over at his audience, and mumbles Marivaux's lines, his French language and literature teacher grows increasingly perturbed. It is clear that her calm yet pointed commentary to the young actor in an earlier scene has not registered; Krimo's performance remains uninspired.

Soon, however, this monotony is interrupted when Kechiche's camera swings from Krimo to the teacher, just in time to catch her thunder at her student: "Have fun!" (*Amuse-toi!*). As Krimo turns to her with a look of panicked heartbreak, the teacher's monologue builds to a feverish pitch: "Try to leave yourself behind and go toward a new language [*aller vers un autre langage*]!" A few moments later, she adds, "Change your language, change your way of speaking, change your way of moving, have fun!" The word *plaisir* permeates her tirade as she reminds her terrified student that this should be a pleasurable exercise. She concludes in the imperative: "Liberate yourself [*libère-toi*], give yourself, have fun!" Krimo, unable to face either Marivaux's lines or his amused classmates, flees the room.

In his commentary on *L'Esquive,* Ari Blatt engages in the allegorical interpretation that Kechiche's scene so clearly invites: "In tracing Krimo's failed attempt to act the part," he writes, "the film dramatizes a young man's struggle to come to terms with a way of being that is not his own. Furthermore, it designates the theater as the site where this struggle is, quite literally, played out."[2] Indeed, Krimo, Lydia, and their mixed group of friends live in a housing project in the Parisian *banlieue* (suburbs), where Marivaux's language is both a source of fascination for the theatrically inclined and an irrelevant reference point for a generation of multicultural youths whose own language is rich with the slang inversions of *verlan*, Arabic, and the occasional English. Yet the tensions of the French classroom and Krimo's humiliation therein serve as reminders, in Blatt's words, of "anxieties about the current state of national identity in France" and of the relationship that immigrants and their descendants can have to the French national heritage.[3] My interest in this scene, however, stems less from the question of French identity and belonging (although this is undoubtedly part of it as well) and more so from the precise role that *theater* plays as the site where this belonging is displayed, confirmed, or alternatively deemed absent. What is it about theater that allows this domain to function as both a *representation* of a certain identity and the space where that identity is openly understood to be the outcome of social *rehearsal*? Asking this question requires that we, like Kechiche, momentarily shift our lens away from Krimo and toward his inexorable teacher.

Over the course of the teacher's monologue, theater takes on a number of connotations. First and foremost, Krimo's inability to lift his body and voice out of their corporeal architecture is understood as an inability to enjoy himself, to have fun. Amusement is associated with "going towards a new language," a reference to the unfamiliarity of Marivaux's tongue as well as the bodily language of the agile Arlequin. The physical zaniness of the servant-disguised-as-master requires a particularly heightened alertness on the part of the young thespian. As the teacher illustrates the adjustments that such a character requires, she cannot help but associate this change with fun, pleasure, and ultimately, freedom ("*libère-toi*"). Thus, when Krimo is unable to release himself into Marivaux's words or Arlequin's body, it follows that he lacks enjoyment, pleasure, and the ability (or willingness) to abstract himself from his own "language" to embody the joyful norm of eighteenth-century French theatrics. And it is precisely Krimo's *willful refusal* to embody this theatrical norm that is interpreted as unliberated, and thus somehow restricted, behavior. When considered in light of Blatt's allegorical reading, such connotations take on additional resonance as both the signs and the vehicles of French identity. Krimo's failed performance reveals his seeming inability to belong, but also his seeming unwillingness to undertake the forms of rehearsal that may ultimately produce the belonging in question. On both counts, Krimo cannot "act the part." And "the part" is to be assumed in the presence of spectators.

Kechiche's scene illustrates a series of dynamics that pervade this book and compose its central questions. For starters, what is the relationship between theater and belonging? In Kechiche's scene, the links between theatrical practice, national identity, and civic participation prove explosive in part because they are imagined to be both self-evident and in need of illustration.

Underlying this paradox is a broader concern regarding the nature of theatrical activity. Is theater a primarily semiotic practice that transmits a series of meanings? Or is theater a space of subject constitution that foregrounds its habit-forming capacities? At the same time, these theoretical distinctions become meaningful only insofar as they are endowed with specific sensibilities and stakes. Signification, embodiment, and their corresponding models of theatrical action mobilize specific visions of the body, as well as of the self to which that body is attached, and the collective to which that self belongs. What then are the unique meanings associated with these distinctions in the context of French debates on immigration? With what meanings are theater, collective identity, and bodily life endowed in contemporary France?

Aesthetic Citizenship seeks to answer these questions by exploring the role that theatrical performance played in how immigration, citizenship, and national identity were addressed in Paris at the dawn of the twenty-first century. Through an ethnographic study of the use of theater by Paris-based organizations interested in immigrant rights, from neighborhood associations to humanitarian alliances to arts organizations both large and small, I examine how theater emerged as a practice with the perceived capacity to address immigrant rights, integration, and experience. Taking the lead from Krimo's scene, my central premise is that national participation, belonging, and citizenship are spheres of experience that require rehearsal, and that theater is a particularly apt space through which to understand the complicated relationship between ideal and enactment. I suggest that a closer look at activist and arts practice displays how early twenty-first-century French public discourses on immigration were not only rendered meaningful and tangible, but were also inhabited and modified in the course of theatrical activity. Throughout, my goal is to examine the relationship between these embodied acts and the political personhoods that they are imagined to negotiate. Thus, at its core, this is a study of the relationship between aesthetics and politics, and of the unique way in which this relationship was construed by a group of artists and social workers in early twenty-first-century Paris.

Contemporary France is an exemplary site to examine the relationship between immigration and theater practice. Immigration has played a central role in French politics and society since the nineteenth century. Beginning with the early 1970s, however, references to immigration have had less to do with the management of migratory flows than with the French state's perceived inability to integrate a multicultural polity. This is reflected in how immigration policies have been repositioned to address cultural plurality and national identity; the not-so-subtle suggestion has been that immigrants integrate into French society by downplaying public signs of cultural and religious difference. The focus on public behavior and *bodily conduct* is often linked to a republican tradition that views compulsory primary education as the guarantee of cultural unity. An oft-cited example of the spatial significance of the republican school and the symbolic significance of bodily conduct are the public debates that began in 1989, when three female students in Creil entered their school with headscarves. This minor event generated a wide-ranging and ongoing debate on French secularism, multiculturalism, and different sets of *bodily* practices.[4]

Kechiche's portrayal of the French classroom as a space of bodily consciousness is thus not an arbitrary choice. The fact that *theater* is the vehicle for this embodied learning is further linked to the practice's unique role in the French cultural imaginary. French cultural policies, legendary for their insistence on cultural democratization as a public service, initially stemmed from a postwar concern with reintegrating formerly German-occupied territories. Throughout the 1960s and 1970s, the Ministry of Cultural Affairs portrayed theatergoing publics as engaged in acts of citizenship. For France's first minister of culture, André Malraux, "the highest and most lasting forms of artistic achievement of the past" could serve as "a means of national cohesion, creating a sense of belonging to a community of shared values."[5] Meanwhile, in the visions of the performance artists that matured alongside the mass political events of the era (wars in Vietnam and Algeria, the extended general strikes of May 1968, and later labor movements), theater was increasingly assigned the role of cultivating awareness, giving voice to the transnational oppressed through public visibility.

The theatrical work that I explore in this book represents the complicated and often contradictory fusion of these two cultural legacies. For the artists and social workers with whom I spoke, theater served as a vehicle for rendering the realities of immigration visible. At the same time, theater retained the connotations of cultivation and belonging that it had inherited from a national context where aesthetic practices continue to serve as the safeguards of national identity. Theater was, in other words, both inherently anti-institutional and institutionally situated; it required both militantly political participants and at the same time, decidedly centralized ones. In the chapters that follow, I explore these tensions in a variety of geographic and institutional contexts and with the aid of a variety of interlocutors. The often-anonymous voices that permeate my study (more on this later) belong to individuals who have imagined and implemented theatrical projects that seek to address the lived reality of immigrant experience in France. These include the former members of the 1970s Arab-French theater troupes Al Assifa and La Kahina; artists who participate in the annual women's art festival called Festival au Féminin as well as nongovernmental workers associated with the organization Accueil Goutte d'Or, both based in the historically immigrant-heavy Paris neighborhood Goutte d'Or; the coordinators of the theater activities organized by the Paris branches of the immigrant aid organizations Réseau Education Sans Frontières (RESF) and La Cimade; the members of Quelques unes d'entre nous, a women's theater collective based in the Paris suburb of Blanc-Mesnil; and the artists behind a range of projects addressing the experiences of undocumented immigrants, refugees, and asylum seekers, from small local performances to the transnational work of the Théâtre du Soleil.

Whether in the context of French language classes for first-generation immigrant women in underprivileged neighborhoods, as part of a series of activities facilitating asylum seekers' cultural and socio-professional integration into French life, or embedded in larger performance-based activisms celebrating immigrant cultural expression, these voices illustrate the ways in which discourses on republicanism, immigrant integration, racial and gender difference, and finally, humanitarianism were rendered tangible as well as altered and quite literally acted upon, through theater. At the same time, this range of contexts signals the proliferation of categories associated with the term *immigré* or "immigrant," and therefore the difficulty of settling on a unified rubric with which to designate the theater produced in these contexts. Indeed, as Emma Cox has shown, this methodological difficulty is not unique to France, but global.[6] In France today, references to "immigration" implicate populations ranging from newly arrived refugees and asylum seekers to long-term residents whose residency statuses are subject to constant changes, to third and fourth-generation citizens of immigrant ancestry. Over the course of this book, I hope to illustrate the widely divergent experiences that are often amalgamated under this rubric, even as I illustrate key points of convergence.

My approach to theater practice takes its departure from the basic theoretical insight structuring Krimo and his teacher's encounter: theater is not merely a representational medium but an embodied social practice. Over the course of my conversations in Paris, this was a duality that I encountered often. For the majority of the artists and social workers with whom I spoke, theater served as a medium for the communication of messages. This representational and expressive understanding of theater was coupled, however, with the expectation that it would also serve to cultivate certain forms of comportment, thus enacting changes whose imagined scope could range, as with Krimo's teacher, from the immediacy of corporeal pleasure to the abstractions of human emancipation. Put differently, the link that they made between outer form and inner substance positioned embodied activity as both *representative* and *constitutive* of inner life and thought. Such an approach blends together two distinct ways in which anthropological and performance studies scholarship have approached the study of ritual and performative action. Briefly put, the first of these is characterized by a sharp distinction between thoughts and acts, where the latter are expressive of the former. The second considers ritual actions to be generative practices that do not necessarily represent an interior self but rather endow it with specific skills. The conceptual challenge posed by my interlocutors thus necessitates an understanding of their work as *performance,* an act that is "furnished forth"[7] into observable public space even when its primary work resists symbolism.

As a discipline premised, in Tracy Davis's words, on the notion that "'bodies' are corporeal not merely textual,"[8] performance studies offers useful conceptual frameworks here. Indeed, throughout this book, *performance* will emerge both as a locatable event and an implied logic structuring individual and institutional encounters. However, it is equally important to stress that my use of this vocabulary stems less from my own theoretical commitments than from the fact that I found myself studying a context that repeatedly thematized human *enactment*. At a moment in recent French history when political and public discourse positioned citizenship and belonging as elusive character traits, my interlocutors worked with the notion that theatrical performance could instill specific modes of interaction and specific understandings of the self. If citizenship is, in May Joseph's instructive terms, "a performed site of personhood,"[9] my interlocutors took theater to be a site where such personhood could be embodied through repeated practice and rehearsal. Ultimately, my argument is that these theatrical practices were neither simply a representational by-product of political shifts, nor an expression of a broader cultural pattern; rather, the relationship between theater and immigration in early twenty-first-century Paris pointed at a differently configured relationship between aesthetics and politics. In this introduction I offer the political, cultural, and theoretical frameworks necessary for understanding *why* this came to be the case, and *how* these processes eventually transpired. Focusing on late twentieth-century immigration policies, public debates on integration, and the postwar history of theatrical decentralization and cultural policy-making, we will see that theater has long been a site where the question of immigration has encountered the human immediacy of aesthetic negotiation and interpersonal engagement.

Immigration: Policy, Politics, and Integrating the Body

When I arrived in Paris to begin my research in early 2008, many of my interlocutors repeated the refrain that French immigration politics had entered a period of crisis. Former Minister of the Interior Nicolas Sarkozy had been elected president the previous year, and his law-and-order campaign platform had begun to show its effects: annual naturalization numbers were already showing signs of dropping and the streets of Paris were as habituated to the daily arrests of undocumented persons as they were to protests by immigrant rights groups. When considered against Gérard Noiriel's panoramic history of immigration in France, we might understand such moments of crisis as part of a broader dynamic of calm and emergency.[10] After all, during the three decades of economic and industrial growth that followed the Second World War in France, labor immigration was largely a question of political economy, responding to immediate market needs and barely registering as a phenomenon of symbolic import.[11] Following the first signs of employment shortage in the late 1960s, however, legal measures began to restrict both labor immigration and the rights available to migrant families. Immigrant populations in general and North African and Algerian immigrants in particular served as the targets of xenophobic language peppered with references to incommensurable cultural difference, delinquency, and disproportionate dependence on the benefits of the French welfare state. Studies have shown that the marginalization experienced by Algerians was nothing new;[12] indeed, colonial Algerians' accession to full French citizenship had been one of French colonialism's most vexed negotiations.[13] What was unique to this particular iteration of immigration "crisis," however, was that it followed on the heels of the Algerian War (1954–62) and the decolonization of a territory that had once been considered seamless with metropolitan France. By the mid-1970s, repatriated French-Algerian landowners and army officials dotted the French suburban landscape, living side-by-side with Algerian immigrants. One such figure was Jean-Marie Le Pen, whose right-wing Front National would eventually spearhead immigration's transition from a technical question to a phenomenon implicating French national character, rendering *intégration* into a hot-button issue.

This shift was nowhere more visible than in legislative developments. Throughout the late 1970s, intermittent restrictions on familial reunification and the delivery of residence permits were coupled with financial incentives designed to encourage reverse migration. The Socialist Party's 1981 victory slowed some of these developments but not without resistance from the Right. Finally, in 1986 and again in 1993, the Loi Pasqua authored by Minister of the Interior Charles Pasqua offered the most concrete link between immigration policy and national identity, as well as a significant intervention into the republic's historical commitment to *jus soli* or territorial citizenship. Whereas children born in France to immigrant parents had previously acceded to French citizenship automatically when they turned eighteen, the Loi Pasqua required that they "manifest their will to acquire this nationality."[14] This measure was overturned in 1998, but its brief tenure is indicative of the degree to which national identity had become a political concern, visible everywhere from debates surrounding the Nationality Code to the formation, in 1990, of a Haut Conseil à l'Intégration or High Council of Integration. Indeed, for many immigrant rights groups, the Loi Pasqua signaled the beginning of a trend whereby the traditional republican emphasis on nationality via schooling and socialization was replaced by a more elusive definition of cultural citizenship. Looking back in 1999, Étienne Balibar had these developments in mind when he identified an emergent discourse of "national republicanism."[15] For Balibar, the implicit "defense of the Republic" built into legislative changes such as the Loi Pasqua negotiated a broader range of anxieties that emerged over the course of the 1990s. Globalization and European unification, perceived increases in cultural communitarianisms, and the crisis of undocumented immigration all contributed to a political landscape that congealed around the idea of French national identity.

The civic actors with whom I spoke routinely denounced these developments. At the same time, they were aware of the messy nature of social work and its questionable autonomy with regard to official bureaucracies. In other words, the changing semantic domain designated by the French state had permeated their nongovernmental vocabulary. For example, nongovernmental organizations RESF and Cimade aid undocumented immigrant youth and asylum seekers during the process of applying for residency permits. When I began to research the theater activities that had comprised one dimension of this aid work, it was clear that the notion of integration had come to define theater's capacities as a social practice. Theater was not a mere artistic exercise that accompanied the more significant work of juridical aid, as I will show in chapter 3. Rather, theater had become an important domain in which both aid workers and participating individuals tested the meanings of notions of integration, citizenship, and national belonging.

Immigration in the Era of Nicolas Sarkozy

If French national identity had already emerged as a question of "manifested" will in the 1990s, it was under Nicolas Sarkozy's tenure as minister of the interior (from 2002 to 2004 and again from 2005 to 2007) and later as president (2007–12) that the precise nature of the bonds between a foreigner and the French nation became the stuff of policy-making. A good example of this development is the Contrat d'Accueil et d'Intégration (CAI) or the Integration and Welcome Contract. A literal contract that was rendered obligatory in 2006, the CAI defined the relationship between a residency candidate and the French state, outlining the candidate's responsibilities toward his potential host country and the deeply affective engagement through which local administrations were asked to evaluate his or her receptivity to republican values, however ill-defined.[16] Indeed, the Loi Sarkozy of 2003 and 2006 were premised on a distinction between *immigration choisie,* migrants who could be selected by the French state, and *immigration subie,* migrants to whom the French state was "subjected,"[17] a distinction that resulted in ever-harsher conditions for residency, familial reunification, and political asylum. With Sarkozy's election to the presidency in 2007, these trends culminated in the founding of a new Ministry of Immigration, Integration, National Identity and Co-Development, which delegated the widespread political management of immigration to a single structure, and institutionalized what had thus far been a largely discursive connection between immigration and French national identity.

This, in a nutshell, was the "crisis" to which my interlocutors referred. In many ways, this crisis was a mere sequel to the "national republicanism" of the 1990s, yet where immigration was concerned, the transformations of the early twenty-first century also resonated with global trends. The events of September 11, 2001, in particular, resulted in increased border controls and repressive immigration policies across the Euro-American world. In France, these trends were reflected in tougher anticrime measures, harsher residency requirements for nonnationals, and increased stigmatization of communities of immigrant descent, particularly those crowded around the emergent "ghettos" of urban peripheries.[18] And throughout this period, protests in largely immigrant neighborhoods resulted in new forms of racialization in a society where difference had previously been framed as a question of culture. The immigration crises of the Sarkozy era, in other words, were multiple and often unique, even as they connected to earlier practices and discourses.

Aesthetic Citizenship's timeline mirrors these dynamics. Whereas the book's focus is on the first decade of the twenty-first century, it will make repeated reference to defining moments from the 1990s and in fact begins in the 1970s, the period that witnessed the introduction of the first laws curtailing labor migration to France. At the same time, recent developments have directly impacted my research. During the early 2000s, nongovernmental organizations were recruited to participate in the management of immigration in new and often expanded ways, a dynamic that is visible throughout this book. The changing landscape of immigration policy not only impacted my interlocutors, it resulted in specific theatrical aftereffects. For example, although the Loi Sarkozy made residency permits harder to obtain, political discourse placed equal emphasis on maintaining France's image as a nation of human rights, one that supported political asylum and welcomed the persecuted, particularly women. Coupled with increasingly affective criteria premised on identifying an "essential quality of integratability,"[19] such principles resulted in what my interlocutors called a "case-by-case" approach. For organizations like RESF and Cimade, this meant that their advocacy strategy often concentrated on the affective potential of singular stories, rather than evaluating these vulnerabilities within the framework of human rights violations. One RESF worker explained that this was how they sought media sponsorship: if the French state promised to honor the particularity of human life, stories that captured the imagination triumphed over the seemingly banal realities of asylum and migration. Theatrical representation, not surprisingly, was one way in which such unique narratives could be presented, all the while signaling the participants' receptivity to this highly symbolic cultural practice.

At the same time, the turn to "particularity" was one that I encountered well beyond the theater activities of immigrant rights groups. As we will see in chapter 2, the emphasis on unique experiences of pain and suffering was a unifying theme among many activists and artists engaged with the question of immigration. These individuals may not have recognized themselves as partaking in either formal or thematic affinities; nonetheless, I often encountered a shared sensibility that understood theatrical performance, particularly when undertaken by immigrant women, as an event that could transition an individual from the particularity of an injured life to universal personhood. Indeed, the tension between universality and particularity, a central dimension of republican nationality and citizenship, was central to how many artists articulated the functions of theatrical performance.

Integration and the Tensions of Universalism

At this point, it will be useful to clarify the precise connotations of *intégration* in France. Contemporary French discourses on immigrant integration are indelibly linked to the republican model of citizenship and to the role that universality has played in its historical construction. Briefly put, the universalist philosophy of French republicanism is premised on the principle of a direct political relationship between the nation and its citizens. In other words, the republican model of personhood is characterized by the autonomy of individuals from the constraints of particular identities such as race or ethnicity, religion, or as some have argued, regional locality.[20] As abstract human subjects, individuals are unmarked by such attachments; their primary affiliations are to the French national community and to the universal, secular, and abstract values that it encapsulates. The eighteenth-century French philosopher Jean-Jacques Rousseau is often credited with outlining the political order that would come to characterize both the French Revolution and French republicanism: in Rousseau's social contract (as it was taken up by the revolutionaries) citizenship was organized by a centralized state, which was itself recognized as the manifestation of "the general will," the collective interests of all citizens.[21] Unlike the Anglo-American tradition of guarding individual liberties against political tyranny, Rousseau's abstract individualism was imagined as a guarantee of the citizen's ability to adhere to the general will, rather than the particular interests associated with a concrete cultural category.[22]

As Gary Wilder has argued, however, understanding republicanism through a clear-cut distinction between the universal and the particular risks blurring the complexities of French political history. The historian writes that "insofar as citizenship was a function of one's abstract human rights, it expressed universality, and insofar as it was secured by membership within a concrete national entity, it expressed particularity."[23] The universality of humanity and the particularity of French nationhood, in other words, were not only compatible but served as the marker distinguishing the national and the foreigner: "Given that all human beings were supposed to be free and equal members of a self-governing nation-state, political exclusion was henceforth only legitimate for those groups whose members did not meet the new criteria of individuality, rationality and autonomy."[24] A brief glance at recent immigration policies reveals that the continuity between universality and particularity remains relevant. As I will demonstrate in chapter 5, during the first decade of the twenty-first century, the political discourse on asylum articulated French citizenship as the symbol for a set of universal values (such as a commitment to human dignity, autonomy, and rights) applicable to all humanity. Such discourses, however, were attached to policy changes that increasingly policed immigrant integration, distinguishing between asylum seekers via approximations of their "integratability" to French norms. Acknowledgments of abstract and universal humanity, in other words, found expression in practices that sought concrete and particular identities.

The notions of immigrant integration that have emerged in France since the 1970s have borne the traces of a political tradition that identifies citizenship as a *moral* project, premised on individuals' self-government vis-à-vis the associative organizations in which they take part. "An idiom for emancipatory action," in Wilder's words, self-government implies autonomous, rational, and secular personhood, manifested through an attachment to French national identity.[25] Beginning with the 1980s, these were the historical and highly abstract reference points that undergirded heated discussions of immigrant integration in France. The political discontent surrounding the Socialist Party's reforms, which included overturning a long-term ban on immigrants' right of association, resulted in accusations of *communautarisme*: a reference to visible signs of an individual's attachment to a particular community and thus of the perceived compromise structuring that individual's relationship to the French state.[26] Whereas the intensity and range of references to *communautarisme* have varied since the 1980s, the term continued to retain its ubiquity during the period of my research. Many of the artists with whom I spoke, particularly those involved in projects that sought to valorize immigrant cultural expression, noted that they had to tiptoe around the term, aware that it was positioned as the counterpoint to national citizenship and integration. In chapter 4, I will show that this political background is central to understanding why terms such as "community-based theater," so prevalent in both the self-conceptions and the scholarly approximations of grassroots theater projects in the United States, remained absent from the vocabulary of local artists and activists in Paris. References to community were laden with unease.

The Immigrant's Body

Whereas the relationship between individuality and community was one of the central rubrics through which the question of immigration entered public discussion, a significant dimension of integration debates focused on *bodily practices*. Jacques Chirac's well-known and oft-recalled remarks from 1991 are exemplary of this dynamic. Addressing a crowd in Orléans, the soon-to-be president would declare that he empathized with the plight of the prototypical "French worker" who lived across from an immigrant family with "a father, three or four spouses and twenty kids who made 50,000 francs in social benefits without working. If you add to this the noises and odors [*le bruit et l'odeur*], then of course the French worker across the landing goes crazy."[27] Such statements revealed that while the conceptual threat posed by the immigrant made reference to his seemingly advantageous relationship to the welfare state, the visceral experience of cohabitation was corporeal: the "French worker's" frustration stemmed from his neighbor's sensory, *bodily* productions.

Chirac's statement was equally prescient of the role that sexual politics would play in the stigmatization of immigrant bodily practices over the course of the 1990s and early 2000s. The "twenty kids" to whom Chirac referred were cast as the joint reproductive product of "three or four spouses," a passing comment that reveals how anxieties over cultural difference and bodily conduct have been anchored around gender and sexuality. Indeed, since the early 1990s, sensationalized media accounts of immigrant bodily practices have focused on identifying polygamy, female circumcision, and gang rape in particular and sexual violence in general as uniquely racialized phenomena that are endemic to urban peripheries populated by Arab and African (and particularly Muslim) men. Nacira Guénif Souilamas and Eric Macé note how such representations not only obscure the demographic realities of sexual violence in France, but also contribute to the portrayal of immigrant subjects, particularly those who are descended from formerly colonized populations, as deviant bodies whose indigeneity cannot be civilized.[28] Elsewhere, Souilamas has noted that integration debates are premised on a dichotomy between the aberrant sexuality and domesticity associated with immigrant bodily practices and the sexual emancipation and equality underpinning French (heterosexual) norms.[29] As Joan W. Scott's work has shown, republican history has in fact had a deeply ambivalent relationship to the feminist struggle for gender equality.[30] For Souilamas, however, what such dichotomies solidify is a dynamic wherein the figure of the immigrant is fundamentally understood through corporeality, first as a *body*, and second as a *sexed body*, one that is either the perpetrator or the receptacle of sexual violence.

By far the most prominent example of the role that gendered corporeality has played in French integration debates is the proverbially named headscarf affair (*l'affaire du foulard*). This issue's decades-long duration offers a chronology of how immigration has become increasingly central to discussions on national education, gender politics, and the uniquely French brand of secularism, *laïcité*. The *foulard* debates began in 1989, when three young women in Creil entered their middle school wearing headscarves. Principal Ernest Chenière's decision to expel the women ignited a controversy that soon dovetailed with the era's popular interest in immigrant youth and Islamic practice to become national in scope. The question of whether these women undermined the separation of church and state by wearing symbols of their religious affiliation on school grounds would continue to occupy public debate for decades to come. In 1989 the case was referred to the Conseil d'Etat, the highest judicial body in France, and resulted in a ruling stating that the laws on *laïcité* banned religious proselytism, not religious insignia.

The matter remained relatively dormant until 1994, when Minister of Education François Bayrou issued a circular in which he noted that headscarves, unlike crucifixes or yarmulkes, were "ostentatious" signs of belonging and therefore, in Joan Scott's words, "transparent acts of proselytizing."[31] By the early 2000s, as President Jacques Chirac established a research commission to prepare the groundwork for legislation banning the headscarf, the issue was indelibly linked to larger debates surrounding immigration and republican citizenship. Chirac signed the bill banning ostensible signs of religious belonging in public primary and secondary schools on March 15, 2004.

L'affaire du foulard has been widely studied within the frameworks of Islam, secularism, and French public space. Less attention has been paid, however, to what it revealed about the French state's relationship to immigrant bodily practices. A closer look at the discussions that surrounded the republican school reveal that the tendency to identify the headscarf as a constraint often centered around bodily activity, particularly sports practice. The 2004 publication *L'Une voilée, l'autre pas* (*One Veiled, the Other Not*) is a good example. A nuanced text authored by the Lyon-based activist Saïda Kada and an anthropologist and educator working for the government, Dounia Bouzar, the book chronicles a dialogue premised on the fact that while both women are practicing Muslims, Kada wears a headscarf and Bouzar does not. Their discussions over a narrative that Bouzar collected during her fieldwork with immigrant youth is useful for understanding what the headscarf debates reveal about the relationship between bodily practices, moral behaviors, and immigrant integration.

One of the narratives that Bouzar presents is that of Nassera, a nineteen-year-old who notes that she stopped wearing her headscarf in order to be able to attend her public school. Nassera adds that her religious practice compels her to seek educational opportunities, thereby allowing her to suspend dimensions of her religiosity, such as wearing a headscarf, for specific durations when necessary. Upon graduating, she begins to wear the headscarf again, telling Bouzar: "my headscarf never left me" (*il ne m'a jamais quitté mon foulard*).[32] In her response to this narrative, Saïda Kada notes that an educational system that seeks to legislate students' spirituality compromises their access to public education. In turn, Bouzar notes that the state's pedagogical project is premised on "constructing the conditions so that the youth do things together, sweat together, construct together."[33] She adds that limitations on cohabitation compromise the republican school's central objective, a process of socialization that is meant to cultivate identification across difference.

Bouzar's example for the kind of sharedness offered by the republican school is a swimming class. Since young women with headscarves choose not to share this space with their male classmates, the swimming pool emerges in Bouzar's commentary as the necessary limit of multiculturalism. For Bouzar, it is not the symbolic import of the headscarf that poses a problem so much as the practical impossibility of cohabitation. In response, Kada notes that a practicing young Muslim's faith should be considered as legitimate a reason for participating in separate physical education classes as other rationales that students offer for not participating at all, adding that the school could "recognize a doctor or psychologist's attestation when he feels this situation provokes real psychological suffering in relation to their identity construction."[34] Bouzar's reply is that where the common law is concerned, standards regarding the "physical and psychological well-being" of the youth are set by the World Heath Organization, not Islam.[35]

I summarize this conversation at length because it encapsulates the complicated and at times incongruous assumptions that underlined the headscarf debates. Bouzar's comments are premised on the expectation that the manner in which human corporeality is lived and experienced stands at a distance from that human's religious or ethical affiliations. Thus it follows that the French state's universal institutions are charged with keeping young bodies healthy, even if the methods for doing so risk inducing other kinds of rupture in that individual's particular life. At the same time, however, Bouzar's arguments are premised on an acknowledgment of the connection between bodily life and moral sentiments. For example, communal physical education classes are imagined to bring about interpersonal identification, social equality, and a degree of cultural homogeneity. Bodily practices, in other words, are understood to engender social and ethical sensibilities, particularly where the relationship between the individual and the collective is concerned.

Here it should be noted that Bouzar's reference to the emancipatory potential of sports practice is not a coincidence. Sports were a frequent reference point during the integration debates of the 1990s, ranging from celebrations of the upward mobility of immigrant sports heroes like Zinedine Zidane to the summer camps instituted by urban reform projects such as the ones chronicled by Paul Silverstein. The anthropologist notes that such projects targeted working-class and immigrant suburbs in metropolitan areas and sought "to retrain Muslim bodies away from religious practices."[36] These projects, like Bouzar's vision of the republican school, were premised on the notion that the human body and its ritual habits held the potential to engender certain forms of moral sensibility and discipline, and took immigrant Muslim difference to represent an incommensurable form of embodied particularity. Over the course of the 1990s, then, mainstream theorizing about immigrant integration viewed bodily practices through a holographic lens: depending on one's angle of vision, they were either understood as a neutral and relatively universal dimension of human life or as the grounds from which a particular kind of human could be cultivated. Likewise, bodily conduct was considered the outward expression of an inner disposition, even as bodily action was identified as a privileged space for the cultivation of emotional and moral sensibilities.

These complex discussions surrounding bodily life, moral attitudes, and social integration were not unlike the theatrical discussions related to me by my interlocutors. Indeed, over the course of my conversations in Paris, I found that the relationship between theater and immigration was premised on a shared recognition that theatrical practice constituted a "work on the body," a project whose perceived reach ranged from the coordination of disorderly arms and legs to that of social and emotional dispositions. Over time, I concluded that changing immigration policies, integration debates, and the role that the immigrant body has played in constructions of republican subjectivity and national morality were central to evaluating how theater was used to address immigration. This is not to say, however, that I consider the theatrical practices that I examine in this book to be mere nongovernmental extensions of the broader and historical "control of immigrant bodily practice."[37] Such an evaluation would negate the degree to which my interlocutors were not only critical of this history but often entirely conscious of how their own civic and artistic vocabularies drew from the semantic repertoire of republicanism. What remains to be understood, then, are the complex ways in which they both related to *and* distanced themselves from this legacy, thereby reflecting *and* refracting it in new and unique ways. I am particularly interested in how the embodied and collective resources of the theater became the environment for this dual project. If integration debates approached bodily practices through a holographic lens, what transformations did these understandings of the body undergo in the context of theatrical rehearsal and performance?

Theater: Policy, Politics, and Representing the Body

The artists and social workers with whom I spoke referenced two dueling ideologies of the theater. For the majority of my interlocutors, theater was a medium of public recognition for those who lacked visibility. Taking the lead from a lengthy tradition of what is often called militant theater, these artists identified theater as an "emancipating" mechanism.[38] At the same time, their understanding of the practice retained the traces of a legacy that had imagined theater doing a slightly different sort of emancipatory work: postwar French cultural policies had positioned arts practices as *habit-generating phenomena* that participated in the creation of cultured citizens. Education and sports were not the only domains in which something akin to Durkheimian collective effervescence was imagined to take hold.[39] Participating in, observing, and frequenting arts practices were equally laden with moral expectation. The contemporary relationship between theater practice and immigration, in other words, was shaped by the historical development of theatrical decentralization and struggles over the reach of cultural policy, even as it sought to rethink the terms of earlier debates.

Although the linkage of culture with the idea of the nation is not a uniquely French phenomenon, the degree to which the French state has intervened in the realm of cultural life marks what is often referred to as *l'exception française*, a national context where state subsidies for the arts have been uniquely robust. This financial support is a largely postwar trend, but the concern with culture has far lengthier historical roots; indeed, culture has been a significant domain through which the French state has undertaken, in Norbert Elias's terms, a "civilizing process," a broad-based transformation of feelings and attitudes with regard to social propriety.[40] If the Third Republic's centralizing tendencies were premised on the oft-remarked "revolutionary myth of a single cultural heritage,"[41] they were equally insistent on cultural democratization and decentralization as a popular right on a par with national education. In fact, decentralization was a theme that permeated cultural politics in France in the twentieth century, both establishing a degree of state monopoly over questions of national arts heritage *and* allowing popular sovereignty, in Loren Kruger's words, to serve as "the discursive formation that legitimates the republic *as* tradition."[42]

A brief glance at the immediate postwar period demonstrates that questions of citizenship and integration have been central to the decentralization of theater. This process was managed by Jeanne Laurent, a policy-maker for the Ministry of Beaux-Arts who drew up a long-term plan for establishing financially autonomous regional theaters throughout France. The first Centre Dramatique National (CDN) or National Center for Drama was founded in 1946 in Alsace. Municipalities in the formerly German-occupied region had filed requests with the ministry, bemoaning "the germanization of the spirit of our provinces" and preoccupying local officials with bringing "the masterpieces of French culture to the Alsatians."[43] Heterogeneous geographies, in other words, were central to the impetus behind theatrical decentralization. Pascale Goetschel notes that in certain cases, an equally significant (and related) ideological dimension was "the necessity to go to the working masses," with a particular focus on immigrant working masses. For example, a 1948 report drew attention to "a strong proportion of workers of foreign origin who need to be made to benefit from our culture so that they become true [*véritable*] French citizens."[44] The foreign origins in question here were mixed, referring to the European as well as non-European immigrants composing the postwar labor force, such that reaching the working class inevitably meant reaching foreigners.

If such remarks were peppered with references to workers, however, Goetschel is quick to note that this did not always result in "a theater of class struggles."[45] Likewise, Jean Vilar, whom Jeanne Laurent appointed to head the Théâtre National Populaire in 1951, sought to reach the working-class public that the term "popular" invoked, yet he did so through a theatrical repertoire largely celebrating the canonical classics of Molière and Racine.[46] References to democratization during these years had less to do with encouraging theatrical work that addressed social stratification and more with facilitating contact with a centralized arts heritage. Laurent referred to interventionist cultural policy as a form of "spiritual life"[47] offered by a secular state, a statement that reveals how the framing of theater as a public service was part of a broader postwar effort positioning the arts as a *civic religion.* The notion of civic religiosity is a common one in analyses of transitional periods in French history, and is perhaps most famously associated with Mona Ozouf's study of how the postrevolutionary period witnessed a transfer of sacred attachment from Catholicism to the Revolution itself.[48] In the postwar period, the most significant architect of *civic religiosity* through the arts was André Malraux. Appointed by Charles de Gaulle as the first head of the newly established Ministry of Cultural Affairs in 1959, Malraux drew from Laurent's map of CDNs to create a supplementary structure of cultural diffusion, the Maison de Culture (MC) or House of Culture. Much like the CDNs, the MCs served as regional nodes where the French public could access a variety of cultural products and leisure activities.

André Malraux and the Maison de Culture

Central to Malraux's vision of a cultured, arts-appreciating citizenry was the idea of "aesthetic shock,"[49] the assumption that the French public's experience of art would be so transformative that it would shun the need for intermediary agents, those who could facilitate the relationship between individuals, artworks, and the institutions that housed them. The MCs, in Dominique Darzacq's pointed words, were to function as "secular cathedrals, destined to permit all citizens to access the masterpieces of humanity."[50] If such descriptions illustrated the civic religiosity that filled the moral vacuum of postwar France, they also revealed the seeds of a renewed notion of secular French "civilization" premised on cultural proficiency and arts appreciation.[51] Speaking at a 1966 colloquium, Malraux compared the MC to the university, constrasting their respective claims to the cultivation of proficient citizens:

> The Maisons de Culture do not bring about knowledge [*des connaissances*], they bring about emotions, works of art rendered live, to people who are facing these works of art. The University must teach what she knows, the Maisons de Culture must make others love [*aimer*] what they themselves love.[52]

In moments such as these, Malraux's comments revealed the paradoxical underpinnings of aesthetic shock. On the one hand, the cultured citizens of postwar France were to experience the arts through a secular spirituality. On the other hand, the arts were distinct from the university precisely because they retained, in Herman Lebovics's words, "the dissipated aura of religious rites,"[53] safeguarding an element of human life that the academic quest for "knowledge" could not address. Cultural proficiency was an elusive ability, in other words, framed as a question of love even as it necessitated centralized action. A remark made during a plenary session of the Commission for Cultural Facilities and Artistic Patrimony in 1961, chronicled by Vincent Dubois, perhaps best summarizes this dynamic. The politician Georges Combet noted that culture "corresponds to the health, to the morale, to the security of man and of the collective and if we have created social securities [*assurances sociales*] to protect man from illness and from accidents, then we also have the duty to protect him against accidents of civilization, born of this period of disorder and disequilibrium."[54] In retrospect, Combet's reference to "disorder and disequilibrium" signals a broader theme of postwar cultural policy-making in France, the tendency to position cultural development as a defense against the economic, technological, and social transformations associated with American capitalism. What is significant here, however, is the discursive formula through which cultural policy-making becomes a question of civic spirituality and civilizational security.

If language such as this recalled the historical project of the civilizing mission, the resonance was less coincidental than one might imagine. A reference to the cultural dimensions as well as the racist projections of French colonialism, *la mission civilisatrice* was premised on the notion that the French tradition of republicanism and the nation's cultural heritage could serve as a model to the indigenous societies with whom colonial administrators and civil servants came into contact. Lebovics notes that during the early years of the Ministry of Cultural Affairs, which coincided with the decolonization of many of France's global territories, large numbers of colonial civil servants were employed by the ministry to carry out what he terms "the metropolitan *mission civilisatrice*."[55] The historian notes that Malraux's goals were as international as they were domestic and that decolonization served as the background against which notions of French colonial management were transformed into the apparently benign project of *cultural* patronage and leadership.[56] Indeed, Malraux's comments on the MCs as institutions responsible for emotional life were pronounced in Dakar, at the opening colloquium of the first World Festival of Negro Arts. The cultivation of an arts-appreciating French citizenry existed on a continuum with France's cultivation as an international patron of the arts.

It is important to note that this mid-twentieth-century cultural policy heritage did not have a direct impact on my early twenty-first-century conversations. Not surprisingly, references to a singular cultural heritage, secular cathedrals, and civilizational security hardly permeated the vocabulary of my interlocutors. These were individuals who were entirely cognizant of what we might term, following Paul Silverstein's reference to "top-down sports development,"[57] a sort of top-down theater or culture development. Rather, they had inherited theatrical and cultural legacies that had emerged as a critique of the Malraux approach. At the same time, however, it would be a mistake to state that the legacy of aesthetic shock was entirely absent from our conversations. My interlocutors rarely assumed that the desire, willingness, or ability to engage in arts practices, and specifically theater, were predetermined. They knew that these experiences required a certain apprenticeship, mediation, and even at times a historical imagination. Nonetheless, I often heard theatrical self-expression referred to as an inherently human need and emancipatory labor. "Being onstage," as one theater workshop leader told me, "is speaking in a space of liberty, where one is listened to." In moments such as these, theater's progressive potential became legible through reference to a series of historically informed capacities and categories. Such expectations meant that when workshop participants, like Krimo, registered nervousness or unease with regard to their time onstage, workshop leaders, like Krimo's teacher, drew from a wide array of somewhat morally tinged vocabularies to mediate this discomfort. Their encounters thus resulted in complex configurations of the relationship between individual agency, moral life, and artistic practice. I pay sustained attention to these configurations throughout the book but my goal will not be to fault these approaches; rather, I wish to show that my interlocutors' tendency to understand theater as one of a series of "everyday moments of national-cultural interpellation and identification,"[58] to borrow Marilyn Ivy's formulation, was not a chance occurrence. At the same time, such moments were often permeated with a self-reflective critique, recognizing that emancipation was not a self-evident category of human experience, and that participation in and enjoyment of aesthetic practices required the prior cultivation of a set of complex dispositions.

A Critique of "Aesthetic Shock"

My interlocutors' critique mirrored that of the sociologist Pierre Bourdieu, whose 1969 publication *L'Amour de l'art: Les musées d'art européen et leur public* (*The Love of Art: European Art Museums and Their Public*), coauthored with Alain Darbel and Dominique Schnapper, proposed an alternative to Malraux's theories of cultural consumption. Commissioned by the Ministry of Cultural Affairs, this study of European museums and museum-going publics explored themes that have been central to the sociologist's later work. Unlike Malraux, Bourdieu argued that the symbols and rules structuring the encounter between an artwork and its observer were far from second nature:

> An act of deciphering *unrecognized as such* . . . is possible and effective only in the special case in which the cultural code which makes the act of deciphering possible is immediately and completely mastered by the observer (in the form of cultivated ability or inclination) and merges with the cultural code which has rendered the work perceived possible.[59]

The act of interpretation, in other words, as well as the pleasure and enjoyment that could follow this act, were contingent upon the observer's having internalized two parallel sets of "codes": the code structuring the artwork itself (thereby allowing it to be understood as an example of a genre, school, or period) and the code governing the work of interpretation (thereby allowing the observer to situate their own estimations in relation to a "scholastic culture").[60] Bourdieu argued that educational institutions were the only spaces where these codes could be assimilated, ultimately functioning akin to his notion of bodily *habitus,* as "a durable and generalized attitude which implies recognition of the value of works of art and the ability to appropriate them by means of generic categories."[61] Museums were not spaces where such dispositions could be cultivated; rather, art institutions were spaces in which only those who had already cultivated such dispositions could enter. It followed that the MCs were participating in a broader preservation of social inequality, circulating symbolic goods among those with the ability to recognize such assets while downplaying questions of access and mediation.

Bourdieu's comments coincided with the broader political upheavals of May 1968, as a general workers' revolt was joined by critiques of bourgeois and Gaullist culture to result in massive disruptions to everyday life. Toward the end of the month, heads of CDNs and MCs gathered at director Roger Planchon's theater in Villeurbanne to craft a response to the political instability. Francis Jeanson soon coined what would become the gathering's most memorable critique, the question of accessing the "non-public." Looking back in 1994, the philosopher argued that

> it was necessary to call into question, very seriously, the relationships between theater and the Maisons de Culture and the population, in its totality and its diversity. Beyond the potential public, it was necessary to take into account the existence of a non-public, composed of the fringes of the public [*marginaux de la chose publique*], citizens who did not have available the real means of citizenship [*citoyennisation*]. An undertaking of politicization, in the sense that it meant helping them to self-politicize, to become effective members of the city.[62]

As Jeanson's comments clearly foreshadow, the eventual Villeurbanne declaration of May 25, 1968, explicitly politicized the work of culture and carved out a privileged role for theater in the work of politicization. Indeed, as cultural action, the declaration announced theater to be "a privileged form of expression out of all the forms of expression as it is a collective human work offered to the collectivity of men."[63] Villeurbanne, in other words, positioned theater not only as a public service but as a vehicle of political protest, arguing that these two functions could be folded together if they acknowledged the work of mediation and politicization. In retrospect, May 1968 was evidence of how wide-ranging theater's connotations could be. On the one hand, rioting students would identify and occupy the Parisian national stage Odéon as an emblem of bourgeois ritual, evidence of the limits of theatrical decentralization. On the other hand, theater-makers imagined the working classes as insurgent audiences, increasingly reflecting the influence and orientation of the German director and playwright Bertolt Brecht.[64]

If these were the theatrical legacies that my interlocutors combined, then their immediate historical reference point was the tradition of *animation* that developed over the course of the 1970s. *Animation* was a preliminary vocabulary for understanding the work of mediation or what the Villeurbanne declaration labeled the self-politicization of others. *Animateurs* were cultural organizers who were charged with facilitating the relationship between artworks and disadvantaged or rural populations, the explicit purpose being to rejuvenate such quarters in much the same manner that previous iterations of popular education had sought to provide educational resources. Throughout the 1970s, *animation culturelle* became the groundwork for a series of fraught discussions, ranging from the relationship between popular education and artistic professionalism to that between centralized support and militant aesthetics. In chapter 1, I will examine the connection between these debates and the meanings they acquired in the context of an emergent immigrant theater. The salient point for now is that the 1970s witnessed a veritable explosion in theatrical activity, even as cultural policy lost luster under less interventionist political leadership. Whether redressing the center-to-periphery tendencies of theatrical decentralization or turning to *animation* to valorize previously unrecognized cultural traditions, amateur theater troupes, including the many that would be founded by immigrant groups, contributed to the growth of a robust civic sphere.

This sphere, one which combined the forms of cultural legitimation produced by centralized cultural policy with the political tendencies of *animation*, served as the broader historical background against which my interlocutors endowed theater with abilities and potentials. Theater, in other words, was both a force for cultivation *and* a space for aesthetic militantism. In turn, these dual tendencies paralleled two specific ways of conceptualizing theatrical practice. Theater historian Olivier Neveux's description of immigrant theater encapsulates these dual capacities:

> The participation of individuals who are not actors, who are socially stigmatized, in an artistic creation/production—as in immigrant theater—shows theater being assigned an immediate function: the space for a singular expression that bears witness to what one is, one's pride, one's dignity, to break with invisibility. Playing becomes the vector for a transformation of self, for a laying bare of the oppression that one has been subjected to, and of the ways of emancipating oneself from it.[65]

In Neveux's approximation of militant immigrant theater, the dual tendencies of bearing witness to oppression and achieving dignity through artistic creation correspond implicitly to two different visions of the work that theater does. On the one hand, theater is a mechanism of witnessing, the bearer of a message; on the other, it is the means to a transformation of self. Indeed, the visions of theater that animated my interlocutors' work were roughly grouped around these dual objectives.

Performance: Representation, Embodiment, and Enactment

A momentary return to Krimo's scene of humiliation will help provide a broader conceptual framework for situating these visions of theatrical practice. Let us remember that Krimo's teacher is frustrated with her bad actor for a number of reasons. On the one hand, this frustration is premised on the expectation that Krimo's performance is being registered as meaningful action. In an earlier scene, which presents Krimo's first attempt at acting in front of his classmates, the teacher interrupts his rhythmically unvaried monologue with a brief grammar lesson. Reminding her student that his spoken text contains commas, she cautions her classroom that in the French language, the written comma corresponds to a pause in speech. In moments such as these, we are reminded that Krimo's performance is being perceived as more than a series of bodily actions; his rhythms of speech are thought to be expressive of his habituation to the national language. On the other hand, theater's capacities are perceived in such a manner that this habituation is not necessarily logically prior to its expression in performance. Theater, in other words, is understood as an efficacious space, where this habituation can be generated through practice. It is Krimo's seeming reluctance to engage with the *embodied* dimensions of theater that results in the teacher's ultimate frustration, as she mutters: "I don't know anymore how else to tell you this."

Over the course of my conversations in Paris, I often heard theatrical practice referred to as "a work on the body." Not every interlocutor reached for this formulation for the same reasons, yet the image of this ever-elusive, receding body referred to a shared understanding that the human form registered the effects of theatrical practice on levels that were not entirely cognitive. Theater, in other words, was understood to be symbolic *and* pragmatic, expressive *and* constitutive. This dual understanding of theater practice has explicit parallels with dominant theoretical approaches to the study of stage and world. More specifically, anthropological approaches to ritual practice and theatrical debates on the nature of stage action have engaged with the question of whether human enactment should be understood as signifying or embodied. Although a quick glance at these debates reveals the sharpness of such a distinction to be misleading, the dichotomy itself has nevertheless produced distinct theoretical approaches.

In her overview of theories of ritual and ritualization, the religious studies scholar Catherine Bell identifies this dichotomy in the "initial bifurcation of thought and action."[66] Suggesting that theoretical approaches to ritual characterize repeated or routinized behavior as actions that proceed from prior concepts, Bell notes:

> Beliefs, creeds, symbols, and myths emerge as forms of mental content or conceptual blueprints: they direct, inspire or promote activity, but they themselves are not activities. Ritual, like action, will act out, express, or perform these conceptual orientations.[67]

Bell further argues that the distinction between conceptual orientation and expressive act can result in understandings of ritual that pivot around the relationship between thinking and acting, rather than a focus on the manner in which ritual acts can be efficacious, particularly where the attainment of certain sensibilities or skills is concerned. At the same time, Bell is quick to note that an approach to ritual activities as textual artifacts that can be deciphered (a paradigm often abbreviated as culture-as-text) unwittingly replicates an approach that views ritual as the dramatization of a set of preexisting beliefs. Clifford Geertz's well-known analysis of the Balinese cockfight, in which the anthropologist identifies the practice as "a metasocial commentary"[68] on Balinese social life ("it is a Balinese reading of Balinese experience, a story they tell themselves about themselves"),[69] is one example of an approach that privileges meanings over strategies. Where theatrical analogies are concerned, Victor Turner's movement from ritual to "social drama,"[70] a movement that accompanies the later stages of the anthropologist's career and is often identified as the result of his collaboration with performance studies pioneer Richard Schechner,[71] results in an understanding of ritual that foregrounds performance and enactment. Yet Bell is wary that such a move gives undue centrality to audience, reducing ritual to symbolic acts that communicate with and demand the interpretive labor of spectators.[72]

Not surprisingly, the question of whether ritual and performance should be understood as primarily communicative phenomena often emerges in theoretical debates on the theater, particularly as a critique of the prevalence of semiotic frameworks that stress theater as "a communicative event."[73] Indeed, European theater studies continues to bear the traces of a semiotic approach that originated with the interwar Prague school and continued in the later work of scholars like Patrice Pavis, Keir Elam, or Erica Fischer-Lichte, where the space of the theater is understood as a system of signs. This system is complex, as it negotiates the theatrical sign's signifying potential, the manner in which it repeats prior theatrical conventions, its reception by a heterogeneously situated audience, and its "cultural placement," its precise relationship to the ideological structures that surround and suffuse the theater.[74] Supplementing rather than opposing the semiotic approach is what we might call a phenomenological or embodied emphasis, with its reminder that "the phenomenal body resists the epistemological model of a corporeal object yielding its meanings to a decorporealized observer."[75] The twin projects of theatrical semiotics and phenomenology mirror Bell's question with regard to the habit-forming dimensions of ritual practices, extending the inquiry to account for the sedimentation of racialized, gendered, and sexual axes of difference. If theatrical practices involve the kinds of instrumental, habitual, and routinized behaviors associated with ritual, what might it mean to suggest that theater has the ability to impart skills that are imbued with moral value?

Embodied Practices

These questions underpinned my interlocutors' practical, everyday decisions. As I noted earlier, many of the artists and activists that I met understood the embodied nature of theatrical work to be generative of emotional, physical, and even linguistic skills. But theater did not consist of scattered instances of rehearsal in the company of fellow actors; it involved performances destined to reach far larger, and anonymous, crowds. Thus although their work was underwritten by a pragmatic understanding of theatrical labor, its culmination in a public spectacle merged this understanding with symbolic concerns: How would certain actions *read* on stage? Of what would they be considered the signs? Would they be recognized as the habit-generating practices that the rehearsals took them to be, or would they be considered enactments of social reality that weren't even that *good*? My interlocutors were concerned with process, in other words, but like most theater practitioners, they were driven by the demands of product. Aesthetic considerations often meant that different and indeed, contradictory, understandings of theater had to cohabit.

A quick clarification is necessary here. In noting that my interlocutors balanced different and even contradictory understandings of theatrical practice, my goal is not to identify such differences as organic, nor to institute a strict separation between communicative practices, whether theatrical or more broadly social, and embodied, habit-forming practices. Whereas I share Paul Connerton's skepticism toward approaches that identify the body through a purely representational model of language, "reduced to the status of a sign,"[76] I am equally wary of concluding that understanding corporeal practices requires eclipsing meaning and signification entirely.[77] Rather than reifying such a binary, my goal in this book is simply to show how my interlocutors' thoughts regarding the theater *worked with* this separation, rendering it meaningful in the context of the work that they performed. Thinking with their words, therefore, has pushed me to understand the body as an object constituted by social discourse, even as I recognize the ways in which it is shaped by corporeal practices.

In recent anthropological scholarship, scholars like Talal Asad and Saba Mahmood have questioned the view that all bodily practices are necessarily *representative* in character. Focusing on disciplinary regimens of bodily training in different religious traditions, they suggest that embodied activity's relationship to thoughts and beliefs can be constitutive as well as signifying. In her study of ritual worship among pious Muslim women in contemporary Cairo, Mahmood notes that "ritual is not regarded as the theater in which a preformed self enacts a script of social action; rather, the space of ritual is one among a number of sites where the self comes to acquire and give expression to its proper form."[78] Likewise, Asad argues for an understanding of ritual behavior as a series of "apt performances": "Apt performance involves not symbols to be interpreted but abilities to be acquired according to rules that are sanctioned by those in authority: it presupposes no obscure meanings, but rather the formation of physical and linguistic skills."[79] Crucially, both Asad and Mahmood's formulations depart from the vision of an interior, intending self whose private feelings and desires are manifested in exterior actions. Building on the work of Marcel Mauss and Aristotle, respectively, these scholars argue that it is through the technical efficacy of bodily practices that subjects come to acquire intentionality.

The above description of apt performance is equally resonant for a number of traditions of theatrical apprenticeship, as well as for a broader understanding of theatrical intentionality and action. The acquisition of abilities, the sanctioning role of authority, and the privileging of skills over meanings are central dimensions of the theatrical analogy that *performance analysis* has brought to bear on the constitution of the social world. The performance studies scholars Joseph Roach, Shannon Jackson, and Diana Taylor follow earlier calls to lift the boundary between the stage and the social world, yet do so specifically to ask how the material and embodied life of aesthetic forms are imagined to cultivate moral sensibilities.[80] Departing from approaches that identify thoughts and beliefs as the outcome of conceptual reflection, they examine how aesthetic forms entail "transformation in sensibility and behavior."[81] Jackson's study of the embodied nature of social reform in turn-of-the-century Chicago, Roach's analysis of the relationship between gestural reproduction (what he refers to as "the kinesthetic imagination")[82] and historical remembering in circum-Atlantic performance cultures, and Taylor's focus on embodied performance as revelatory of how Latin American individuals come to know a set of historical truths, values, and attitudes demonstrate how a focus on aesthetic practices can illuminate discussions regarding the relationship between ritual activity and political personhood.

Nervous Enactment

At this point, let us undertake one final return to the scene of Krimo's humiliation. As I noted earlier in this section, the teacher's frustration results from the fact that Krimo cannot recognize theater's twofold ability to both *represent* and *engender*. He seems unable to perform *or* to rehearse his performance. Yet the sheer intensity of the teacher's outburst is evidence that something slightly more complicated is taking place, that the teacher's frustration stems not from what Krimo is *not* doing but from what he *is* doing: rendering Arlequin into a shy teenager who is perhaps unable to communicate Marivaux's lines but is quite apt at communicating his attraction to Lydia/Lisette. If, once again, we engage in the allegorical reading that positions Marivaux's lines as French cultural heritage, then Krimo's enactment reveals the multiple ways in which (aesthetic) citizenship can be inhabited, and that citizenship itself, as May Joseph notes, is contingent on repeated "expressive enactments."[83] Joseph's specific interest is in the forms of performed citizenship that pattern east African Asians' experience, first as the "inauthentic"[84] citizens of east African states, and later as migrants in Euro-America. Yet I find her notion of a "sphere of nervous enactment"[85] to be useful in understanding the French context, where recent discussions around immigration and citizenship inevitably point to anxieties regarding the transmission of national culture and the perceived failure of the project of national integration. The teacher's frustration has as much to do with her recognition that expressive enactments can depart from prescribed theatrical/national roles as it does with bad acting.

This is perhaps so apparent a point that it risks stating the obvious. When considering the relationship between ritual activity and political personhood, to subscribe to the notion that bodily practices can sediment certain sensibilities requires recognition of the fact that such sedimentation is rarely linear, unidirectional, or absolute. Recognizing the inevitability of transformation in the process of sedimentation recalls Judith Butler's discussion of how the possibility of change and alteration is often built into the very structure of social norms, as well as the process of iteration that maintains them. Butler's theory of performativity originates with J. L. Austin's theory of the linguistic performative, which depends on the presence of appropriate circumstances, as well as an observer's approximation of the distance between a speaker's "outward utterance" and their "inward performance."[86] Butler's understanding of performativity is based on Jacques Derrida's reading of the Austinian performative, a reading through which Austin's emphasis on convention and circumstance gives way to a recognition of the broader iterability of speech and finally emerges in Butler's work as a reference to linguistic *and* bodily acts.[87] Butler famously identifies gender performativity "not as a singular or deliberate 'act,' but, rather, as the reiterative and citational practice by which discourse produces the effects that it names."[88]

Butler's understanding of the relationship between discourse and the body has been placed into productive conversation with the notions of bodily materiality that have animated the literature on ritual practices.[89] I reference the theory of gender performativity here, however, to recall that the way in which Butler theorizes *challenges* to iterativity and citationality produces complicated understandings of agency, both allowing for Derridean breaks with context *and* recognizing the "peculiar bind" that renders authority the very condition of agency.[90] I find this complexity particularly important to remember when considering theatrical norms and practices, as notions of authority, malleability, sedimentation, and agency take on specific meanings in aesthetic contexts where discipline and spontaneity are not automatically opposed. Put differently, the allegorical reading of Krimo's refusal could be understood as a rejection of the particular "national-cultural interpellation" Marivaux's play performs. As such, it is a spontaneous break with a context that beckons particular forms of comportment. Yet a surface-layer (and more theatrical) reading of the scene positions Krimo's spontaneity differently, since spontaneity is precisely what the teacher seeks. The difference is that she seeks the kind that can only result *from* disciplined repetition, not the kind that constitutes its impediment. The simultaneous availability of these two layers of meaning is what draws me to this scene: Krimo and his teacher's encounter constitutes a merger between performance as staged event and performance as a structuring logic of social life. In examining how theater practices can serve as the grounds for social work, my goal in this book is to highlight moments where such mergers are not the exception, but quite literally the norm, thus illustrating "the continuity between the noticeable and public performance of cultural performances, and the spontaneous, unscheduled, optional performance contexts of everyday life."[91]

Recent scholarship on citizenship has underlined a similar continuity, arguing that the term "citizenship" exceeds a reference to legal status, as well as to the basic political duties performed by citizens as rituals of democratic participation. Particularly as supranational formations like the European Union witness a parallel strengthening of national allegiances, "citizenship" has been broadened to refer to the social, cultural, and moral dispositions associated with any given national culture. While many critique the link between nationality and citizenship, national bureaucracies often enshrine such connections through specific ceremonies, illustrating the proliferation of conditions surrounding the offer of democratic citizenship. The fact that these conditions filter into daily existence is evidence of how the "optional performance contexts of everyday life" are often less than elective. At the same time, the malleability of "noticeable and public" displays of cultural performance reveal spaces of engagement that do not fall into immediately identifiable categories of enactment. As recent work by Emma Cox, Charlotte McIvor, and Alison Jeffers has shown, performative engagements with citizenship and the question of migration are multiply inflected.[92] Representations of refugees, asylum seekers, and immigrants have been central to delineating the borders between the citizen and the noncitizen, challenging as well as solidifying singular constructions of national identity, and probing the limits of theater's emancipatory potential. Likewise, Engin Isin has called for care in how we identify "acts" of citizenship, drawing specific attention to ruptures that "create a scene rather than follow a script."[93] Understanding the continuity between these two performance modes ("creating a scene" vs. "following a script") reveals as much about the process of negotiating norms of democratic citizenship as it does about theater-making.

Challenges, Choices, and Organization

This book is based on both ethnographic and archival research. The fieldwork vignettes that permeate its pages are the results of my conversations with theater practitioners, social and humanitarian aid workers, and political activists. The vast majority of these in-depth interviews took place in 2008, with follow-ups conducted in 2009 and 2012. At times, I enjoyed the good fortune and the generosity of interlocutors who allowed me to visit rehearsals for theatrical performances that were underway. At other times, I benefited from family albums and carefully preserved newspaper clippings in reconstructing events at which I was not present. And more often than not, I found myself conducting something akin to ethnographic oral history, as I would find out about a performance long after the sounds of applause had faded, when my understanding of the event was limited to the form in which my interlocutors recalled and narrated it. These limitations are by no means foreign to theater historians, yet where performance ethnography is concerned, they result in a text whose chapters do not enjoy the luxury of methodological consistency. Certain chapters therefore draw from a more robust store of archival materials, whereas others benefit from the fleeting, informal insights and exchanges that characterize participant observation and ethnographic presence. Virtually all of the chapters, however, are saturated with the contents of my open-ended interviews, conversations which went anywhere from an hour to several hours to multiple meetings across a number of months.

The vast majority of my conversations have been with the organizers, directors, or leaders of theatrical projects engaging immigration, rather than with the participants for whom migration was a daily reality. At times this was a reflection of practical availabilities, as participants would have moved away by the time I approached a specific organization to inquire about a past project. At others, my desire to exhume a past performance was tempered by the sense that the experience may have been a discomforting one for those involved. In moments like these, I chose not to pursue conversations with individuals who were negotiating undocumented status or in the process of applying for asylum. At the time, I rationalized this choice with reference to the very real vulnerabilities that lay at the perimeter of my ethnographic field. In retrospect, I am deeply aware that this choice reveals as much about my own readiness to attribute certain patterns of vulnerability as it does about whether these individuals would in fact have preferred a conversation. My methodological choices, in other words, are imbricated in some of the very dynamics that I examine, and critique, in this book.

A related choice has been to retain the names of institutions and organizations while omitting or altering the names of individuals. This is a reflection of what Micaela di Leonardo identifies as a key divergence of ethnography and oral history. Whereas the tradition of ethnography places a premium on privacy, oral historical interviews are often undertaken precisely for the public record.[94] I have chosen to navigate this conundrum by treating the vast majority of my interlocutors within the framework of the former, while placing the two historical voices from chapter 1, with whom I was fortunate enough to exchange feedback on my written material, in the framework of the latter. These choices inevitably evoke the question of authority that has structured theoretical literature on ethnography since the 1980s, and its call to make explicit one's narrative strategies and choices. That this mixture of privacy and publicity participates in generating its own truth claims goes without saying; my hope is that I am able to make these dynamics explicit throughout.

In the end, to ask what worlds result from a series of individuals acting on their artistic, moral, and political intentions is also to ask where my narrative stands in relation to theirs. My original intention in Paris had been to study the ways in which contemporary theater addressed the Algerian War. Yet the leaflets, posters (and soon, e-mail announcements) that crossed my path all demonstrated the presence of a multidimensional link between theater and the question of immigration, asylum, and exile. As I began researching the work that produced these performances, I found that their relationship to ongoing public debate on immigration was neither entirely critical (although it was often that) nor entirely suffused with its logic (although it was also often that). What emerged then was "a space of contestation"[95] where the terms of these debates were *worked on*. I found this to be a rich arena for research, but I remain acutely aware that, to extend Catherine Bell's analysis of how ritual theory has reorganized the thought-action dichotomy, such a project integrates *my* thoughts with *their* actions.[96] I will endeavor to remain mindful of this dynamic throughout the book.

In the pages that follow, I begin by identifying a series of precursors to the early twenty-first-century relationship between immigration and theater. Chapter 1 focuses specifically on the 1970s Arab-French theater troupes Al Assifa and La Kahina. Founded by a group of North African and French laborers, Al Assifa performed sketches on immigrant workers' experiences in France, while La Kahina gathered a mostly second-generation North African community to address the gender bias that plagued immigration politics. When examined together, their work illustrates that 1970s theatrical immigration activism provides an excellent site for tracking a series of social and political transformations. The 1970s are typically referred to as an era that witnessed symbolic transitions in the figure of the foreigner: as the postwar economic boom came to an end, *immigrant workers* began to be perceived as *immigrants*, residents who now constituted a social and cultural problem for the national community. This shift signaled transformations in activist and artistic sensibilities, and coupled with a post-1968 turn to human rights and identity politics discourses, fundamentally changed both immigration activism and its accompanying aesthetic practices. Using archival materials as well as oral historical interviews, I show that Al Assifa and La Kahina's theatrical work reveal how an emphasis on classed labor struggle slowly morphed into a tendency to view immigrant cultural production as a claim to difference. Throughout, I note how the themes that structured immigrant aesthetics in the 1970s, such as the challenges associated with representing racial and gender identities onstage, laid the groundwork for more recent iterations of immigration and theater activism.

From the early 1980s I move to the early 2000s, turning my lens to contemporary practices. In chapter 2, I focus on the prevalence of personal narrative performance in immigrant women's theater. Drawing on the Festival au Féminin, an annual women's art festival based in the immigration-saturated Paris neighborhood of the Goutte d'Or, I show how the idea of theatrical spectatorship in immigrant women's theater is premised on the assumption that the narratives of immigrant women are driven by the urgency of suffering. At the same time, performance is viewed as a vehicle that releases the performer from the particularity of their racial and gender identity. While I highlight some of the aesthetic underpinnings of this work, I also place immigrant women's theater in conversation with late twentieth-century French racial discourses and the broader tensions between French republican universalism and racial difference. In the second part of the chapter, I switch my lens from professional artists to Accueil Goutte d'Or, a Goutte d'Or-based civic association, to focus on how theatrical self-narrative is further framed and conceptualized in nongovernmental contexts addressing immigrant women. Throughout, I analyze personal narrative performance in conversation with the dynamic of universality and particularity that is central to French republicanism.

Chapter 3 extends the focus on nongovernmental contexts to two humanitarian organizations engaged in providing juridical and social aid to undocumented immigrants and asylum seekers in France, Réseau Education Sans Frontières and La Cimade. I specifically draw attention to the role that ideas of immigrant integration have played in how these organizations have conceptualized their theatrical "aid" work. Noting that both *La Plume sans papier* (*The Pen without Paper*), RESF's 2007 play featuring undocumented immigrants, and Cimade's annual theater workshops (2003–7) posit theater as a practice of integration, I examine the ways in which their aid work construes the relationship between bodily life, moral autonomy, and social integration. In sociological scholarship, the term "integration" generally refers to the process by which the members of a collective acquire shared values and norms. In the context of French immigration debates as they have developed since the 1990s, however, integration to national norms is more than a matter of shared affiliations: integration implies an individual's moral autonomy and individual rationality, best exemplified by the notion that abstract individualism can serve as a safeguard against communitarian tendencies. I propose that both RESF and La Cimade have positioned theater to respond to this twofold understanding of integration.

Leaving Paris for its suburbs, I turn in chapter 4 to Quelques unes d'entre nous, a women's collective of the Maison des Tilleuls (MDT), a social center located in the small, northeastern Paris suburb of Blanc-Mesnil. Composed of first-generation immigrant women from North and sub-Saharan Africa and the Middle East, as well as second-generation residents of Blanc-Mesnil from equally diverse origins, Quelques unes d'entre nous grew out of a series of civic activities that were held at the MDT in the early 2000s. The seeds of the collective's theatrical work were sown during the fall of 2005, when the highly publicized riots (*émeutes*) that began in neighboring Clichy-sous-Bois spread to Blanc-Mesnil as they made their way across towns and urban centers throughout France. Although the unrest began as a reaction to police violence in Clichy-sous-Bois, it was fueled by a broader dissatisfaction with the chronic unemployment, racism, and discrimination that is shared by a wide segment of *banlieue* residents. The collective's first play, *Le Bruit du monde m'est rentré dans l'oreille* (*The Sounds of the Crowd Entered My Ear*), was composed of the women's reactions to the violence that engulfed Blanc-Mesnil. I suggest that *Le Bruit du monde* is exemplary of how theater can be endowed with meanings and capacities relative to its political contexts. My goal in this chapter is to ask what this insight might mean for our understanding of theatrical rubrics like community-based or intercultural theater. Specifically, I argue that the use of terms like "community" and "culture" prove challenging in the French national context, where the deeply fraught history of associationalism has resulted in a political culture unconcerned with communal categories and identities.

Finally, in chapter 5, I extend my analysis of the relationship between politics and aesthetics to the theatrical representations of migration, exile, and asylum that have emerged in Parisian theater over the course of the last decade. These performance projects, ranging from small neighborhood-based productions to the transnational work of the famed Théâtre du Soleil, reveal a shared tendency to represent notions of universal humanity over political or geographic specificity. I propose that these aesthetic tendencies are related to what has been called the humanitarian turn in French immigration policy, whereby the moral imperative to relieve human suffering has replaced long-standing political criteria in the evaluation of migratory flows and political asylum. I argue specifically that the medical humanitarian practice of *témoignage*, or "witnessing," has resulted in changing artistic vocabularies and changing imaginaries regarding the capacities of political art. To demonstrate these dynamics, I focus my analysis on a small theatrical production sponsored by RESF, a performance by a prestigious and relatively well-known arts center in Paris, and Théâtre du Soleil's epic 2003 spectacle *Le Dernier Caravansérail* (*The Last Caravansary*).

Although these case studies will prove representative of the myriad ways in which theater practice has responded to questions of immigration, citizenship, and national identity at the dawn of the twenty-first century, they cannot exhaust the sheer variety of artistic and nongovernmental work taking place in Paris today. Nonetheless, it is my hope that these choices do justice to the complexities and contradictions that structure the relationship between theater and immigration, complexities and contradictions that are so well captured in Krimo's scene.

Chapter 1

✦

On the Paris Stage

By 1975, Al Assifa was showing signs of wear and tear. The Paris-based Arab-French theater troupe had been touring their immigration-themed play throughout France. In a meeting on October 12, a troupe member looked back, diagnosing the group's problems: "We often lived as though we were a community, but it is a community that was in fact a fiction . . . This is probably the most important reason as to why we had crises, crises which erupted over the smallest details."[1] While this member dispelled the notion that immigration activism sufficed to unify a group composed of French nationals and North African immigrants, troupe member Mokhtar went further in another, undated meeting: "Often, it is only the acting that brings us together. That is insufficient and dangerous for our continuation."[2] Later in the conversation, another voice added: "We must install ourselves in a neighborhood, take it, and then animate it."[3]

Today, these voices illustrate a series of questions that vexed 1970s theater practitioners, cultural policy-makers, and immigration activists. Of what did *animation*, the strengthening of communities through arts practices, consist? How were cultural activities to be implanted in low-income, disadvantaged neighborhoods and rural regions across the nation? Of what did community consist? If political goals were shared by individuals with radically different political statuses (e.g., citizens vs. temporary residents), how could they rally for the universality of labor injustices while honoring the particulars of the era's social discriminations? Of what did theatrical acting consist? An intimate endeavor that could provide the illusion of community, what role did this aesthetic practice have in denouncing social conditions? Did actors simply "take" neighborhoods and cultivate stories from their struggles, or did actors have a story and struggle of their own, as these brief exchanges immediately reveal? On whom then, was the work of acting spent?

In this chapter I arrive at these questions, and thus the particulars of 1970s theater activism concerning questions of immigration, via the Arab-French theater troupes Al Assifa and La Kahina. Founded in Paris by a group of North African and French laborers and students, Al Assifa performed sketches on immigrant workers' experiences in France, from encounters with institutional racism to workplace and housing conditions. They toured until the group's 1977 dissolution, reaching audiences that ranged from trade unions and humanitarian groups to rural agricultural communities. La Kahina was founded in 1976 by Salikha Amara, a young woman of Algerian origin whose family had settled in the northeastern Parisian suburb of Aubervilliers. Troubled by the gender bias that plagued immigration politics, Amara organized friends, family, and other activists and wrote a series of plays that portrayed Algerian women's lives on both sides of the Mediterranean. Examined in unison, Al Assifa and La Kahina's theatrical work are dually revelatory. On the one hand, they reflect the rapidly changing sociopolitical terrains of their era, for the references to community, solidarity, and theatricality related above are indelibly linked to the role of the "immigrant" in an evolving polity. On the other hand, the troupes' work outlines the manner in which these changes manifested themselves in theatrical practices, rendering the theater into a space where strategies for empowering immigrant political subjects revealed their potentials, contradictions, and limits.

Al Assifa and La Kahina's work serves as a useful historical background for understanding the aesthetic forms and social contexts of contemporary theater and immigration activism. For example, questions that beset theatrical representations of immigration in the 1970s, such as the ambivalent portrayal of racial or ethnic difference, set the terrain for later practitioners. Likewise, transformations in how this era understood the social dimensions of artistic self-expression resonate with recent debates among nongovernmental organizations devoted to cultural activism. These continuities will become apparent throughout the chapters that follow. That said, this chapter is devoted to a set of contingencies that were unique to 1970s France, however ongoing their effects. I will argue that the era's theatrical immigration activism bore witness to a transition from a form of politics that underlined the racial division of labor and the gendered histories of migration, to a politics of difference premised on the recognition of (an often singularly defined) immigrant identity.

To be clear, this was a transition that took place both beyond the domain of theater and beyond the national borders of France during the 1970s and 1980s, eventually forming the backbone of the feminist debates of the 1990s. Scholars like Nancy Fraser, Judith Butler, and Axel Honneth approached this dichotomy through the rubrics of redistribution and recognition, with Fraser often identifying the unequal distribution of resources as the heart of social injustice,[4] and Honneth and Butler drawing attention to the injurious effects of the lack of cultural recognition.[5] Whereas the basic terms of these debates appear throughout this chapter, I suggest that Al Assifa and La Kahina's work is significant precisely because it bears witness to a period when recognition-based and redistributive political strategies had not yet arranged themselves into a strict dichotomy.[6] The troupes' work thus resulted, on the one hand, in theater that negotiated the representational dilemmas of identitarian politics (thereby revealing both universalist and particularist tendencies) and on the other, in activism that embraced militant working-class politics (thereby forging complicated relationships with changing cultural policies and imperatives).

Before turning to specifics, however, my decision to locate Al Assifa and La Kahina within a tradition of political rather than theatrical labor deserves some clarification. After all, both troupes performed at a time when Parisian theatrical practices overflowed their "bourgeois" stages.[7] This movement would result in ubiquitous street-theater enterprises and newly institutionalizing performance venues such as the Cartoucherie, which housed the collective creation-oriented Théâtre du Soleil, Théâtre de l'Aquarium, and Jean-Marie Serreau's Théâtre de la Tempête. Serreau in particular sought the "institutional existence of a decolonized theatre" in the early 1970s, following earlier collaborations with the Martinican poet and playwright Aimé Césaire and the Algerian Kateb Yacine.[8] The latter himself toured his immigration-themed play *Mohamed prends ta valise* (*Grab Your Suitcase Mohamed*) throughout France in the mid-1970s. In fact, scholarship on the decade often underlines Kateb Yacine's extensive tour as the beginning of a "theater of immigration" (*théâtre de l'immigration*) in France.[9] This theatrical landscape certainly served as the background to Al Assifa and La Kahina's work, as did the sheer multiplicity of Spanish, Portuguese, Antillean, and West and North African immigrant theater troupes that emerged over the course of the 1970s, and gathered together in 1975 at the first Festival de Théâtre Populaire des Travailleurs Immigrés in Suresnes.

My conversations with Tancelin and Amara, however, revealed another set of orientations. Emergent immigrant labor movements, cultural policy turns toward the needs of disadvantaged communities, and newly acquired political rights of association for immigrants all served as the divergent sources from which the troupe's aesthetic practices drew their principles. While the broader sphere of 1970s theater (itself enmeshed within labor movements and associational contexts)[10] certainly influenced the troupes' work, at times it was precisely their isolation from dominant registers of theatrical practice that generated specific techniques, discourses, and practices. In this chapter then, my goal is to place Al Assifa and La Kahina against the background of immigration politics while recognizing where the troupes' work stands in relation to theater historical developments. To do so, I draw primarily on oral historical interviews with Al Assifa's Philippe Tancelin and La Kahina's Amara. Neither individual was able to supply me with their original performance texts, yet a series of fragmented archival materials provide a sense of the broader sociopolitical networks within which the artists functioned. In what follows, I begin with a brief overview of 1970s immigration politics in France, examine the troupes' work first as theater practitioners and then as community activists, and end with a brief glimpse at theatrical representations of immigration in the early 1980s.

From *Travailleur immigré* to *Immigré*

Al Assifa and La Kahina emerged during a time that would prove decisive for French immigration policy. Immigration from former colonies had been central to French social life throughout *les trente glorieuses*, the thirty "glorious" years of economic expansion that followed the Second World War. But the early 1970s increase in unemployment (joined by the increase in oil prices that had begun with the OPEC crisis) soon resulted in immigration's emergence as a political issue. In 1974 President Valéry Giscard d'Estaing announced the suspension of labor migration to France, including therein a ban on familial reunification. This second prohibition was overturned four years later, yet by then France's essentially "laissez-faire" postwar immigration policy was driven by a stronger emphasis on reducing the number of migrants living on French soil.[11] As single male workers were joined by women and children, familial reunification contributed to the perception that immigration signaled the end of postwar prosperity. In effect, the transitory *travailleur immigré* or "immigrant worker" of the metropolitan French imagination became the *immigré*, or "immigrant," detached from one qualifier only to be exposed to the assortment of others that permanency entailed.

As urban reforms struggled to contain this shift from "labor" to "settler" migration,[12] housing became immigration's most politicized dimension. Public resources that had funded hostels for foreign workers were increasingly redirected toward *grands ensembles*, the French state's postwar public housing projects that had been built to house a mix of social classes.[13] Abdelmalek Sayad notes that immigrants' transition to suburban housing carried a strong moral dimension, as "a mark of civilization" that contrasted with the cramped homosociality of laborers' residences.[14] Public housing not only quarantined families to urban peripheries, however, but the symbolic distance between French social norms and the Arab-African body soon eclipsed the ideal of social proximity.[15] These developments did in fact coincide with the significant antiracism legislation of 1972, yet the model of racialization evoked by these laws was primarily Vichy anti-Semitism, with less emphasis on anti-immigrant discrimination in housing, workplaces, and schools.[16] In this newly sedimenting racial order, North African and Algerian immigrants in particular suffered the effects of an ongoing "colonial" racism,[17] exacerbated by the memory of the not-too-distant Algerian War (1954–62).

If such developments were to prove decisive, however, the emergence of the *immigré* drew on more than policy changes. This figure was equally inflected by transformations in what we might call the moral relationship between French citizens and the Third World, a geography that encompassed both former French colonial territories and newer zones of war and occupation. While the protests of May 1968 and their insistence on joining the workers' uprising to intellectual reform would impact the French cultural landscape for many years to come, early 1970s political activism carried a new component:

an interest in subaltern subject positions as a question of human rights and identity politics. Kristin Ross has suggested that this development had both domestic and transnational dimensions. As the humanitarian leanings of former Leftists provided an ethical framework for understanding suffering abroad, the legacy of 1968 was reinterpreted as manifesting the "identity" of a particular collective, at home.[18] The notion that political action could only happen on behalf of the interests of a specific group dovetailed with the configuration of certain groups' interests around the theme of suffering. When "the colonial or third-world other of the 1960s," Ross notes, shifted "from militant and articulate fighter and thinker to 'victim' by a defense of human rights strictly identified as the rights of the victim,"[19] this transformation had implications for a variety of relationships marked by *difference*, including immigration. For Ross, earlier figures of social protest were subsumed beneath "'the plebe,' a spiritualized and silent figure of helplessness,"[20] less significant for its relationship to civic life and material existence than for its importance as a source of moral truth and knowledge, a trope that has been key to French humanitarianism.

This multidimensional shift from "immigrant worker" to "immigrant" is well captured in the evolution of Al Assifa and La Kahina's work, as I will soon show. A fuller understanding of how the troupes sought to render immigration *politically visible,* however, will benefit from a glance at how the larger world of collective dissent positioned both French colonialism and the immigrant body. The forms of protest action that emerged from May 1968, as well as those that characterized the 1970s Mouvement des Travailleurs Arabes (MTA) or Arab Workers' Movement, provide especially fruitful contexts. Although May 1968 is often recognized for having linked metropolitan workers' conditions to a critique of French colonialism, during the 1960s, representations of colonial others avoided easy identification between the two categories. These political and artistic disidentifications provided later artists with a rich understanding and allowed Al Assifa and La Kahina to imagine performative engagements that did not make a straightforward claim to difference. Meanwhile, the bodily nature of hunger striking, the MTA's emergent tradition of immigrant labor protest, resonated with the question of universality and particularity that haunted the portrayal of the immigrant's body in performance.

Protest Action and Disidentification

The general strikes of May 1968 are often underlined for the novelty of having gathered multiple grievances beneath the umbrella of one extended social uprising. Indeed, the targets of the protests ranged from President Charles de Gaulle's support for the American presence in Vietnam to French factory administrations skeptical of proposals for workers' self-management. Yet the day-to-day experience of protest action was perhaps not as new, resonating with the experiences of Algerian War protesters in 1961 and 1962, a phenomenon largely due to the presence of colonial militarism in the practices of urban police forces.[21] What was significant about the language of protest characterizing 1968, however, was that the colonial dimensions of class struggle rarely resulted in demonstrations *on behalf of* the Algerian people. This is a stance that Ross reads via Jacques Rancière's comments on political disidentification.[22] Rather than identify with the suffering of a tortured other, Rancière suggested that protest action could spring from a disidentification with the *torturer*, the French state, thus alienating "the 'French' political subject from him or herself."[23] In this scheme, ethical recognition did not begin where political action met its limits; rather, ethical limitations beckoned different kinds of political action: "the cause of the other," Rancière wrote, "exists only within politics, and it functions there as an impossible identification."[24]

Indeed, a panoramic view of the metropolitan effects of the Algerian War during the 1960s reveals a series of disidentifications, both political and aesthetic. For example, the Manifesto of the 121, or the "Declaration of the right of refusing to serve [*insoumission*] in the Algerian War," was drafted in 1960 and signed by 121 intellectuals, artists, and theater practitioners. The manifesto famously criticized the French army for forcing French citizens to experience their citizenship as a "shameful submission."[25] Absent from the declaration was a reference to Algerian victims; instead, war made victimhood and injury available to all and could thus serve as the context for rekindling a broader *proletarian* politics.[26] Meanwhile, Jean Genet's *Les Paravents* (*The Screens*) stood out in the pre-1968 aesthetic landscape as an example of *theatrical* disidentification. Staged in 1966 at the state-subsidized Théâtre de l'Odéon, Genet's play was based on the story of Saïd, a young and poor Algerian around whom the seventeen episodes of the play grew in concentric circles, encompassing the multilayered state of Algeria in war. Predictably, public reaction was mixed, ranging from spectators who applauded to protesters who set the Odéon's carpeting on fire, hurled smoke bombs, and injured actors. Throughout the period of turmoil that surrounded the play, Genet denied the play's connection to colonialism. "The Algerian war? I don't know about you but me, I am not Algerian," he wrote pointedly in his prescriptions to director Roger Blin, later adding that "[this play] does not address Algerians any more than *Les Nègres* [referring to his earlier play *The Blacks*] addressed black people."[27] These instances reveal that the playwright not only invited audience members to disidentify as French subjects vis-à-vis Algerian ones, but that he had an acute sense of the publics his work *could* occasion, underlining the possibilities of political action that could unfold in the absence of the "Algerian" addressee. Tom McDonough has shown that such explorations were not limited to institutional spaces but emerged in avant-garde experimentation as well.[28]

In many ways, these traditions of disidentification provide a counterintuitive framework for understanding 1970s theater activism concerning immigration. Whereas Genet refused to frame his work as a naturalistic rendering of colonial trauma, Al Assifa and La Kahina insisted on the coincidence between the material realities of their actors and the social injustice they sought to depict. For them, the persons on stage were not merely symbolic vehicles but participants in the world they portrayed. Similarly, Al Assifa and La Kahina were invested in the actual presence of immigrant addressees in the audience, as the structural inequalities of immigration concerned both French and immigrant communities, two entities they often bound together in a proletariat "without borders."[29] As empowering as such investments could be, however, the troupes were equally aware of the limits of insisting on authentic identities: both Al Assifa and La Kahina experienced the difficulty of transcending an identitarian model of theatrical action to make either aesthetic claims or to argue for the importance of the practice's nonrepresentational, embodied dimensions. These alternative investments, I suggest, are best understood in light of these earlier traditions of collective dissent, traditions that depended less on recognizing or speaking on behalf of difference than on enlarging the possibilities of action available to the members of an audience, whether political or theatrical.

The Mouvement des Travailleurs Arabes

If such legacies served as one strand of the troupes' intellectual heritage, then the Arab workers' movement served as another. On a logistical level, labor activism and activist theater were practiced in intersecting spheres, often depending on each other's networks for circulation. When it came to the question of rendering the immigrant body politically visible, however, there were conceptual resonances as well. Founded in 1972, the MTA focused its call for reform on the Circulaires Marcellin-Fontanet, which made the delivery of an immigrant's residency permit contingent on a work contract and "decent" lodgings.[30] Paving the way for nationwide protests, the bill also laid bare the need for immigrant activists to create a movement that met the increasing specificity of immigrant needs. The prominent activist Saïd Bouziri, who led a well-publicized hunger strike in 1972, recalled that "immigrants had to be autonomous, create their own movement, and they could not organize from within existing structures."[31] The hunger strike soon became this autonomous action. As a political act that highlighted individual corporeal experience, self-starvation was meant to show that "one plays with one's body to say that one cannot take it."[32] Soon hunger striking became a model for the MTA's protest actions, with the immigrant body central to its message. A mid-1970s MTA pamphlet, for example, clarifies the focus on the bodily life of immigrant labor: "A shocking example: every morning at the Carpentras market, bosses choose from the workers who have lined up, waiting to be recruited according to their 'physical form' exactly as it was during the good old times of slavery."[33]

It is tempting to label spontaneous hunger striking an "autonomous" response to such labor conditions, yet the practice did negotiate a challenge. On the one hand, MTA activists underlined their particular identity as a foreign labor force exploited in specific ways; on the other hand, they were hesitant to emphasize racial or ethnic identity as the core of their struggle, opting instead to emphasize the universalist reach of working-class mobilization.[34] Within this fraught context, hunger striking was a response to the conundrums of universality. As a bodily act, hunger striking could function as universal, as harm done to that body would be recognizable to all. Yet it also marked that frame as particular, because the immigrant's "physical form" was uniquely central to his livelihood, one which fell outside the protections offered by citizenship.

Whereas hunger striking negotiated the fraught autonomy of immigrant labor activism, it was equally imbricated in the changing models of political action available to immigrants. Despite the labor politics that formed the core of its struggle, Johanna Siméant has suggested that these practices mirrored "a 'humanitarian' approach centered above all on the question of 'dignity.'"[35] Indeed, Saïd Bouziri himself remarked that "the hunger strike had proven to be something about identity, a form of recognition."[36] Whereas it would be shortsighted to claim that these forms of recognition obscured the racial division of labor to which the activists drew attention, it is equally important to note the resonances between the sensationalizing of the immigrant's body and the increasing prevalence of recognition central to identitarian politics and human rights discourses. The MTA, in other words, vacillated between different forms of protest politics.

What was the relationship between hunger striking and theatrical practice? Theater, much like hunger striking, disrupted "both the hyper-visibility of the immigrant (the fears and hatred that he/she engenders, the caricatures that specify him/her), and the immigrant's political invisibility."[37] Theater, in other words, negotiated the same challenge as labor activism in seeking a form of protest that both resisted the stigmatization of the *immigré* and sought to render *immigré* experience visible. While the MTA positioned the immigrant body as a site through which to address the paradoxes of universalism, Al Assifa and La Kahina struggled to generate what we might term an *immigrant aesthetic*, building new aesthetic categories around the performing immigrant body, while nonetheless participating in the wider world of cultural resistance in Paris. For both of these body-conscious protest formats (hunger striking and theatrical performance), representing the immigrant revealed the difficulties of addressing racial and ethnic difference in the French context. Additionally, both practices laid bare immigrant activists' vacillation between protest tactics that were motivated by class-based "politics" and those that revealed an "ethical" turn, emphasizing the recognition of a specific social experience, and often one of suffering.

Before examining these dynamics in detail, however, it is important to note that the resonances between hunger striking and theatrical practice need not obscure our understanding of the differently privileged bodies that undertook these corporeal practices. In fact, the high point of immigrant labor activism in 1970s France coincided with a major shift in the theater. A development often identified as a turn to "total theater," this shift undermined the traditional prominence of playwrights, giving way to greater experimentation with directing and collective creation and bringing a renewed focus on the actor's body.[38] Where bodily experience is concerned, the relationship between the theater activist and the hunger striker are striking in the recollections of one activist interviewed by Siméant:

> Before 68, I was a really cynical guy; I was passionate about dadaism and surrealism. . . . I did theater, but not street theater and not popular theater, I had met people who were coming back from Roslow in Poland, who had worked with [the experimental theater director] Grotowski, and the big question that we were passionate about at the time was the work on the body. And it's true that working on the body and then finding oneself supporting people who weren't eating, who used their bodies as their principal support for their demands, this was no coincidence. And this work on the body, research on the work on the body as a means of expression, a body not used by a doctor or a director, it's in a sense the actor king [*c'est l'acteur roi en quelque sorte*].[39]

For this activist, the resonance between the body as a means of theatrical expression and the body as a political instrument was clear. What remained opaque was the structure of privilege that underwrote the desire to juxtapose these different models of "work on the body." The use of the language of theatrical agency and artistic sovereignty (the avant-garde "actor king") to characterize the possibilities of action available to *social* actors shows that theater and hunger striking were uneasy partners in embodied activism.

Al Assifa's New Cultural Identity of Resistance

Al Assifa (Arabic for "storm") was founded during the Lip watch factory strikes that took place in Besançon in 1973, an occasion that joined immigrant workers with a heterogeneous Left. "On our way to Lip," founding Al Assifa member Philippe Tancelin remembered, "we decided that we wouldn't simply arrive with tracts but that we would quickly put together a series of sketches."[40] With connections and audiences that soon ranged from the MTA to the assorted corners of the French Left, Al Assifa reflected a broad spectrum of tendencies. For example, while its name referenced the Palestinian

Fatah movement and the MTA's strong links to the Palestinian cause, it also reflected Palestine's broader and more abstracted significance as "a beacon of revolutionary resistance" (Tancelin) for the French Left. This merging of political positions that were at once domestic and transnational, concrete and abstract, was visible in brochures presenting the troupe's theatrical work. As one pamphlet made abundantly clear: "The idea was born of the need for communication and exchange between our struggles as immigrant workers and the struggles of French workers. The working class is without borders."[41] Al Assifa's imagined addressee could range from North African immigrant workers to the French working class to an international proletariat, joined together through the era's emergent rhetorical formation, a world "without borders."

If Al Assifa addressed a borderless working class, however, it was equally aware of the fractures that underlined such universal calls to mobilization. Much like the MTA, Al Assifa emphasized the specificity of the immigrant laborer's condition but sought to maintain a link to the broader labor struggles of the 1970s. In a scene from their first play *Ça travaille, ça travaille, ça ferme sa gueule* (*It Works, It Works, It Shuts Its Mouth*), a character identified in the printed text as "The Worker" is tossed from one official counter to another, alternately being told by his boss, the bank teller, the government official at the national employment agency, and the landlord outside his hostel that he lacks the necessary paperwork. This classic scene of bureaucratic struggle is complicated as he crosses paths with the police, greeting them with "Hello, police who are gentle with Arabs."[42] The worker's Arab identity, established through the threat of police violence, is further emphasized in linguistic routines whereby he repeatedly mishears his interlocutors. Meanwhile, his own and bare use of the French language highlights another dimension of his presence in the scene. Walking up to a government official, he introduces himself with "me work" (*moi travailler*), eclipsing the ethnicized uptake that follows as the official responds, "Hello, Mohammed."[43] In moments like these, the failure of the worker's universalizing gesture mirrored the limitations on Al Assifa's own search for a "working class without borders." Such claims to proletarian universality, as I will soon show, were repeatedly compromised by questions of racial or ethnic particularity. Yet the social uptake of scenes like these held out the promise of another kind of recognition, encapsulated in an older immigrant audience member's reaction: "It has been five years since I've been back to my country, tonight, I am there."[44] Recognition, in other words, functioned on levels for which the French working class was not always the primary referent.

During my conversation with Tancelin, the activist identified Al Assifa's larger goal to be "the affirmation of a new cultural identity of resistance and of immigration by way of aesthetic work, theatrical work that claimed its own aesthetic categories." In the years that preceded the creation of its first play, this new cultural identity of resistance manifested itself in a desire to "take the streets" (*prendre la rue*).[45] Marked by a May 1968 sensibility, this call resonated with street theater projects that were emerging throughout metropolitan France in the mid-1970s, as a wide variety of artists "appropriated the street without any prior authorization, [the street] suddenly transformed into a forum" on social injustice.[46] In their book *Les Tiers Idées*, Tancelin and Al Assifa co-activist Geneviève Clancy chronicled an example: a troupe member would run down an unspecified street while two others yelled "Stop him, stop him, he stole yogurt, it's an Arab."[47] The chaos that ensued would eventually be settled with a public conversation on the biases underlying the crowd's reaction. Identifying this strategy, the authors asked: "*Théâtral invisible*? When those who walk by do not know that what is happening is a representation, an intervention."[48]

In retrospect, this "intervention" echoed not only the era's street theater, but a broader panorama of mid-century, site-specific sensibilities, ranging from Allan Kaprow's late 1950s Happenings to Guy Debord's Situationist critiques. While theoretically divergent, these pre-1968 activities nonetheless situated "the viewer-participant's activities between an unfolding artwork and everyday activity."[49] Augusto Boal, who developed the methodology known as Forum Theater and maintained an intermittent presence in Parisian performance activism during the 1970s, is perhaps an even closer fit. In *The Theatre of the Oppressed,* the Brazilian director would notably call on spectators to intervene in the development of the dramatic action they were witnessing, suggesting that this intervention functioned as "a real act even though he [the spectator] does it in a fictional manner."[50] In the same way, when the spectator-actors involved with "Arab man with yogurt" complained to troupe members that they had been misled into participating in a false scenario, the group would reply that "what is true is the reaction that everyone had, as if this were really happening."[51] This dismissal of the event's frame in favor of the actor's intentionality recalled Boal's thoughts on Théâtre Forum: "Within its fictitious limits, the experience is a concrete one."[52] The origins of Al Assifa's new cultural identity of resistance thus shared an intellectual repertoire with a wide range of artists interested in the relationship between spectatorship and social action.

Les Tiers Idées, however, did not encourage these resonances. The authors often rejected street theater idioms, asking instead: "What will differentiate us from the culture of the left? From troupes that stage spectacles on current events, on the fight?"[53] The urgency of differentiation was visible many years later during my conversation with Tancelin, as I sought to identify a relationship between Al Assifa's work and that of contemporary troupes like the Théâtre du Soleil. For example, the famed company's 1975 production *L'Âge d'or* featured the Algerian immigrant worker Abdallah as a central character, and drew on the company's tradition of physical dexterity to recount the discrimination he faced in France.[54] Moreover, much like Al Assifa, the Théâtre du Soleil had gathered performance material from their own fieldwork, chronicling the lived experiences of factory workers and strikers.[55] When I asked about these resonances, Tancelin replied that "Al Assifa was a militant troupe, the Théâtre du Soleil is a troupe that holds certain political positions, it's not the same thing." These differentiations, whether between politics and militancy (or street theater and "taking the street"), revealed the broader cultural dynamics surrounding Al Assifa's work. As wide-ranging as theatrical militancy could be in 1970s France, the racial politics of immigration activism and the changing place of *animation* in cultural policy-making would circumscribe the possibilities of an immigrant aesthetic.

Militancy, Racial Authenticity, and Animation

When Philippe Tancelin differentiated between theatrical immigration militancy and theater troupes that advocated on behalf of specific political causes, this distinction rested on a perceived difference between laborer-actors implicated by the injustices they decried, and artists whose political sensitivities included the recognition of immigrant struggle. In Tancelin's words, "there was no separation between the Al Assifa actor and the identity that he represented." The coincidence between actor and role implied that the individual embodying labor struggle on the stage did so in the social world as well, the performance functioning as merely one node in a broader effort to "carry Assifa with us and let it live everywhere."[56] At the same time, this militancy was marked by the complicated relationship between embodiment, racial identity, and ideals of community. However adamantly Tancelin insisted on the non-separation of actor and role, his own status as a white Frenchman recalled this chapter's opening anecdote: Al Assifa was a community whose political ideals were manifested in widely varied lived experiences. As logistically useful as this heterogeneity could be, it set limits on the troupe's claim to authentic actorly representation. Furthermore, Tancelin's comments on the *embodiment* of political struggle rarely referenced the ethnic composition of the group, yet the new cultural identity of resistance was not divorced from the performativity of immigrant difference. For Tancelin, Al Assifa's success with immigrant audiences was rooted in the kind of "family recognition" and "relationships of affinity" that he felt it provided, namely, the literal presence of Arab performers in their midst. Immigrant aesthetics was dependent on the bodies of Arab laborer-actors who, after all, *looked* Arab and often delivered lines in Arabic. Theatrical immigration militancy, in other words, was premised on the perception of racial or ethnic authenticity.

Indeed, the question of authenticity structured a terrain that stretched beyond the viewing experience of other Arab spectators. A reviewer for *Le Monde* was equally seized by the seeming candidness of immigrant aesthetics: "They are present there, normally, we perceive them in their usual circumstances [*conditions habituelles*], there is nothing they are hiding [*il n'y a rien dans les manches*], no finesse in the setup, no special effects in the sound."[57] For both Arab and French audiences, in other words, the Arab bodies on stage functioned as evidence of theatrical transparency, of the coincidence between actors and roles, and of the minimal role of stage aesthetics. In these instances, the presentation of a collective racial identity could waver between its emancipatory potential and the overdetermined dimensions of the spectators' reception. Additionally, the imagined transparency of the Arab laborer-actor implied a parallel negation of the theatrical apparatus, an imagined transparency (or absence) of aesthetic labor.

What was at stake in these notions of authenticity? If highlighting racial or ethnic difference in the theater was a complicated matter in 1970s France, this dynamic was related in part to the era's cultural policy developments. During the postwar period, cultural policies had been marked by an effort to decentralize theatrical and cultural production, an impulse that had resulted in regional structures like the Centre Dramatique National and Maison de Culture, respectively. These centers were to increase public access to artworks, generate a set of nationally recognizable cultural sensibilities, and in Minister of Cultural Affairs André Malraux's vision, humanize the masses. Needless to say, such efforts were called into question during the mass upheavals of May 1968. The cultural activist Francis Jeanson famously addressed the artists' assembly at Villeurbanne with reference to the "non-public" of cultural policy, referencing working-class audiences that advocates for cultural democratization routinely bypassed.[58]

Jeanson's warning resonated with a practice that was institutionalized in the 1970s: *animation culturelle*, or the invigoration of low-income and rural communities through the promotion of cultural activities. Throughout the 1970s, *animateurs* or cultural organizers worked as mediators between amateur populations and arts practices, serving as the latest in a series of policy frameworks designed to promote cultural decentralization. By the middle of the decade, however, *animation* acquired political connotations and its status came into question. At this point, cultural policies revealed "a sharper distinction between professional creation and amateur creativity, art and *animation*."[59] Minister of Cultural Affairs Maurice Druon underlined the politically charged dimensions of *animation* when he famously stated in 1973 that he intended to dismiss those who approached his ministry with a "begging bowl" in one hand and a "Molotov cocktail" in the other.[60] While this declaration was motivated by the evident end of *les trente glorieuses*, it was also the harbinger of soon-to-be President Valéry Giscard d'Estaing's emphasis on professionalization in the realm of culture.

This development emerged in Al Assifa's experience in unexpected ways, underlining the fraught racial politics of an immigrant aesthetic, as well as the limits of immigrant actors' access to the kinds of dispositions that Pierre Bourdieu would broadly label "cultural competence."[61] Tancelin noted that the majority of their "militant" audiences felt that "yes, we support the workers, but culture? That's another thing . . . when immigrants, when workers want to work aesthetically, no!" These statements revealed that in a climate that separated art from *animation*, aesthetic creation and the cultural work of resistance were increasingly irreconcilable. Militancy on behalf of immigration, in other words, could not claim aesthetic achievement. At the same time, this disavowal could work both ways. Well before Al Assifa's official formation, a number of its soon-to-be members had themselves labeled aesthetic success irrelevant. In a 1971 interview they asked: "Why do we refuse to talk about street theater? Because for us the notion of theater is still too ambiguous."[62] In these early discussions, "theater" was considered too rooted in the cultural rituals of the bourgeoisie. Meanwhile, the avant-garde tended to subsume political questions to a purely formal inquiry. Theater was thus painstakingly separated from political action that happened to have dramatic qualities: the goal was to "take the city, not the stage" (*prendre la ville, pas la scène*).[63] A few years later, however, the distinction between immigration militancy and aesthetic practice carried new connotations: amateur agitprop vs. professional creation. Thus, theater's connotations changed as well. In a 1976 Al Assifa pamphlet, the practice was reclaimed as a cultural good in need of democratization: "We have taken the stage, not because theater would be easier, or because it would be a militant mode, but because the stage, like the street, was forbidden us."[64]

Tancelin's discourse of embodiment and authenticity is perhaps best understood in the context of these rapidly changing dichotomies. Racial authenticity rendered the exhibition of this body aesthetic by way of *moral* criteria: this was a body in the know, the Arab laborer-actor. Whereas racial authenticity could not redress the unequal distribution of cultural privilege or capital, it could generate access to limited forms of majority recognition, premised on the perceived transparency of a minority collective's experience or identity. This meant that the proletarian universality of a new cultural identity of resistance could not be dissociated from the particularity of racial or ethnic authenticity in performance. It also meant that Al Assifa would confront the complexities of having been assigned a unitary identity.

Technical Competence and "Enunciation of Self"

As is clear from the anecdotes I relate above, the relationship between minority experience and majority recognition was central to the reception of Al Assifa's work. Not surprisingly, this theme is also present in scholarship on 1970s immigrant theater. For example, the theater historian Olivier Neveux suggests that in works resembling Al Assifa's, "competence would no longer be technical or academic, but it would be of the order of knowing [*de l'ordre d'un savoir*], of biography or of the survey—a process of the enunciation of self."[65] Neveux's statement alludes to the era's dominant methodology for the procurement of social "truths," the survey (*enquête*). The practice of surveying or investigating emerged during May 1968 and flourished among artists and scholars alike. But the historian's emphasis on biography exceeds a mere reference to methodology, as the suggestion seems to be that where immigrant theater was concerned, personal *experience* ("knowing") dislodged aesthetic *expertise* ("competence") from its prioritized position in theatrical practice. An emphasis on the authenticity of the actor's personal experience, in other words, engendered a renewed plane of personal expertise, rendering aesthetic criteria and aesthetic achievement irrelevant. Certainly, Neveux's distinction does not seek to mirror the exclusivity that Tancelin attributed to the French Left, yet the historian's celebration of "biographic" competence unwittingly reproduces a parallel binary.

The question remained, however, as to whether Al Assifa experienced biographic competence and technical expertise as mutually exclusive. While "enunciation of self" was significant to Al Assifa's practice, the distinction between expertise and experience was not quite as delineated. However bare and uncomplicated their stage setups and costumes, actors remained conscious of the technical expectations trained on their work. In fact, the discussions surrounding their second play, *C'est la vie de château, pourvu que ça dure* (*It's a Fancy Life, Provided It Lasts*), revealed the troupe's growing interest in symbolic representation and the desire to generate a surreal atmosphere on the stage. In the play, the immigrant worker Mohamed was drawn toward France by a woman's voice and proceeded as though in a dreamlike trance. Yet troupe members repeatedly underlined the need to balance this atmosphere with factual details, because Mohamed's dream was "not a dream but a nightmare with dreamlike overtones."[66] Working toward both objectives required a sense of how realism could function on stage, and the kinds of strategies that could be put to use to evoke that genre while both abstracting from it *and* avoiding overt theatricality. The notes from a 1975 meeting reference an event at the Cartoucherie (the rehearsal and performance space of the Théâtre du Soleil) and further reveal the troupe's increasing insistence on the cultivation of theatrical skills. The note-taker's narrative of what seems to have been an unsatisfying performance elucidates the role of technical competence:

> All forms of struggle implicate the mastering of its techniques. Some fight with submachine guns against the enemy. If they don't know how to use it, the enemy, he will know and shut down their voices.
>
> The same thing when one is fighting on the cultural front [*sur le front culturel*] with the arm of theater (last year's example from the Cartoucherie is clear: at the last minute, the Arab comrades who were present were all enlisted. The result: chaos on the stage. The newspapers the next day: They [Arabs] would do better to learn French before throwing themselves in to the theater).
>
> Every time we forget this, we do our cause a disservice.

> However, careful: "technique" must not be the tree that hides the forest from us. Two things are important to note.
>
> The bulldozer can construct or destruct; it all depends on the driver.
> Technique is not frozen. With our creative imagination, it renews itself.
>
> This concretely implicates a certain way of engaging and investing in order to acquire all the technique to put it at the service of what one wants to say.[67]

In this passage, references to technique were dually significant. On the one hand, artistic technique was necessary to the theatrical struggle. Yet it also had the potential to become a "bulldozer." Mastering the bulldozer, rather than rejecting its extra-daily force entirely, was key to militancy. On the other hand, technique carried broader connotations in the context of immigration; its absence could imply both the absence of a minimum of stage vocabulary (for example, avoiding turning one's back to the audience) *and* adequate knowledge of the French language. The "chaos" at the Cartoucherie revealed that the absence of theatrical technicality could signal a blatantly racist query: could Arab immigrants participate in *any* form of cultural action? Both avowed and disavowed, technique thus encapsulated the basic stakes of an immigrant aesthetic. Immigrant laborer-actors, barred from the domain of the cultural, would inadvertently rely on the visuality of difference. Yet it was this reliance that then drove their desire for technique, belying dissatisfaction with the "enunciation of self." The relationship between expertise and experience, in other words, was far from static, revealing a flexible connection that shifted alongside the materialities of their performance contexts.

La Kahina and Theatrical Self-Work

While Al Assifa's experience with immigrant aesthetics was defined by the members' dually politicized identities as immigrant workers, La Kahina's experience developed in conversation with a different yet equally restrictive duality, their status as women immigrants. During my conversation with founder Amara, I found that La Kahina (like Al Assifa) manifested this duality in the thematic content of their work, as well as through the experience of performing in the militant theater circuit of the 1970s. In ways that both paralleled and exceeded Al Assifa's experience, however, La Kahina members faced a terrain that demanded singular identities, eschewing the forms of plurality highlighted by the era's burgeoning immigrant women's collectives and portrayed by Amara's troupe. A closer look at the challenges that La Kahina faced in depicting the simultaneity of identitarian experience reveals the historically specific constraints on immigrant women's experience in the French public sphere.

During our conversation, Amara noted that she had founded La Kahina in order to bear witness to the gendered dimensions of postwar immigration from North Africa to France. The writer, actor, and director added: "I was frustrated by the discourse that said that in France immigrants are men, they come here to work, they don't come with families, they have one suitcase. How could we show that we exist in this country?"[68] In fact, the mid-1970s witnessed a number of contradictory developments when it came to the question of women in immigration. Familial reunification and the presence of women and children were central to mid-1970s perceptions of the permanence of migrant communities. Yet as Jane Freedman notes, "political representations of immigrants in France . . . often ignored women's varied migratory projects and trajectories."[69] Partly in response to this marginalization, the era witnessed the emergence of a number of immigrant women's collectives, organizations that maintained conversations with but remained autonomous from the larger political movements founded by immigrants. These movements were often oriented toward their constituents' national identities of origin.[70] Amara's choice of the name La Kahina, a nod to the much-mythologized seventh-century Berber warrior, revealed the hybrid position immigrant women activists could occupy in relation to such political formations. On the one hand, they identified with a historical figure from the North African nationalist imaginary and celebrated the story of a woman "who took up arms to defend herself and her people." On the other hand, they repurposed the figure of La Kahina as a symbol for the empowerment of immigrant women, underlining the figure's feminist potential. Despite these multiple investments, however, Amara noted that she felt sequestered among the various collective groupings with which she could identify: Algerian immigrant, woman, second generation, *banlieue* (suburban) youth, and so on. These particular identities experienced their exclusion from their respective universals through practices that were often barred from merging with other forms of mobilization.

Consider the case of Amara's first play, a trilingual production that mixed French, Arabic, and the Berber language Kabyle, *Pour que les larmes de nos mères deviennent une légende* (*So That Our Mothers' Tears Become a Legend*). Debuted in 1976, the play was composed of dimensions of Algerian women's lives in both France and Algeria, with a focus on traditions of forced marriage, repudiation, and divorce, as well as violence and torture during the Algerian War. Amara laughingly described this production as "too visual," since it included imagery that troupe members knew would surprise their immigrant audiences, such as a bedsheet stained with virginal blood on an Algerian couple's wedding night. This example of an "immigrant aesthetic" was enthusiastically invited to a feminist celebration at the era's progressive and experimental Faculté de Vincennes. When the troupe arrived, however, they found that the organizers were reluctant to let the men inside. Amara remembered: "we explained to them that we were a theater troupe and we needed to act, the men had roles, and it was precisely to denounce their roles that they were acting." The show began smoothly, showcasing female actors for the first couple of scenes. However, with the arrival of a scene depicting a French officer torturing an Algerian woman, Philippe Tancelin stepped on to the stage, in the role of the torturer. "The audience began saying," Amara told me, "'Men outside! Men outside!'" The actors' pleas were rejected and the troupe left the stage. Later that day, Amara was watching the press conference that had been arranged to advertise the celebration, when she noticed male press members in the hall. She remembered: "I ran onto the stage, grabbed the microphone and yelled, 'You wouldn't let us speak about the condition of the immigrant woman because we have four male actors, and here, men are everywhere.' From then on, we left the French feminist realm." In relating this anecdote to me, Amara was frustrated with the identity categories she felt "French feminism" upheld. Indeed, these recollections revealed that her troupe's inclusion at Vincennes was premised on a parallel exclusion with regard to the content of the theatrical representation: the celebration's desire to create a space for La Kahina involved censoring the depiction of the gendered violence of French colonialism. The Algerian woman's emancipatory political activity existed among a constellation of related positions, some undertaken by men, and the gendered mixity of this constellation had confounded the spectatorial imagination at Vincennes, pushing spectators to demand Tancelin's absence from the stage.

In retrospect, we can only speculate as to the ephemeral dimensions of this theatrical conflict. After all, the audience's chants had halted a scene featuring the white, French-born Tancelin in the role of colonial torturer. In 1976, such an image may have ignited a whole range of racial identifications and political desires; the affective outpouring of these experiences did not necessarily foreground the complexities of the feminist struggle but rather those of a newly postcolonial polity. Where feminism was in fact concerned, the objections may have been to a theatrical world that presented a victimizer-victim scenario, one in which the French torturer embodied the outermost ring of social suffering to surround the Algerian woman. Tethering what Wendy Brown would call "the political significance of their difference [to the] white masculine middle-class ideal,"[71] was perhaps construed as an attempt to link her social emancipation to his theatrical presence. This male presence differed from those of the reporters, yet their uninhibited entry had outraged Amara, who experienced their refusal of her work as a denial of her community's existence in the French militant landscape.

Immigrant Aesthetics or a Work on the Self?

In many ways, La Kahina's struggles with French feminism resonated with Al Assifa's negotiation of universal categories. Both troupes found that their theatrical work allowed them entry into the era's established idioms for collective militancy: the French proletariat, French feminists, and their rapidly growing repertoire of aesthetic by-products. Both troupes also found, however, that the manner in which these contexts addressed North African immigrant difference placed limitations on how they were to conceptualize their publics, whether aesthetic or ethnic. La Kahina's theatrical work in particular allows insight into how immigrant expression was framed in the public sphere.

For the immigrant women's movements of the 1970s, disentangling the question of gender from existing frameworks of struggle (often class-based or national and anticolonial in orientation) proved challenging. After all, this was a historical moment that had just begun to transfer immigrants' political investments from their countries of origin to their conditions of life in France. Yet immigrant women had to negotiate their relationship with mainstream feminist movements as well, often finding themselves facing what Claudie Lesselier has called "insufficient or ambiguous solidarities."[72] For La Kahina, these ambiguous solidarities resulted in a set of imperatives that were particularly visible in cultural products dealing with immigration: immigrant self-expression was understood as a relationship between performer and spectator, rather than one internal to the persons onstage. Indeed, the refusal at Vincennes assumed that La Kahina's theatrical work primarily engaged those outer rings of social grievance in which the immigrant woman met the French torturer. The fact that La Kahina placed young men of immigrant origin onstage, denouncing the patriarchal structures of their community in front of members of the same immigrant group, went unnoticed. In contrast, the 1979 documentary *Larmes de sang* records La Kahina actors insisting that the significance of their work was in the context of the larger immigrant community: the political project was premised less on the claim to a feminist identity than on the public revelation of new relationships between women and men, mothers and daughters, fathers and sons.[73]

The image of the stained bedsheets was a cornerstone of this effort. When read in relation to the mainstream and exclusionary tendencies of contemporary French feminism, such scenes might resonate with a familiar scenario that solidifies the incommensurability of immigrant difference through reference to sexual oppression. Where La Kahina is concerned, however, this reading would offer only a partial, and somewhat anachronistic, explanation. In contrast, Amara remembered that the scene of the *nuit de noces* or wedding night was both targeted to and drew the most protest from their immigrant audiences. On various occasions, these audiences had called them "prostitutes . . . not from good families, for daring to say what we said." Amara's earlier references to excessive visuality resonate with what the sociologist Adil Jazouli has called a "cultural laboratory."[74] Drawing on interviews with different groups that had been active during the 1970s and 1980s, Jazouli has suggested that immigrant youths' theatrical work "was lived as a rupture, full of doubt, psychological instability, or solitude."[75] Far from the confident cries of a militant machine, troupes like La Kahina provided both actors and spectators with discomforting moments, the stained bedsheets only one in a series of what many, according to Jazouli, considered "a shameful 'strip-tease' "[76] of a marginalized community's strained inner workings. Smiling, Amara remembered during our conversation: "With the blood, my mother was shocked. My mother came to all of our showings and she saw everything, everyone was shocked." Later, she added, "it took a lot of courage to get up on that stage." These comments resonate with what Jazouli has called "a work on the self,"[77] referring to forms of collective social action whose addressee and outcome are less premised on spectatorial identification than on developing an embodied vocabulary with which the self can experience and absorb the "shock" of others.

Framing La Kahina's work via reference to semiotic structures (such as an "immigrant aesthetic") as well as embodied capacities (such as a "work on the self") is useful insofar as it allows us to complicate the dichotomy of personal experience and aesthetic expertise. At the same time, this distinction reveals the limits on immigrant theater's conceptual framing: participants occupy an aesthetic field where they either communicate via token visual signs deemed typical of their racial or ethnic collective (such as the connotations of sexual alterity underlined by the bloody *nuit de noces*) or they are imagined to be engaged in endless iterations of self-work vis-à-vis the (unmarked) French gaze. As Jazouli notes:

> On the one hand, there is the necessity to witness [*témoigner*] and analyze familiar and interpersonal relations, but on the other, there is the need to exit from these old schemes, imposed by a certain "militant" theater, where the immigrant is often presented in a miserable fashion, as a "poor victim of the system."[78]

An actor quoted by Jazouli further maintains that the actors wanted "real theatrical roles" rather than "our 'own roles.' "[79] These comments point to how the distinction between militant or politically engaged theater and theater premised on the display of aesthetic and communicative skill generated a wider field of discursive oppositions in 1970s France. One's "own role" could not transcend the "poor victim" genre, as self-expression necessarily implied the narration of injury. In "real" theater, conversely, the coincidence between actor and role was not the primary axis of engagement with an audience. Militancy, in other words, could not reconcile personal experience and artistic achievement.

Personal Experience vs. Real Theater

Scholarship on La Kahina's work often underlines the perceived power of experience: "Guided by a will to biographic representation and cultural valorization," Jeanne le Gallic writes, "this theater of immigration [referring to La Kahina as well as to 1970s immigrant theater more broadly] is an instance of witnessing the reality of immigration, with all of its elements."[80] Without a doubt, *témoignage* or bearing witness to a certain sliver of social reality is a significant element of this work. Yet the desire to draw a parallel between self-knowledge and the valorization of *culture* remains somewhat opaque. Is the will that underlines public biographic or autobiographic representation the same will that structures a desire to present or valorize a certain collective way of life, whether aesthetic, material, or spiritual? Is the passage from biography to culture, what Anthony Appiah has called the "personal" and the "collective" dimensions of individual identity, simple and unidirectional?[81]

Such questions are preceded by a concern with the status of *experience* more broadly. As Joan W. Scott has noted, experience has occupied an unsteady position in scholarship devoted to historical difference, for it tends to weaken the mechanisms of contestation that accompany the search for knowledge regarding the past. The "authority of experience,"[82] Scott notes, serves as evidence of the truth of difference, while establishing visual input and seeming transparency as the foundation for comprehension. Scott's visibility metaphor is a particularly useful one when considering the case of the theater spectator or historian. Theatrical spectatorship can suffer from a particularly robust propensity to overlook the constructedness of the auditory and visual encounter on offer, even as the practice itself calls attention to its apparatus. Scott's cautions draw attention to the ambiguity of what is learned by those sensory faculties, as well as how that learning can foreclose an examination of the broader social systems that have produced a seemingly *personal* experience. In the context of immigrant theater, an emphasis on the transparency of difference can render *aesthetic frames* irrelevant and beyond reach. Thus, real theater becomes the aesthetic act that escapes the immigrant.

This yearning for real theater, much like Al Assifa's search for technique, was one that Amara knew well. During our conversation she stressed that the troupe's second play, *La Famille Bendjelloul en France depuis 25 ans* (*The Bendjelloul Family, in France for 25 Years*), on generational conflict in an Algerian-French family, was a more professional effort than *Pour que les larmes*. Indeed, *La Famille Bendjelloul* traveled along the networks that had been established with the first play, as well as to Algeria during a summer tour. A professional actor was cast in the central role of the father, and his domination was depicted via methods slightly more conceptual, such as showing the rest of his family as marionettes manipulated by his hand. Nevertheless, La Kahina members often found during their habitual post-show debates that audiences overlooked professionalism. Amara remembered being approached by an older gentleman who wished to speak to her "father," only to find that the actor had washed the white streaks out of his hair and transformed back into his daily self, thus frustrating the audience member who felt implicated and wished to intervene. The fact that Amara still finds herself approached at gatherings as "a La Kahina girl" (*une fille de la Kahina*) is indicative of how overdetermined the contrast between *témoignage* and real theater could be. First, it was assumed that real stage action would be registered as unreal by all involved, which was not uniformly the case. Second, *témoignage* was assumed to be a plea for recognition from French civil society, while doing real theater meant entering an expert domain. Neither assumption correlated with the lived experience of theatrical activity.

Social Work, from *Animation* to *Intégration*

While Al Assifa and La Kahina's theatrical work resonates with the politics of representation that structured the 1970s, their social work further illustrates how the era's cultural policies transitioned from the democratization of access for disadvantaged communities to a concern with their identity and integration into French social life. During the early 1970s, the immigration-saturated Parisian neighborhood of Barbès emerged as an important activist front. Al Assifa presented some of its landmark performances in the neighborhood and sought ways to enter its daily rhythms, both mirroring and modifying the era's principles of *animation culturelle*. Slightly further north in Aubervilliers, La Kahina's theatrical work slowly gave birth to the Association de la Nouvelle Génération Immigrée (ANGI), the Association for a New Immigrant Generation. Founded in the immediate aftermath of the Socialist reforms of 1981, the association's work with local youth reflected both the influence of policy changes on conceptions of immigration and the role of theater in social practice as the decade drew to a close. Considered together, the troupes' social work reflects the tensions that characterized the negotiation of redistributive and identitarian political strategies.

In the early 1970s, Barbès served multiple functions. A site of initiation for newly arrived immigrants, it was also the locus of larger communal gathering for North African populations, particularly on weekends. Moreover, the neighborhood had, since the upheavals of 1968, served as a magnet for militants and intellectuals who wished to understand its tightly knit structure and its relationship to racial violence and the police forces.[83] To Al Assifa, Barbès partook of a different set of "habits," "traditions," "principles," and "freedoms."[84] The familiar formula of "taking a neighborhood, taking the terrain, taking a space" had to be modified, as it had the potential to be experienced by resident communities as a "*coup de force*."[85] Doing theater in Barbès thus meant asking a question that was central to the era's discourses of *animation culturelle*: "What is a true activity of implantation and popular creation in a neighborhood?"[86] As Al Assifa searched for the parameters of such "true activity," however, it was equally cognizant of the forms of solidarity that already structured the neighborhood. Tancelin and Clancy wrote that

> to animate a neighborhood is not to drive a specific content, a program, however eminent it may be. It is far more substantial, and humble, politically, to respond in precise terms to the difficulties that people encounter, the needs that they express and to respond to these along with them. Such neighborhoods might not have any cinema, any center for activities or community/leisure center [*centre de loisirs*]. If certain elements are missing that would help the neighborhood access leisure practices, then these are elements that need to be found together, and constructed.[87]

Taken from *Les Tiers Idées*, this passage illustrated a number of key dynamics. On the one hand, it revealed how Al Assifa merged an *animation* sensibility focused on the creation of leisure practices with the sensitivities of the survey (*enquête*) tradition of May 1968. The survey borrowed a methodology attached to market research yet used it to cull, in Kristin Ross's words, "revolutionary aspirations existing in a latent state, encouraging their expression, then synthesizing them and returning them in the form of political propositions."[88] The approach outlined here resonated with a desire for communal authorship, for leisure practices had to be "found together, and constructed." On the other hand, the passage revealed the contradictions associated with the process of synthesizing and returning to the people of Barbès their own thoughts. While the authors wished to answer the neighborhood's needs "along with them," the leisure practices to be constructed were already somewhat defined: they generally referred to arts practices, *creation* rather than *recreation*. With concrete examples, however, such a distinction itself began to fall apart; arts practices were imagined to cultivate specific kinds of sociability. This was manifested in the authors' desire to turn their neighborhood performance space (borrowed from a local parish, the Salle Saint Bruno), into a regular destination outside of the twice-weekly performances of Al Assifa's second play, *C'est la vie de château, pourvu que ça dure*.

Aware of the hazards of "driving a specific content," yet intent on responding to a specific set of (at times imagined) leisure needs, Al Assifa's negotiations revealed a key dynamic of cultural action in the 1970s. The anti-institutional impulse that underlay "taking the street" nonetheless maintained an ambivalent relationship with the French state, *animation* being a concern that bridged militant activism and the administration of culture. "We would like to insist on terms that will permit us to differentiate such an initiative of animating a neighborhood," wrote Clancy and Tancelin, "from other animations that have been attempted numerous times and that have proceeded from the same intention."[89] Their concerns, however, were ultimately not different from those of other *animateurs*. For example, they emphasized the need to proceed cautiously, for *animation* consisted of "giving the first impulse"[90] and then allowing for these cultural activities (theater, film projections, debates, and weekend festivals) to adapt to the conditions of life in the neighborhood. In fact, this caution mirrored the sensitivities of an assortment of cultural activists, both institutional and independent. As advocates of professional creation and the autonomy of art downplayed the role of *animation,* the perils of the over-involved *animateur* were evoked in a range of contexts, often with differing political orientations.

A good example is the cultural theorist and *animateur* Pierre Gaudibert, who voiced the conundrums of animation as such: "The objective is to help this population to take their own development into their own hands, to master and control its daily life; at the limit, once the impetus is given, it should no longer function as animation, self-management [*autogestion*] being the act of a population that 'animates' itself."[91] Cautioning against a heavy-handed approach, Gaudibert suggested that genuine self-expression and artistic creation were the groundwork for civic participation, that social development was a matter of self-management. His use of the term "self-management," or *autogestion*, referred in part to its usage in contexts like the Lip watch factory strikes, where *autogestion* denoted the institution of workers' committees in the place of the Lip administration. However, references to self-management also resonated with Giscard d'Estaing's neoliberal tendencies, which included withdrawing institutional support from the realm of culture. Debates on *animation*, in other words, masked larger questions on the public use of creativity and self-expression. And activists and administrators often found themselves using analogous terms.

La Kahina's associational work reveals the extent to which the construction of leisure practices and popular expression became connected to self-management as a social goal. In the early 1980s, La Kahina members ceased their theatrical activities and directed their efforts at forming a nonprofit organization, the ANGI. For Amara, this closure was less a comment on the efficacy of theatrical militancy than a direct response to the social reality that troupe members encountered: the precarious situation of young North African women who had fled their homes. In his dissertation on the ANGI's work with these populations, La Kahina member Youcef Boussaa connected theater and social aid:

> Every presentation is followed by a debate, sometimes bitter, between the spectators and the actors/actresses. These debates provide an opportunity for people to narrate their personal experiences, experiences of constraints that were imposed on them, of being runaways, and the outcome of this for both them and their families. These [debates] also constitute a time for meetings, prompted by [the exchange of] secrets and requests for help: "I saw your piece, I recognize myself in it, it's my history, I ran away as well, and now please help me for I am alone, sometimes I feel lost but it has done me good to meet you."

> And so the reality leaves the stage and enters back into the everyday. Thus, it is necessary to respond to these demands, to respond fast and above all respond well, to the degree that that is possible.[92]

Theater, in other words, had the ability to recall and make witness events, sensibilities, and expectations that may or may not have been shared, but whose unfolding could provide the groundwork for communication. When the newly elected Socialist government granted immigrants the right of association in 1981, ANGI applied for associational status. Two years later, they established a hostel that provided temporary residence for North African immigrant women who were runaways.[93]

While associational work replaced theatrical work, a *performance* sensibility nonetheless permeated ANGI's activities. During the summer of 1984, ANGI established a Université d'Été Beur, a summer school for North African immigrant youth from Seine-Saint-Denis, the department situated to the northeast of Paris. Located in the eastern mountain range of the Jura and animated by association members and professionals of North African origin, the goal of the school was to provide "the means for each [student] to develop his or her confidence in themselves by the research of an individual performance."[94] For the Université d'Été Beur, performance implied both social comportment and theatrical enactment. The summer school's pedagogical units began with arts and sports activities, followed by a section titled "Does a social movement exist?" whose subtitles included "Searching for a new communication" and "Creating/inventing new kinds of behaviors" before proceeding to writing and film workshops and culminating in the creation of a theatrical presentation.[95] The goal, Boussaa wrote, was to "attempt to enter or reenter these youth into a global historical dynamic, while taking into account the modifications brought about by immigration,"[96] placing their individual performances in step with those of the society in which they lived.

This language is a good indicator of how the discursive repertoire of the Université responded to changing cultural imperatives. In the early 1980s, personal expression and personal performance were increasingly placed in the service of professionalizing the desires and comportments of immigrant youth imagined to be "in a state of failure."[97] François Mitterand's wide-ranging reform platform included a political agenda now referred to, in shorthand, as *droit à la différence*: the state's recognition of cultural plurality and the right to difference. When it came to the question of immigration, a significant component was the lifting of the ban on immigrants' right of association. Although driven less by a desire to rethink republican universalism than to control the French state's relationship to existing forms of cultural and ethnic mobilization, this shift nonetheless merged with developments like the 1983 antiracist protest Marche de Beurs to co-create a new era of immigration politics. The term "Beur" (the inverse of the French *Arabe*), and more specifically the Beur movement, denoted the variety of political projects that had begun to emerge from within second and third-generation North African communities at the dawn of the new decade.

Droit à la différence reverberated in the cultural realm as well. Vincent Dubois identifies the practical initiatives that were designed to broaden and decentralize the parameters of legitimate artistic production as "cultural rehabilitation" projects geared to jump-start "integration."[98] While cultural practices continued to be linked to the issue of social justice, terms like *autogestion,* or the self-management of populations, were replaced with references to *individual* integration. As the management of immigration shifted from an emphasis on the welfare and labor conditions of immigrant working classes to their cultural identity and integration into French social life, "an elite stratum arising from within the Maghrebi minority"[99] was increasingly charged with privileging individual identity over collectivity, diffusing ethnic communalism and facilitating social integration.[100] ANGI's militants were neither state-appointed nor recent transplants to Seine-Saint-Denis; they possessed a far more organic connection to the needs of northeastern Parisian *banlieue* populations. Yet the turn to the primacy of the individual, and of that individual's social performance, revealed that ANGI's conceptual strategies resonated with the era's emergent "cultural policy of integration."[101]

Conclusion

What, then, were the emergent theatrical sensibilities of this new era? Published in 1984, Chérif Chikh and Ahsène Zehraoui's *Le Théâtre Beur* provides a few clues. The volume, one of the few that documents theatrical texts from the period, contains the scripts of three plays that were written and performed by North African immigrant youth during the late 1970s and early 1980s, often in associational contexts. In his preface, Guy Jacquet wrote:

> Actors. They want to be actors. This doesn't necessarily have to do with theater but simply with no longer being objects of our indifference, of our contempt or, even better, of our "benevolence." The actors of their lives. This is what they would like to be first. And because acting also means climbing onto a stage, speaking out [*prendre la parole*], they will also be that kind of actor. But their theatrical reality is that the two kinds are intimately related.[102]

In their introduction, Chikh and Zehraoui echoed Jacquet's themes, adding that "what animates the girls and boys making up these troupes is a profound desire to narrate stories [*raconter*], to narrate their own stories [*se raconter*], a desire to analyze and denounce."[103] Although these comments echo Al Assifa and La Kahina's earlier articulations, in retrospect, it is equally clear that a new set of terms are being privileged. First, *prendre la rue* (taking the streets) has given way to *prendre la parole* (speaking out). The basic idiom of theatrical immigration activism has transformed from a May 1968 sensibility making a claim for public space to an emphasis on self-narration that presents *personal speechmaking* as political action. Indeed, the following chapter will examine the contemporary manifestation of these dynamics through a focus on the prevalence of personal narrative in contemporary immigrant women's theater. Second, Jacquet positions theatrical agency and social agency as parallel projects and both require spectators that are referenced via the plural possessive "our." Being an actor is indelibly linked to the presence of an unmarked white French audience, one whose celebration of agency no longer seems to reference collective solidarities. Instead, the focus is firmly on self-expression and personal identity.

Without proposing too strict a contrast, it is worth remembering that Al Assifa and La Kahina emerged at a time when the links between theater, immigration, and immigrant identity were only beginning to sediment, generating complicated and contradictory impulses. While both troupes professed to belong to a variety of universalizing categories, such belonging was often ruptured by the particularity of their North African identity. At times, this rupture resulted in a desire to further highlight the racial or ethnic particularity of the performing immigrant body and the "family recognition" that it had the potential to generate for immigrant audiences; at others, it necessitated the turn to a discourse of technique that could shed the particularity of a "poor victim" theater by way of professional expertise. Professionalism itself remained a contested domain, as the parameters of artistic and social work resonated with centralized practices and the French state's cultural policies, rendering anti-institutionalism an ambivalent claim. Finally, these policies changed from prioritizing the invigoration of communities to positioning artistic self-expression as a rehabilitative practice that could secure self-management and social integration, fundamentally altering the principles framing immigrant expression in the public sphere.

The manner in which Al Assifa and La Kahina negotiated this complicated, transitioning terrain cautions against positing too seamless a history for immigration activism utilizing the theater. Yet Al Assifa and La Kahina also complicate a theater historical narrative that often positions 1970s French theater as dominated by the self-determining, heteronomous spirit of collective creation. This is not to say that the troupes' works were not improvisational or communal in nature, but that the explanatory models to which they turned did not always correspond to the proper objects of theater history. While collective creation could be considered novel within a theatrical lineage whose precursors were single-authored works, it was perhaps less of an innovation when positioned against a history of messy, flexible, and collaborative political and cultural action. Similarly, heteronomous artistic practice undid the authorial stability of the theatrical script, yet immigrant actor-agents dealt with both theatrical and social scripts that already placed them at a distance from an autonomous ideal. In other words, 1970s France harbored a range of relationships between theatrical creativity and collectivity. By accentuating their specific sociopolitical imaginaries, Al Assifa and La Kahina reveal the complexity of engaging in immigrant aesthetics at a time when both immigration and aesthetics evolved in rich, multidimensional ways.

Chapter 2

✦

Prendre la Parole

In an early moment from the popular stage actress Rachida Khalil's one-woman show, *La Vie rêvée de Fatna* (*Fatna's Dream Life*), the young Moroccan woman Fatna boasts to her neighbor that her husband is off arranging visas for them to immigrate to France. Their destination, she notes enthusiastically, is "the country of the rights of man."[1] Undeterred by her invisible neighbor's blasé reaction, she repeats the phrase and adds that in France "a word that is given is a word that is respected" (*une parole donnée est une parole respectée*). As she utters this line, Khalil releases a peal of laughter that breaks the imagined wall separating the diegetic world from the auditorium and reveals the Moroccan-French actress's own amusement at Fatna's assertion. France, the country of the rights of man? France, the land where a word given is a word kept? Over the course of *La Vie rêvée de Fatna*, these assertions are both evacuated and confirmed as the show counterposes Khalil's alter ego, the emancipated Moroccan-French actress Karima, and her childhood friend and aunt Fatna, whose parallel life in a small village in the mountains of Rif haunts her for illustrating what her own path could have been: an arranged marriage during her teenage years, early motherhood, and limited participation in public life. Needless to say, the show is rife with the problems that underline the binary positioning of these two women, yet it is also often the first to question it, pushing both stereotypes to their limits. Fatna's emotional life proves richer than the imagination of the producers with whom Karima battles for non-typecasted roles, and the country of human rights is depicted as presiding over a crumbling and cruel welfare system. Given this commentary, Khalil's amusement at the suggestion that in France "a word that is given is a word that is respected" can be read as a reference to the nation's unkept promise to its immigrant population. Yet the line also begs to be read in a self-referential manner, highlighting the premise of the performance itself: that the words given out to the audience will be *kept* and respected by them, "integrated into public memory and social knowledge in such a way that, directly or indirectly, it will make a material difference."[2]

Khalil's ambivalent commentary on the theatrical "word" foreshadows a series of dynamics at the intersection of immigration, personal narrative, and theatrical performance in early twenty-first-century Paris. In the phrase "*une parole donnée est une parole respectée*," the term *parole* constitutes a reference to a word that is given, a promise that has been made. The term's everyday usage, however, can vary from designating the literal *words* that exit the mouth of a speaker to that individual's *speech* more broadly, the particular snippets of communication that they send into the world. In certain instances, it can designate the sum total of the communication that that individual has with the world, a sphere that is assumed to have an authoritative link to that individual's interiority and that thus references a meaning akin to an individual's *voice* (as in the phrase "I want my voice to be heard"). Over the course of my research on immigration and theater in Paris, the phrase *prendre la parole* (literally "taking the word," or taking speech) was one that I encountered often. Depending on the context and the emotional force with which it was spoken, I translated the phrase as speaking, speaking up, taking the floor, making one's voice heard, and seizing speech. The connotations that *prendre la parole* could carry thus ran from a reference to an enunciated word to the entirety of a person being thrust into the public eye, an experience often glossed as synonymous with that person's experience of their personal agency. In turn, this wide spectrum was reflected in the ease with which theatrical orality was endowed with moral meaning, and nowhere more so than in immigrant women's theater.

The polyvalence of *parole* is central to this chapter's claim regarding the relationship between immigration, gender, and theatrical performance. Indeed, my argument is that immigrant women's theater in early twenty-first-century Paris endowed performed personal speech with an imagined urgency, and identified public recognition as its moral mandate. In the process, self-narration, racialization, and theatrical and moral spectatorship were linked in specific ways: personal narrative performance, particularly when undertaken by a racialized woman, was imagined to be driven by the urgency of that woman's suffering. Performance, however, also served as the vehicle for this suffering's remedy. As a public venue, it guaranteed an acknowledgment of this pain and also signaled the speaker's liberation from it, allowing her to accede to universal personhood. Personal narrative performance, in other words, was premised on the tensions of universality and particularity.

In many ways, this joining of narrativity and urgency may not seem particularly worthy of note. As Susan E. Chase has noted, research on personal narrative has drawn attention to the political functions of narrativity, both to underline the often unequal distribution of storytelling privileges and to highlight the process by which narrative inquiry has been included within the fold of academic research. Where narrativity and political praxis meet, Chase notes, is in the "urgency" of narrative: "the urgency of speaking, the urgency of being heard, the urgency of collective stories, and the urgency of public dialogue."[3] This has been particularly true with regard to populations whose access to public dialogue has historically been compromised. In proposing to think through the imaginary of urgency that undergirds immigrant women's theater in France, my goal is not to undermine the relationship between narrative and social justice. Rather, I hope to show that attributions of urgency and necessity may themselves be motivated by highly complicated political impulses that deserve closer attention. The category of the "urgent" is hardly transhistorical; therefore, what is understood to function as imperative speech at any given moment reveals as much about its cultural context as it does about the inherent significance of its narrative content. Since the specific form of urgent personal speech in question here is personal narrative performance, my discussion will dovetail with theoretical approaches in performance studies that have been concerned with the imperative to perform, whether that imperative is connected to the question of performance's live immediacy or its political efficacy.[4]

In what follows, I focus on two contexts: the Festival au Féminin, an annual women's arts festival run by professional artists; and Paroles de Femmes, an amateur theater workshop that was organized by the civic association Accueil Goutte d'Or (AGO) or Goutte d'Or Welcome. Of significance is the fact that both theater practices have taken place in the Goutte d'Or. A Paris neighborhood of historic significance for postwar immigration, the Goutte d'Or's identity has shifted in recent years from its traditional North African connotation to one that underlines the heterogeneity of immigration to France. Equally known for its history of civic activism, the neighborhood has been at the center of immigrants' rights struggles, from attracting prominent intellectuals to the immigrant cause in the aftermath of May 1968 to serving as the site of the 1996 occupation that carried undocumented immigrants' struggle into the French headlines. When I visited Goutte d'Or in 2008, the neighborhood had been designated a *zone urbaine sensible*. Referencing an at-risk territory marked by high levels of unemployment and unsatisfactory housing conditions, the *zone urbaine sensible* offered a political framework for renewed state subsidies, and channeled this funding from the state toward local associations.[5] The Goutte d'Or was thus an exemplary site through which to examine how broader public discourses on women and immigration not only emerged within but also shaped theatrical and civic practices.

The theater company Graines de Soleil was founded in the Goutte d'Or by the Moroccan artist Khalid Tamer in 1998 with an interest in creating a workshop, Paroles de Femmes, that would function as a self-expression atelier and language course for immigrant women living in the neighborhood. Over the years, Paroles de Femmes came under the joint coordination of a number of Goutte d'Or associations and found its main home with the AGO.[6] Meanwhile, the annual performance by workshop participants served as the seed of what eventually became the Festival au Féminin in 2003. While these performance contexts are institutionally and geographically linked, their juxtaposition also highlights the different meanings with which personal narrative performance can be endowed. For the professional artists who perform in the Festival au Féminin, the moral significance of performed personal speech is negotiated in a context where the stakes are largely audience-oriented and aesthetic. In contrast, the AGO is interested in what personal narrative performance can cultivate in the immigrant women who become amateur performers. Their concerns thus lie with the embodied, rather than the symbolic, work of performance. Drawing on interviews, performance texts, and promotional and associational materials, my goal is to explore the range of meanings with which personal narrative performance is endowed in these contexts.

In doing so, I address two of the themes that emerge throughout this book. First, immigrant women's theater evokes the dynamic of universality and particularity that is central to French republicanism. In republican thought, humanity is abstract, universal, and hostile to cultural, religious, or ethnic particularisms that run the risk of mediating the relationship between French citizens and the state. As a number of scholars have argued, however, particularity is also what gives universality its purchase, its ability to gesture at a universal human.[7] Immigrant women's theater provides an especially useful venue through which to trace how French republican universalism accommodates difference. Second, immigrant women's theater often positions performance as a phenomenon that cultivates particular kinds of subjects and the theater as a space of subject formation. In other words, what is at stake in these performance projects is often not a mere representation of self, premised on the referential functions of personal narrative. Rather, the discourse surrounding immigrant women's theater is often about the disciplining of a particular kind of self, a self for whom public, personal speech can entail a transformed world. "That is," in Kristin Langellier's terms, "personal narrative performance *constitutes* identities and experience, producing and reproducing that to which it refers."[8] Taken together, these themes allow us to ask a number of questions: Why have narratives of suffering become key to the forms of recognition that immigrant women's theater is imagined to engender and what are the genres that have been deemed appropriate for such a project? What is the relationship between these theatrical genres and the broader shifts in representations of race and ethnicity in early twenty-first-century France? And finally, how is the project of theatrical self-cultivation related to the themes that have emerged at the intersection of gender and immigration? To answer these questions, I begin by tracing the dynamics of the Festival au Féminin. In the second part of the chapter I will turn to the work of Paroles de Femmes in the context of Accueil Goutte d'Or.

The Festival au Féminin and Direct Speech

The Festival au Féminin is a weeklong event scheduled around March 8, International Women's Day, and dedicated to showcasing women in the performing arts. When I visited the Goutte d'Or in 2008, Graines de Soleil was producing the festival's fifth installment. This included concerts, dance, poetry readings, and story hours as well as theatrical performances, many of which were based on workshops conducted with women in underserved neighborhoods and shaped by their narratives of labor, marriage, domestic violence, and immigration. One such performance was an episodic piece that the playwright Angela had constructed from the many women's narratives that she and her company had collected since the early 2000s. The piece was performed by professional actors and interwove vignettes based on personal narratives with a variety of other kinds of literature. These included UN protocols about discrimination against women, statements regarding women from French literary figures such as Émile Zola, international statistics on conjugal violence and rape, an explanation of non-Western cultural practices involving women (for example, the *sati* tradition of self-immolation), and controversial excerpts on femininity from religious texts. The personal narratives left their speaker's identity ambiguous; however, they at times carried comments that would presumably be taken as signs of the speaker's non-French origin, such as a reference to illiteracy or to the village of one's youth where one is made to marry at the age of eleven. Throughout, one of the actors periodically recited the proper physical comportment for women, while demonstrating and parodying bodily stances from a humbly perched sitter to a demure greeting. Additionally, a number of these episodes were labeled "Interlude-Game" (*Interlude-Jeu*) and structured with a call-and-response aesthetic. For example, the actor would read an excerpt from a holy text that stressed hair covering for pious women, then turn expectantly to the audience, who would proceed to offer the names of religious texts until they could identify the correct one. During the 2008 performance that I attended, the largely female and largely native French audience's sighs, gasps, and audible disapprovals permeated the soundscape of the performance, concluding in a round of fervent applause that reverberated in the small theater of the Lavoire Moderne Parisien, a Goutte d'Or institution partnered with the Graines de Soleil.

In many ways, the heterogeneity of the performance's episodic structure set the parameters for the kind of moral condemnation that it could cultivate in its audience. The juxtaposition of census data and statistics, canonical texts, and personal narratives entered particular articulations of gender into a larger historical process. Violence done to women was rooted in the beginnings of divinely narrated history and presently identified most sensationally, albeit hesitantly, in the non-Western world. This trajectory not only implied continuity between culturally and historically diverse instances of women experiencing discrimination or violence, it also positioned the intended audience, political imaginary, and ethical configuration of each of these texts, traditions, or experiences as synonymous. In short, Angela's text resonated with a tendency that Chandra Talpade Mohanty has identified as "ethnocentric universalism."[9] Talpade Mohanty refers here to feminist scholarship that stresses the "universal cross-cultural operation of male dominance and female exploitation," thereby positing femininity and masculinity as homogeneous, binary givens that precede their formulation in any specific historical or political moment.[10] The play's episodic structure revealed just such an approach, chronicling varied experiences of injustice into a grand narrative of misogyny.

Angela's near-taxonomic approach to the history of women's exploitation revealed a universalizing tendency, yet equally interesting was the manner in which difference was made to emerge *within* this portrait of uniform oppression. For example, certain personal narratives were left unmarked by the speaker's racial or ethnic identity, while others explicitly beckoned a contextualized reading (i.e., the unmarked narrative told of an individual's struggle with an abusive partner, while a marked narrative told of a *culture* of forced marriage). The juxtaposition of universal and particular was further mapped onto the bodies of the four actors. Three of the women in Angela's play were white, while a fourth was of North African origin and it was she who often delivered narratives of forced marriage and illiteracy. The universality of female suffering, in other words, was nonetheless materialized through bodies that were racially marked as particular.

While I was initially tempted to interpret these artistic choices as the blind spots of "ethnocentric universalism," a closer look at Angela's use of *personal narrative* revealed a more complicated understanding of the relationship between pain, universality, and performance. Indeed, Angela's emphasis on personal narrative stemmed from her interest in the theatrical force of what she termed "direct speech." For Angela, direct speech was speech that identified its source as its protagonist. During my conversation with Angela, I found that although the attribution of directness to an individual onstage involved the recognition of particularity, the delivery of direct speech could also serve as evidence of that individual's ability to function as a universal representation. Performance, in other words, was conceptualized as both the presentation of particularity and the vehicle for particularity's erasure. It is worth taking a closer look at this understanding, for it reflects both theatrical and political tendencies that I repeatedly encountered among artists working on immigration.

An experienced actor, director, and playwright, Angela had worked in both highly prestigious theatrical institutions and in the Parisian *banlieue* with, in her words, "a working population of multicultural origins." Her interest in violence done to women had been a constant throughout her career, leading her to identify what she called a kind of "pure theater" premised on the urgency of speech:

> When speech or words that are staged arise out of a necessity to speak and also come from the person who is speaking, a person who

> wants to express all of this, and not from the words of another, but with urgency from the speaker herself . . . what results is much better than the work of professional actors on a piece of fiction.

As these comments immediately make clear, "pure theater" was premised on a rather unique actor-spectator exchange. On the one hand, it was comprised of the personal narrative of an actor who *desired* public self-expression. On the other, it required an audience with the capacity to recognize the actor's narrative *as* personal, as opposed to the scripted "words of another." If both criteria were fulfilled, the anticipated artificiality of theatrical narrative could be interrupted by a personal story. In turn, the power of this performance could exceed "the work of professional actors on a piece of fiction." Pure theater, in other words, was premised on a performance of authenticity with both social and aesthetic stakes: it involved the public recognition of an urgent speech act, and it entailed the aesthetic pleasure of absorbing a "sincere" and thus transparent (calling to mind here Lionel Trilling's seminal definition of sincerity as the transfer of inner experience into spoken words)[11] artwork.

As our conversation continued, it became clear that this performance of authenticity carried a racial dimension. Angela noted that the performance of urgent speech could prompt an entry into a universal narrative, "reciting a history that can itself recite many other histories." Universality referenced a tale's ability to "address everyone" present in the room, while also belonging to a speaker who sidestepped the imperatives of traditional theatrical representation. To illustrate this dynamic, Angela drew on her experience working with amateur performers in the *banlieue*:

> For example, a woman who performed a Kabyle [the language spoken by North African Berbers] song is not entering a relationship of representation, but she is in a relationship to direct speech [*la parole directe*], which is at the same time, you see, a beautiful moment of presentation.

These remarks were striking for the way in which the urgency of an individual's implied suffering (and the desire for public self-expression that was imagined to follow from it) were saturated with *difference*. The aesthetic effect (the "beauty") of pure theater or direct speech was best illustrated through reference to a North African woman. To make matters more complicated, in the performance example that Angela gave, the Kabyle song was untranslated. Thus it followed that for a native French audience, its narrative content and the singer's identity could only be allied in a vague manner, its presumed directness anchored in an ambiguous sense of a human already assembled prior to the speech act in question. Put differently, direct speech was not necessarily a reference to *comprehensible* speech. Rather, it was speech that *is imagined to have originated* in the speaker's lived experience, resulting in a stage presence that Angela labeled both "beautiful" and designated as superior to the work of professional actors on a piece of fiction.

If the audience's imagination was central to their understanding of this directness on the stage, its role was further clarified for me when it became clear that Angela's references to direct speech were not concerned with factual accuracy. Indeed, during her theater workshops, Angela reassured her participants that the theatrical stage was a space that was "sacred and imagined." She added: "I do not want to know the reality of what you are saying, I don't want to know if it is true or not." Rather, Angela's interest lay first in understanding what formal qualities and genre conventions would guarantee the illusion of direct speech and second, what direct speech would secure for both speaker and spectator, namely a sense that the directness in question signaled a universal experience, detached from the racialized identity pronouncing it.

Angela's interest in the formal aspects of staging personal narrative was also important for her understanding of the relationship between actors and spectators. For her, the audience's recognition of a universal experience did not require a factual story, nor its authentic speaker. Rather, of significance was the *skilled delivery* of that story, a delivery that sought a nonrepresentational ideal all the while displaying the physical and emotional dexterity of the thespian. Thus, in her contribution to the Festival au Féminin, Angela had worked with professional actors to portray her workshop participants' narratives. The expressive potential of pure theater posed a significant challenge for the professional actor: finding a set of aesthetic and disciplinary practices through which stage *professionals* could cultivate the nonrepresentational presence of the orator of direct speech.[12]

The Theatrical Voice and Interculturalism

During the months that followed my conversation with Angela, I found that there were multiple ways to contextualize her comments. From a theater historical perspective, Angela's references to *la parole directe* could be placed in conversation with what some scholars have labeled a theater of *la parole*.[13] In commenting on late twentieth- and early twenty-first-century French writing for the stage, theater scholars have referenced the prominence of *la parole* to draw attention to a renewed narrativity in playwriting. Indeed, theatrical textuality is often depicted as having "fallen from grace since the mid-twentieth century,"[14] a victim of trends toward collective creationism and total theater in the 1970s as well as of the broader avant-garde suspicion of language that has resulted in a "postdramatic" theater.[15] Yet scholars like Jean-Pierre Ryngaert and Clare Finburgh note that the renewed attention to voice, lengthy monologues, and conversational excess in the plays of Valère Novarina, Michel Vinaver, and Bernard-Marie Koltès has freed speech from its realist responsibilities even as it has allowed the audience an anchor: in Ryngaert's words, "although utterances no longer build up monolithic identities, a pragmatic analysis of the speech exchanged nevertheless makes it possible to make out identifying profiles, roles, and positions—all in continual interplay."[16] Finburgh credits Valère Novarina in particular with repurposing the theatrical voice in a way that both resists realism and draws attention to its sensuality, adding that for Novarina (as for earlier practitioners like Antonin Artaud) "the actor's voice is appreciated for its immediate concrete materiality, not just for its ability to communicate semantic signification and teleological diegesis."[17]

In many ways, Angela's *la parole directe* participated in the same theatrical project. The playwright's contribution to the Festival au Féminin brought together a variety of narrative voices that remained identifiable even as their plurality resisted a concrete space of utterance. Likewise, the piece developed a story, but without recourse to a logical, linear narrative development. As significant as these parallels were, however, I found over the course of my conversations in Paris that the frequency with which I came across aesthetic choices like Angela's revealed a more complicated relationship between "concrete materiality" and "semantic signification." In fact, far from standing in opposition to one another, I often found that in situations like that of Angela's North African woman, the materiality or musicality of the body/voice and its signification were directly related, and the performer's materiality itself was, to borrow a formulation from Judith Butler, "demarcated in discourse."[18] That is to say that Angela's approach to the Kabyle song posited it first and foremost *as* material and therefore non-signifying. Yet this "concrete materiality" (or physical presence) nonetheless did diegetic work, as it told the story of a somewhat essentialized yet equally ambiguous particularity. Understanding these dynamics requires reference to a slighly different theoretical frame, as well as a different genealogy of French theater history.

How did artists situate women's personal narrative performance in relation to the question of universality and particularity? What I found over the course of my conversations was that in theater like Angela's, the particular performer's claim to universality did not entail what some critics of universalism have called assimilation. Rather, it established universality *as a condition of particularity,* and vice versa. In other words, the tension between universality and particularity structured the model of inclusion proposed by women's personal narrative performance. In this scheme, racial or ethnic difference was often positioned to enlarge the scope of an already known and grieved fact: gender inequality. But difference could also be recuperated as evidence of sameness, even as it began to test the boundaries of ethnocentric universalism, thus revealing that gender is not an ahistorical given but a construct best understood in a specific sociohistorical context. The passage from universality to particularity, in other words, was contingent on the simultaneous production of difference and sameness. This dynamic is equally central to Angela's other theater historical precedent: the lengthy, complicated history that is often studied beneath the heading of theatrical interculturalism.

Indeed, the illustration of nonrepresentational theatrical presence through the body of a non-Western woman can be traced to an era that Ric Knowles calls the "heyday of interculturalism in the West":[19] European modernism's flirtation with the aesthetic and cultural forms of non-Western and pre-historic peoples. In the domain of theater and performance, modernism revealed a particularly primitivist tendency, one which joined a fascination with the seeming alterity of the ritual practices of non-Western cultures with an expectation that these practices also revealed evidence of underlying, universal human commonalities. A central figure in this genealogy, the writer, actor, and director Antonin Artaud, sheds light on the intellectual history that precedes Angela's formulations. As a young actor in the early 1920s, Artaud trained with the famed actor and director Charles Dullin, an artist who maintained respect for dramatic literature but also introduced his students to a variety of corporeally inclined theater traditions. A decade later, Artaud's own aesthetic tendencies had matured, ignited in part by his encounter with a Balinese dance troupe at the Paris Colonial Exposition of 1931. Designed to illustrate the breadth and diversity of western Europe's imperial holdings, the Colonial Exposition presented Artaud with performers that he would later liken to "animated hieroglyphs."[20] Rather than functioning as the vehicles of a dramatic text or the depositories of an intricately psychologized character, these actors generated "the sense of a new physical language based on signs rather than words,"[21] meant to be encountered in a logographic and sensory manner rather than a representational, intellectual one.

Artaud's deep admiration for this theatrical language resulted in prescriptions for his Western contemporaries. He advised his readers that "the Orientals have something to teach us in matters of reality,"[22] that "our theater would do well . . . to ask the Balinese Theater for a lesson in spirituality."[23] As he contrasted the mysticism of Balinese theater with the seemingly dry, literary realism of modern Western theater, Artaud coupled this distancing with a move emblematic of the brand of primitivism that followed the First World War. He noted that the "gestures" of the Balinese hieroglyph were "mysterious signs which correspond to some fabulous and obscure reality that we Westerners have definitely repressed."[24] Invoking the layered, palimpsestic model of the human psyche favored by his earlier colleagues the Surrealists, Artaud identified Balinese gestures as mysterious but also familiar, frolicking somewhere within the collective Western unconscious yet too submerged to be accessed by the fragmented postwar individual.

Artaud's interwar reflections were by no means a direct reference point for the moral-political model of theater invoked by Angela. As Kimberly Jannarone has noted, Artaud's influence in France has largely been within the domain of "radical theory" rather than "radical theater."[25] During my conversations in Paris, however, I found that although personal narrative performance was not modernist in its historical or political imaginary, it recycled the formal tendencies of modernist performance. Rebecca Schneider has noted that aesthetic representations of femininity and primitiveness were central to the "primal, visceral connection"[26] promised to the alienated viewer of modernism. Likewise, in early twenty-first-century immigrant women's theater, the visuality of gender and racial difference was central to the imagined purity and directness of personal narrative performance. Angela's example of *direct* speech was in fact opaque: a Kabyle song that would not allow non-Kabyle speakers to establish the desired alignment between sound and image. The Kabyle song thus functioned in a way that stressed its sensory, rather than conceptual, potential. The imagined "truth" of its speaker could be read into this unmediated sensory encounter, establishing the North African performer *as* a hieroglyph.

When framed via French theater's lengthy history of experimentation with interculturalism, references to the universality of the North African woman push us to ask another kind of question: what is at stake in the positing of this human commonality? Given that it is the very unintelligibility and difference of her song that establishes her pure and unmediated presence in the theatrical encounter, we might note that it is precisely this difference that allows the audience to imagine her as a universal figure. Critics of universalism in modern aesthetic practices have identified the turn to universality as an assimilationist move. For example, Julie Stone-Peters notes that "Western description of non-Western performance as 'universal' is merely a disguised form of orientalism, for in the identification of the likeness of other and self (the likeness of deep structural patterns, the likeness of emotion, the likeness of spiritual force), those ostensible 'others' are simply assimilated."[27] Hal Foster's widely circulated critique of the New York Museum of Modern Art's 1984 exhibition on "'Primitivism' in Twentieth Century Art" is similar: both scholars underline the ethnocentrism intrinsic to positing an all-embracing universal humanity. Such critical moves are both crucial and complicated, often inviting criticism for having engaged in a parallel re-instantiation of "the absolute rupture and transgression of the primitive."[28] My suggestion is that the critical continuum that runs from "likeness" to "rupture" risks sidestepping the political imaginary of artists working on immigration in contemporary France. What I found over the course of my research in Paris was that universality and particularity were forced to remain in constant tension, rendering difference thinkable on the condition of its assimilability, but likewise rendering human sameness representable on the condition of doing so through difference.

Grappling with Difference

If theatrical interculturalism is one context for considering the relationship between women's personal narrative performance and the question of universality, an equally important framework is the broader tension between French republican universalism and racial difference. Theater like Angela's is directly influenced by late twentieth-century French racial discourses, even as it modifies them. Indeed, the tension between universality and particularity in the discussion of the North African woman is emblematic of a broader trend in representations of women and immigration in France. Immigrant women are often viewed through the filter of an imagined, particular violence that both endears them to the compassionate viewer *and* tinges their difference with a threat that is diffused when their experience of violence is reframed as a *universal* reality. This dynamic is well captured in a 2008 interview where Graines de Soleil founder Khalid Tamer comments on the Festival au Féminin's ongoing success. "Above all," the artist notes, "the Festival has grown increasingly open, without communitarianism."[29] Tamer's use of the term "communitarianism" is linked to its recent usage in French integration debates, where it refers to suggestions that immigrants are more committed to autonomous cultural/religious identities than they are to the national community. This comment is striking, for the festival's original installments were focused on the arts of Tamer's own background, North Africa. Yet this rejection of communitarianism has less to do with a denial of difference than with a climate that has equated communitarianism with racism. This requires some unpacking.

The political imaginary of French republicanism has historically been premised on the absence of racial discourses. Humanity is universal and abstract and is wary of the particular attachments that might be occasioned by racial, religious, or regional identities. Although immigration has certainly complicated this picture, it is precisely in the domain of citizenship that universalism is still taken to manifest its promise. National belonging is rooted in political participation and assimilation via national institutions, rather than in an ethno-cultural identity. Race, in other words, is positioned as irrelevant to French identity and in turn is considered central to the communitarian American model to be avoided: "a frightening terrain of warring multiculturalism."[30] In recent decades, however, the racialization of French identity has taken increasingly complicated turns, a development often traced to the emergence of a discourse of *antiracism*. During the early 1980s, the newly elected Socialist government's reform practices were characterized by a vision of France as a multicultural melting pot.[31] Responding to the forms of ethnic mobilization and demands for political rights already emerging from second and-third generation immigrant communities (largely North African in origin), the Socialists positioned these particular affirmations as part of a broader, universal struggle *against racism*. Organizations like SOS Racisme and France Plus, which began as civic efforts but were rapidly incorporated into the government, were largely responsible for setting the political culture of a new, antiracist and anti-communitarian era. Scholars have since suggested, however, that they often linked the struggle against discrimination to the necessity of integration, intimating that "the best way to defend oneself against racism was to avoid behavior drawing attention to differences from the French 'norm.' "[32] Racism, meanwhile, emerged as the central axis for understanding social injustice. For example, the organizations' central slogan "Don't touch my buddy!" (*Touche pas à mon pote!*) positioned the act of being a racialized other's "buddy" as exemplary of citizenly relationships. Racial or ethnic otherness from the "norm" was intimately bound to victimization and suffering, and antiracism was positioned as a relationship that native French subjects could have with one another *on behalf of* nonnative ones.[33]

Not surprisingly, the representations that accompanied antiracism mirrored these dynamics. Pierre Tevanian has highlighted the representational trope of the nonnative, nonwhite French resident, a figure whose emancipation serves as the groundwork for generating community and resolve over brutality.[34] Yet the link between racism and communitarianism in Tamer's comments draws on a number of further developments. In recent years, the dichotomy between antiracism and racism has evolved, with each end of the contrast acquiring new resonances. "Are you universalist or differentialist? Republican or communitarian?" asks Eric Fassin, adding, "Today in France, reflections on racisms and races are most often organized around this conventional opposition."[35] Indeed, the prevailing assumption that the republic has failed to integrate a multicultural polity has increasingly resulted in semantic maneuvers that link signs of *communautarisme* to racism. For example, in the aftermath of the suburban demonstrations of 2005 that protested police violence and unemployment, participating youth were initially accused of communitarian tendencies, then labeled *racists* undertaking "anti-republican pogroms" (*pogroms antirépublicains*).[36] In such a climate, the antiracist position of the early 1980s has been reformulated as a renewed respect for the republic[37] while the racism in question has been attributed to Arab or black youth residing on the peripheries of metropolitan areas. These racial categories are typically textured with what has been called the new Islamophobia,[38] a criminalization of Muslims that increasingly employs a securitarian logic.

However, these stigmas are complex, and they resonate with the question of universality in immigrant women's theater. On the one hand, antiracism has wed the acknowledgment of racial difference to a discourse of victimization. On the other, public affirmations of ethnic belonging can be considered *threatening*. The best example of this dual characterization has been the young woman wearing a headscarf, a figure that has been at the center of French public discourse on immigration since 1989. At times, her headscarf is a symbol of her victimization at the hands of Islamic norms and patriarchal oppression. At others, the headscarf is a sign of her freely undertaken attempt at communitarian separatism and racism.[39] Theatrical performance, like a variety of other media, has contributed to the repertoire of representations fueling this dynamic. What I have suggested about women's personal narrative performance is that it provides a space where this threat is contained by recuperating her imagined suffering as a universal experience. At the same time, the fact that this universality is illustrated through a racialized body contributes to a tendency where, in Miriam Ticktin's words, "violence can be spoken and heard only in certain terms and spaces, requiring specific culturally and racially marked performances."[40] Commenting on how sexual violence has gained visibility in France, Ticktin notes that gender difference and sexual injury are often recognized in relation to other forms of racial or religious particularity, thus revealing "contemporary French republican universalism as a practice that can accommodate difference only in an exceptional, discretionary manner."[41] To note that this dynamic is equally present in the theater, we need look no further than the rest of Khalid Tamer's interview on the Festival au Féminin.

In the interview, Tamer notes that the festival's goal is to "change the way we look at people and try, above all, to understand the other. Humanity is to look at the other without judging it and have the insatiable desire to want to meet it."[42] Further illustrating the festival's focus on violence done to women, Tamer evokes his emphasis on the visual experience of otherness through the figure of an African woman in Paris. This woman, the author of a letter that Tamer has received, has come to France in search of factory labor but has instead found herself engaged in sex work. Tamer adds that "when one sees a prostitute, one can't know where she came from, what her story is."[43] Indeed, the emancipatory potential of speech ("her story") serves as a through-line for the festival, perhaps best encapsulated in the name of the workshop at its origin: Paroles de Femmes. Interestingly, however, Tamer references the significance of this figure through her body: "it is exactly this body, treated violently, violated and sold that interests us this year."[44] Likewise, the festival's program notes counsel readers that "the body can render visible what words cannot say."[45] The figure of the African woman that is meant to encapsulate the goal of the festival thus functions evocatively on two distinct planes: first, as the vehicle of a narrative of violation, and second, as the visual sign of an unpronounced narrative.

This imagined harmony between sound and image is reminiscent of the North African woman's direct speech and presumes familiarity with what Michel Foucault would call "a primary reference that prescribes and classes":[46] a figure that is perennially violated, suffering. In other words, the "insatiable desire to want to meet" that is central to Tamer's definition of humanity is evoked by an entity that has in fact already been met; such a model of spectatorship requires a specific kind of performer and not a very novel one. Tamer's African woman resonates with earlier conventions of racialized theatricality, such as the "nègre" in turn-of-the-century Parisian cabarets and music halls, a figure that accompanied the escalation of colonial conquest and, as Sylvie Chalaye notes, prompted both abhorrence and fascination.[47] Thus, much like the young Muslim woman wearing a headscarf, the contemporary figure of the "African prostitute" joins together different connotations. On the one hand, she is the result of neocolonial and anti-immigrant discourses that have increasingly wed prostitution to migration. On the other hand, her singling out as the recipient of a spectatorial gaze draws attention to the broader tropes through which violence, alterity, and aid are joined. My suggestion is that the link between the trope of (sexual) violence and suffering and the recognition of racial or religious difference is nowhere more visible than in women's personal narrative performance.

Accueil Goutte d'Or and *Prendre la Parole*

The professional artists who contribute to the Festival au Féminin illustrate the ways in which gender, racial identity, and personal narrative performance are imagined to come together in a context where performance carries minimal yet also not negligible commercial stakes. I would like to turn now to how the same dynamics were negotiated by amateurs in a nongovernmental aid context, specifically that of the association Accueil Goutte d'Or. Paroles de Femmes, the annual performance that served as the origin of the Festival au Féminin, was a six-month French language and theater workshop managed by AGO and often run by a member of the Graines de Soleil. The AGO was founded in the Goutte d'Or in 1979 by inhabitants who wanted to create a network of public services aimed at the neighborhood's changing demographic. Over the course of the 1970s, the Goutte d'Or's population of immigrant women increased in line with the government's familial reunification policies, yet AGO's founders noticed that there were few structures that could address their basic needs, from negotiating their complex legal statuses in France to daily life in the densely packed metropolis. Originally partnered with the Secours Catholique, an arm of the French Catholic Church that targets poverty and social exclusion, AGO became an independent nonprofit *association* in 1996 and further earned the title of a *centre social* in 2001, as the recipient of funds directed to groups working within specific localities. The AGO's services include day-care centers, juridical and employment aid services, as well as a series of socialization activities such as a literacy program that culminates in a theater workshop.

When I met with AGO member Delphine, as well as with several of the women who had been responsible for running Paroles de Femmes, it was clear that the workshops often emphasized personal narrative performance, presentations that revealed the women's own life experiences and thus provided them with an opportunity to take the floor (*prendre la parole*). At times, AGO's emphasis on personal narrative echoed the principles that I had heard from professional artists working on immigration: theatrical performance was imagined to have an inextricable relationship to the urgency of suffering, and was thus considered most powerful when it stemmed from the women's personal experience. Yet whereas an artist like Angela was concerned with pinpointing a set of aesthetic conventions for narrating the personal, AGO workers were more interested in what personal narrative performance could cultivate *in the performer*. While cognizant of theater's semiotic dimensions, they stressed the practice's *constitutive* elements, the expectation that its embodied nature could engender new sensibilities, desires, and even actions in those who undertook its routines. For AGO workers, the republican dynamic of universality and particularity emerged *through this emphasis on self-cultivation*: while personal narrative performance privileged the particularity of immigrant women's stories, theatrical practice itself was surrounded with the expectation that the participating women could share a singular, universal vision of bodily self-realization. In order to understand how this expectation came about, it is necessary to introduce the basic contents of the theater workshops as well as to explain how broader public discourses on women, violence, and immigration filtered into the social work of this nongovernmental organization.

Self-Expression and Authenticity

What precisely did *prendre la parole* look like in practice? The AGO's theater workshops generally began in October or November and ended in March with the annual Festival au Féminin, where the participants presented their final performance product. At the time of my research, workshops had had approximately fifteen participants per year, with groups largely divided between women from North and from West Africa. Conversely, with the exception of one person, the workshop leaders and coordinators with whom I spoke were all native French individuals. Workshop themes and improvisational exercises were often built around concrete needs, such as a 2009 installment on getting to know the particularities of employment training and acquisition in France. Stemming from the literacy program's emphasis on linguistic skills, the workshops often began with writing exercises designed to tap into the women's own life experiences. These were followed by physical activities and improvisation exercises which were geared toward the creation of a final product, created and staged by the workshop leader. One workshop leader told me that these activities and exercises constituted a "work on the self," cultivating the kind of confidence necessary not only for voicing one's thoughts but for doing so in French and in front of a French-speaking audience. This interlocutor, like many others, insisted that theater had the ability to influence the participating women's general well-being, level of self-confidence, and sense of autonomy. Yet she also added that theatrical rehearsal could be "upsetting," generating both physical and emotional fatigue. Participants' lives were often harried, divided between caring for children, family members, and homes while negotiating the difficulties of living in a foreign land. While the workshops' theatrical product was identified as a largely positive experience, coordinators and leaders were equally straightforward about the concrete and to-be-expected barriers both they and the participants faced during the theatrical process: absences, reluctance to participate, and confusion regarding the content of the participation.

Despite these occasional and largely practical hurdles, AGO workers involved with the theater workshops were unanimous in their belief in the benefits of personal narrative performance, the stage performance of *prendre la parole*. Delphine explained it thus:

> What we often say is that we would like to change the image people have of these women. Because in public opinion, people perceive them as submissive women [*les femmes soumises*], as immigrants in France. So yes, we tell them: "So what if you did not attend a French school? Today you are here and capable of producing things. You produce texts that are very moving [*émouvant*] and must be known by the broader public." We ask this of them as well, because they are in a sense spokespersons [*porte-paroles*] for all women who do not have the words to express themselves.

Delphine's comments illustrate that while AGO workers recognized theater as an artistic practice, these practical dimensions were joined by the expectation that theater partook of a moral-political project as well. Particularly where audience members were concerned, Paroles de Femmes sought to counter the social and cultural marginalization of the neighborhood's immigrant women by validating their experiences. Furthermore, it sought to do so while encouraging their participation in a medium recognized for its ability to communicate "moving" narratives.

Importantly, AGO had experimented with forms of theater that were not simply geared toward self-expression. In 2008, for example, a workshop leader had chosen to work with a pre written theatrical script that she had adapted from a short story. Instead of building a performance based on the women's own writings, she had opted for a somewhat more traditional process based on casting, memorization, and staging. The project was successful and although it had posed new challenges to the participants, the performance was lauded by all present. Yet when I spoke to those involved with the project, they felt that AGO's preference was for the women to work on their own stories. Theater, Delphine added, asked the women: "What are you capable of doing with your body, what are you capable of saying? As a militant association, we want to give the women a chance to speak." It is clear in comments such as these that for AGO, vocal and physical capabilities were best explored through placing one's speech and body in the service of one's own history, rather than assuming a theatrical role.[48] Faced with a choice between the perceived authority of personal speech and the capacities associated with theater as a recognized cultural practice, AGO workers chose to highlight *la parole* as a form of both self-realization and exchange.

If theatrical *parole* served as a placeholder for the workshop's emphasis on personal immediacy, however, this discourse of authenticity was not without a strategic role. The idea of personal narrative as a separate and secluded realm was due in part to a desire to sidestep the "commodification" of social work in France,[49] the growing expectation that nongovernmental organizations harmonize their goals with those of political structures. In France, the delimitation of *zones urbaines sensibles* in the 1990s is a prime example of this process, whereby the state's responsibility toward urgent problems like unemployment has been transferred to civic associations. Scholars have noted that this shift in the provision of services from the state to local, nonprofit actors in both Europe and the United States has resulted in a romance with grassroots authenticity[50] and a desire to protect bodily life and expression from the market economy.[51] Bemoaning the increasingly expert-ridden tendencies of the social service sector, AGO members have stated that

> the history and the experience of our association Accueil Goutte d'Or teaches us, in contrast [here referring to the turn to expertise], that the first experts of the everyday are the inhabitants themselves and the associations that they give themselves. Consequently, professional expertise cannot in any case substitute for that of the situation in which the inhabitants and their associations live.
>
> . . .
>
> Moreover, we have, multiple times, experienced how much the inhabitants have to say and to share when we give them the possibility to express themselves and to be heard. These are therefore competencies and richness, the fruits of original histories and different cultures that express themselves.[52]

In many ways, then, privileging personal speech was AGO's gesture of inclusion and the theater workshops were one of a number of ways in which they sought to place an emphasis on everyday expertise and cultural diversity. Indeed, the excerpt above is evidence of AGO's desire to affirm individual narratives independent of the political pressures that shape civic activism in France. At the same time, however, the very notion of an "expertise of the everyday" reveals how the category of personal narrative *itself* can be transformed into a question of competence and expertise. Kristin Langellier has noted that when experiential content is transformed into a narrative form, it becomes beholden to "the desires and choices of the teller, to the constraints of the audience, and to the forces of narrative traditions."[53] In AGO's example, a secondary layer of mediation surrounded the very idea of personal narrative's experiential authenticity and political significance. Resonating with what Della Pollock has called "a ready claim on voice and narrative as private property," *prendre la parole* thus functioned as evidence of the authenticity of "original histories" and of the transparency and seeming autonomy of these histories' outward expression.[54]

Finally, in Delphine's comment above, the benefits of self-expression were directly connected to public debates on immigration. Indeed, one of the ways

Delphine explained the necessity of providing the Goutte d'Or's women with a voice was through reference to a public discourse regarding the submissiveness of immigrant women, a prevailing prejudice that the majority of women immigrants in France were forced to submit to a patriarchy inherent to what were variously referred to as their native cultures, religions, and traditions. Delphine's allusion to the image of "submissive women" is intentional and points at a number of complicated discourses concerning immigration, women, and feminist activism. Patterns of postwar immigration to France have generally reflected the host country's changing needs: earlier waves from North and West Africa and parts of Europe were largely composed of single male workers, with women generally joining the migratory flow later than men. As chroniclers of immigration have shown, these women often found themselves in multiply disadvantaged social situations, alienated not only from the dominant culture but from the homes and habits that they had left behind.[55] Yet as Jane Freedman notes, women were also "represented as both the bearers of 'tradition' and agents of 'modernity,' responsible both for perpetuating the boundaries of ethnic groups within France and for ensuring that these boundaries are made permeable to French culture."[56] Since the early 1980s, it has largely been from within the "boundaries of ethnic groups" that immigrant women's lives have been evoked in public discourse, with the imagined otherness of such groupings distilled through "readily recognized tropes of alterity, such as forced marriage, honor killings, or excision"[57] and most recently, gang rape. This particular form of violence against women entered the public sphere in 2002, after the highly publicized murder of Sohane Benziane, a young French woman of Algerian origin who was burned alive by a group of men in the Parisian suburb of Vitry-sur-Seine, and the publication of Samira Bellil's personal account of gang rape and sexual violence, *Dans l'enfer des tournantes* (*In the Hell of Gang Rapes*).[58] The outrage that followed gave birth to Ni Putes ni Soumises (NPNS) or Neither Whores nor Submissives, an association that decried violence against women and was soon supported by political circles, with its most visible spokesperson, Fadela Amara, granted a position as secretary of state in charge of urban policies under then–Prime Minister François Fillon's (UMP) government.

NPNS has provided one of the most visible frameworks through which the images of women immigrants and their descendants in France have been linked to sexual violence. The group's relevance for my purposes, however, is the manner in which it marshals the two opposing terms encapsulated in its title, even as it works to reject them. NPNS states that Muslim/Arab/immigrant women are neither *whores* for adopting French ways of life (a notion that was often evoked as the crime for which the gang rapes served as punishment) nor *submissive* to (Islamic) patriarchy. As Nacira Guénif-Souilamas has noted, however, the slogan perpetuates an uncomfortable dynamic where it is Muslim/Arab/immigrant men who are addressed, rather than patriarchal structures more broadly.[59] Additionally, while NPNS members declare themselves to be *insoumises* and argue against the conflation of this attitude with other injurious epithets, their vision of emancipation has overlapped with their defense of French republican secularism. The group's well-publicized support for the 2004 law banning the wearing of headscarves in public secondary schools often draws a direct link between Islam and violence done to women. For example, Amara has identified the headscarf as "a means of oppression, of alienation, of discrimination, an instrument of power over women used by men."[60] While NPNS is uniquely positioned to speak of the multiple factors contributing to the marginalization of young men and women in disenfranchised *banlieues*, the organization's insistence that republican *laïcité* is the only reliable framework for generating a feminist movement has proven controversial.[61]

Delphine's passing allusion to submissiveness reveals the difficulties of conducting social work in a context where the recognition of racial and gender particularity has been wedded to perceived categories of patriarchal and religious violence. This connection was clarified for me during a conversation with a social worker who had run an association working with Turkish migrants. This person told me that while she had a very difficult time getting the ministry in charge of immigration to fund cultural projects, financial aid was always available to projects addressing domestic violence against Turkish women. Thus, it is not a coincidence that AGO workers used every opportunity to underline the Goutte d'Or women's strength and resourcefulness. Skeptical of the notions of emancipation and submission made available by public debate, they recognized that the primary problems plaguing immigrant women's lives were *practical*. What was significant about their understanding of theater's ability to address these practical problems was how this understanding nonetheless resonated with the overlapping discourses of feminism and republicanism, particularly where the question of submission and authority was concerned.

Theatrical Liberty and the Paradoxes of Universalism

AGO workers positioned the stage as a space of emancipation, "a space," as one workshop leader told me, "of liberty." The fact remained, however, that some women were unwilling to climb onto it. While AGO workers acknowledged that the reasons for these refusals were multiple, the prevailing explanation evoked the women's cultural origins, religions, and traditions. For example, one workshop leader recalled:

> There was one woman who did not play [*jouer*] at all. This was a woman who had really progressed in oral and written work. During rehearsals, she said that she could help with rehearsal but not onstage. I thought that this would change but it did not. Afterwards, I spoke to some of the others and it turned out that she was very, very

> religious. This created problems with some of the other participants, who said, "We are also practicing, but we are going to do this." In the end, she did not play. But she never said it was because of religion. She said it was because of playing in front of others. So I don't know, because she never tried and never played.

Comments such as these revealed the negotiations and improvisations that structured this workshop leader's own possibilities of action. On the one hand, the workshop leader underlined the ambiguity of the situation, the fact that she did not "know" the participant's internal negotiations. On the other hand, she recalled the ease with which both workshop leaders and participants interpreted the refusal to "play in front of others" as the symptom of a religious sphere constraining this individual's choices, as opposed to a pragmatic choice concerning both "play" and "others." During our conversation, this workshop leader was as frustrated by this participant's absence from the stage as she was by the overdetermined nature of the conversations that surrounded her presence in the workshop.

The contrasting models of agency, interiority, and liberty that underline this brief anecdote are worth understanding in detail. Throughout my conversations with AGO workers, theatrical play and theatrical *parole* functioned first as the outward manifestations of interior thoughts and second as placeholders for this inner sphere's freedom from constraint. Thus at times, the inability (or lack of willingness) to participate could be interpreted as religious or traditional forces *constraining* the individual's will.[62] Yet AGO's comments on theatrical self-cultivation revealed a contrasting model of the self, one that is not uncommon in contexts of theatrical discipline: AGO used theater because the practice's embodied dimensions were understood to shape the capacities of participants' bodies and voices. In other words, although AGO workers spoke of theatrical participation as an exercise in liberty, this freedom nonetheless required *compliance* with both theatrical activity and personal speech. Theatrical *parole* was neither an unrestrained, authentic display of personal emotions nor a transparent link between experience and language. In this context, theatrical *parole* developed in relationship to constraints placed by workshop leaders, by theater's bodily conventions, and by other workshop participants. We might even note that the desire for public and personal speech was not a predetermined given but a readiness *cultivated* by the rituals of theatrical practice. In a sense, then, AGO alternated between two models of selfhood. On the one hand, their emphasis on theatrical self-cultivation recognized the fact that projects of self-realization can take place in conversation with forms of authority and constraint. On the other, their understanding of a participant's refusal to do theater drew on the belief that personal freedom and authoritarian constraint exist in a rigid binary, mapped onto an equally static distinction between inner desires and outer acts.[63]

These contrasting notions of the self were connected to the overdetermined relationship between universality and particularity, and of the specific ways in which this relationship emerged in the context of personal narrative performance. Because personal narrative performance could be endowed with the urgency of specifically racialized and gendered suffering, a participant's refusal to conform to the norm of public personal speech left these amateur theater practitioners with a seemingly transparent explanation: that the inability to conform was itself the sign of a will hindered by patriarchy, rather than that of a robust refusal motivated by personal hesitation. This overdetermination was visible beyond the domain of personal narrative. For example, the year that theater workshops were based on a pre-written text, the workshop leader had chosen to adapt the play from the story of a woman experiencing forced marriage. When I inquired as to the rationale behind this choice, the workshop leader told me that her goal had been to present the women with a "familiar" story, even as she sought to step away from the workshop's previous emphasis on *personal* narrative and self-revelation. The theatrical transformation that the pre-written text promised was tempered with an already developed sense of which transformations these women could actually experience. In other words, while the theater workshops' three-dimensional "work on the self" imagined a formula for self-realization posited as a *universal*, this work was nonetheless realized through *particular* articulations, unable to reconcile the imagined suffering of the "immigrant woman" with emancipation in Western terms.

In many ways, these dynamics resonate with the principles that undergird contemporary French debates on multiculturalism and social integration, debates that I will examine in detail in the following chapter. In so far as AGO's work joins a broader array of civic associations premised on creating a shared collective sphere, however, it is worth noting the immediate parallels between the question of theatrical participation detailed above and the question of civic participation as it can be understood by community groups. For example, Beth Epstein's ethnography of civic associationalism and community work in the Paris suburb of Cergy reveals that ideals of collectivity are premised on a distinction between those who participate in (an ambiguously defined) collective interest and those who refrain from engaging with community affairs. Epstein notes that in Cergy, this distinction is weighed with moral value, as "disinterest in civic affairs is considered evidence of an untenable lack of social conscience" and a lack of willingness to work on social bonds.[64] My goal here is not to suggest that AGO's vision of civic associationalism is premised on such a distinction. Indeed, the language I encountered in the Goutte d'Or was far less rigid, far more interested in understanding how their neighborhood's collective interest was defined in the first place. What I found striking in AGO's understanding of theater, however, was in how the perceived collectivity of this embodied practice created a space through which both workshop leaders and participants entered into discussions regarding behavior that they felt was appropriate to collectivity. Theater, in other words, was understood as a space with the potential to maintain or resist existing social arrangements.

Such an expectation will not be news to scholars of performance. The intellectual history of performance studies has been uniquely invested in what Jon McKenzie has called "the challenge of social efficacy,"[65] the delineation of the efficaciousness of cultural performances. Whereas McKenzie identifies a shift in the efficacy paradigms of performance studies from transgression to resistance, he argues that liminality has remained a frequent trope, with the quest for a "liminal-norm" determining "the selection of activities to be studied, their formal analysis and their political evaluation."[66] McKenzie's caution against this narrow and ambiguously celebratory focus resonates with the work of scholars like José Muñoz, who has noted that "not all performances are liberatory or transformative."[67] Muñoz's reference to the "burden of liveness"[68] that haunts the representation, materiality, and temporality of minoritarian subjects on the American stage posits a performance expectation that places Latina performance in the United States in a continuum with the different celebrations of cultural diversity that I encountered in the Goutte d'Or, as well as with the attributions of urgency that can at times mark the politicization of narrative research. AGO's work, and the performance of personal narrative in the Goutte d'Or more broadly, remind us of the complexity of the political and social circumstances that result in the proclaiming (and at times, lauding) of theater's transgressive potential, live authenticity, and politics of urgency.

As a final note, it is important to relate that these dynamics did not run counter to or hinder AGO's nuanced desire to combat negative representations of the *femme soumise* (submissive woman). Rather, my suggestion is that AGO's twofold interest in the representational *and* embodied dimensions of the theater resulted in the rich, complicated terrain that is theatrical immigration activism. Consider a final comment from Delphine, who felt that Paroles de Femmes addressed the increasing austerity of French immigration policies. These changes labeled residence on French soil legitimate only if the immigrant in question displayed signs of a healthy integration into mainstream society. She noted:

> In France, they [the administration] want everyone to be the same. Instead, we want these women to be able to say, "as a human being with all that I am, all that I already have in me, I am capable of living in a society by understanding its codes, their usages and have a place for myself" . . . These are human beings with sentiments and an attachment to France, who have lived through very difficult things, and they have traversed the Mediterranean for the land of their lives [*la terre de leurs vies*].

Delphine's comments elucidate how AGO reconciled their emphasis on what the women "already have" with the possibility of carving out a place for themselves within a complex system of "codes" and "their usages." Acculturation and difference, in other words, were not oppositional concepts, they could coincide. *Theater* served as a venue whose own "codes" and "their usages," when mastered, signaled both acculturation *and* difference. My point has been that when theatrical practice is positioned as both a disciplinary mechanism that can cultivate specific kinds of familiarities and dispositions *and* a representational venue charged with displaying "human beings . . . who have lived through very difficult things," the theater that results cannot but evoke the ambivalence attached to the question of universality. While the theatrical display of "very difficult things" mandates the moral spectatorship of the audience, it is theater's perceived ability to release the individual from their particular difficulty and join them to the larger body of "human beings with sentiments" that is celebrated. And not coincidentally, human sentimentality manifests itself through an "attachment to France."

Conclusion

By way of conclusion, I would like to note the unpredictability of the theatrical container. The majority of the comments that I have relayed here are *theoretical* considerations of theatrical participation and spectatorship: my goal has been to depict some of the principles used by social workers and theater artists working on immigration and gender in Paris. While these comments reveal the political and aesthetic imaginaries that animate this domain, they nonetheless manifest themselves in theatrical products whose sensory strength and experience override the abstractions of dramaturgy. I was present at the 2008 workshop performance of Paroles de Femmes, sitting in the small and overcrowded theater of the Lavoir Moderne Parisien where I had also witnessed Angela's performance. As the women moved about the stage, assembling themselves into their designated spots, their actions seemed imbued with a range of attitudes, at times reluctance or ambivalence, at others determination. Crowd scenes lent themselves well to the actors' tendency to hide behind one another, while scenes featuring selected figures front and center drew the other actors out of the backstage shadows, their interests piqued. At one point, the actor who served as the piece's narrator had difficulty remembering the precise line she needed to deliver: she was recounting the way in which Salina, the main character, had difficulty accepting some of the decisions that her family made in her name. She attempted the sentence three or four times, failing with each attempt and breaking into an embarrassed smile that acknowledged the presence of the anonymous crowd. At a certain moment she took a deep breath, smiled, let go of the sentence that had been plaguing her and stated: "Salina hated that!" At that moment, the audience broke into thunderous applause. The other actors began to laugh and clap at the success of their stage partner while the actor herself beamed at the audience and slowly dissolved into the scene change that followed.

How are we to understand such a moment? The skeptic in me takes note of the fact that the audience followed and supported a declaration whose content aligned with an *insoumise* stance. After all, this was a middle-aged Algerian woman who wore a headscarf that covered her hair, neck, and shoulders and who had been asked to narrate the life story of a character who had rejected patriarchy. Yet the audience had reacted first and foremost to the visibility of the actor's agonizing stage fright and her subsequent triumph over the tyranny of a memorized text. Their approval was of her actorly dexterity, her quick wit and self-acknowledgment in a moment of public humiliation. Perhaps these dynamics do not sidestep the broader categories of representation that had led the play's director to choose this play and cast this individual in this role and the audience to applaud her courage. But something of the very sensory and erratic meeting between actor and spectator had momentarily confused the predictable representation she could have delivered. Her non-rehearsed solution to a *public problem* proved to be the link connecting her to the audience.

Immigrant women's theater exhibits two recurring themes: first, the tension between universality and particularity that is internal to French republicanism and that acknowledges racial and gender difference only under exceptional circumstances, and second, the notion that theater is a space where bodies are disciplined to become a certain kind of public subject, one which internalizes public speech as a privileged venue of self-realization and emancipation. In many ways, my suggestion is that theatrical *prendre la parole* is the genre-correlate of this exceptional acknowledgment of difference, offering the possibility of theatrical self-cultivation as an exit from particularity. If, however, the erratic, unpredictable domain of performance is where these two strands are joined, where the project of theatrical self-cultivation meets the specific rationality through which difference is acknowledged, then immigrant women's theater is premised on the *limits* of both discourses: the limits of republican universality to encompass difference and the limits of theater to render the figure of "the immigrant woman" available to manipulation, whether on a representational or on a disciplinary plane.

Chapter 3

✦

The Integrated Actor

In 2007 Réseau Education Sans Frontières (RESF) or Network for Education without Borders, a web of nationwide aid collectives that support undocumented youth educated in France, produced *La Plume sans papier* (*The Pen without Paper*). A wordplay on the colloquial reference to undocumented immigrants, the paperless *sans-papiers*, the performance was composed of testimonies written by undocumented youth awaiting evaluation of their residency applications. Initiated by RESF 91 of the Ile-de-France district of Essonne, the project had begun as a writing workshop, with an eye to providing a creative outlet for youth struggling with undocumented status. Soon afterward, the young authors found themselves rehearsing for a theatrical performance of their work with the popular film and stage actor Rachida Brakni. By the time I met the North, West, and sub-Saharan African men and women involved with staging *La Plume sans papier*, they had performed their work several times and collected much media attention. At the time, several members of the original cast were no longer with the group and had been replaced by other, eager RESF youth. Sofia, an active member of RESF 91, interpreted this readiness as the reflection of a generalized awareness on the part of the aid community: the efficacy of public performance. Referencing one recently joined actor, a teenager with a few years in France under his belt but grim prospects for his application, Sofia related that he had probably joined because the activity would bolster the chances of his residency application. When I inquired as to why that was, Sofia's reply voiced a belief that became commonplace in my conversations in Paris. For many of my interlocutors, public performance served as the sign of an attachment between the applicant and their social world. One of the key criteria in the French state's offer of residency was *intégration*, an affective attachment to French culture and the outward exhibition of a desire to be enmeshed in its values, ideals, and practices. The teenager's theatrical work wasn't a mere addendum to his application for residency status; rather it would fundamentally shape the process of proving to the authorities that he was sufficiently acculturated. Put simply, theatrical storytelling functioned as evidence of integration.

This connection is clear in *Libération*'s coverage of an early performance of *La Plume sans papier*. As the reporter's narrative demonstrates, political efficacy is uniquely central to the audience's experience of this event:

> On Saturday, the Viry-Chatillon theater (Essonne) played to a packed audience. The program: a performance by eleven undocumented immigrants, aged 16 to 24, whose origins are either from the Maghreb or sub-Saharan Africa, and directed by the actress Rachida Brakni. In the auditorium, the air is festive. The militants of Réseau Education Sans Frontières, a network that defends undocumented youth educated in France and their families, are present, both from Viry-Chatillon and beyond. From one end to the other, they call out to each other and give each other news of foreigners supported by the network. "X did a very stupid thing: he went to the Comissariat without us. He was arrested," says one female spectator to another. "Oh, he was already deported four times and he always came back," replies the other. On the stage, a young black man comes forward: "You, who don't want me, I chose this country, not you." . . . Wednesday, the militants of RESF Essonne are going to submit some fifty-plus applications for regularization to the local police, all of them for youth who have been educated here, including those of the amateur actors.[1]

The particular configuration of theatrical practice that characterized the Viry-Chatillon performance resonates with what I have elsewhere called theatrical aid work, that is, theatrical projects that join a wide range of associated aid practices that seek to support undocumented immigrants' claims to permanent residency in France.[2] Often premised on the delivery of personal narrative, theatrical aid work is permeated by the uneven forms of political and social authority that pattern the relationship between undocumented aid recipients and native aid workers. In the excerpt above, the joining of the aid worker's blasé reference to X and the young actor's defiant address to an ambiguous "you" capture the tensions of this domain. Theater may serve to support this young man's application for regularization, the article seems to suggest, but undocumented status entails vulnerabilities that endure both within and beyond relationships of aid.

In this chapter, I explore the multifaceted, ambiguous, and often precarious connection between theater and integration by considering how two nongovernmental organizations, RESF and La Cimade, configure the relationship between the embodiedness of theatrical practice, the possibilities of aid work, and the process of social integration. Over the course of my conversations with these theatrical aid workers, it became clear that their understanding of integration exceeded the term's oft-cited sociological reference points, such as an immigrant's professional achievements or their community's rates of intermarriage. Rather, integration referenced an immigrant's ability to adhere to

French values, a relatively abstract criterion that the French state's evaluation of residency applications nonetheless measured in concrete ways. Theater, in RESF and Cimade's work, emerged as one such concrete context for thinking about integration. Theater's embodied nature, its ability to endow its practitioners with a heightened sense of bodily presence and its experiential focus on the creation and ownership of a collective artwork positioned the practice as a literal rehearsal for social collectivity. As the above anecdote reveals, however, the content of the theatrical performances hardly demonstrated an abiding relationality; they could range from critiques of the government to narratives of geographic displacement and social isolation. Importantly, such narratives were understood to display the protagonists' individual autonomy, personal empowerment, and self-sufficiency, all the while alleviating their need for public self-expression. For these aid organizations, integration meant both *enmeshment* within a larger collective infrastructure and *autonomy* from such collective formations.

Whereas this dual understanding of integration may appear unique to RESF and Cimade, it has resonated with the term's transformations in French debates on immigrant integration since the 1980s. As migratory flows from beyond Europe's borders became a reference point for both political and social action during this period, the management of immigration was indelibly linked to a republican ideal of citizenship. In its republican formulation, citizenship entailed individual rationality and moral autonomy, with an emphasis on individuals' freedom from nonnational (e.g., religious, racial, ethnic, or cultural) groupings. Although integration continued to reference an individual's degree of adaptation to the cultural patterns of the host society, moral autonomy was often posited as a necessary component of the individual's relation to the universal state, and his or her distance from other collectivist formations. RESF and Cimade's references to autonomy and self-sufficiency emerged in civic contexts that were critical of this political climate, even as their understanding of the capacities of theatrical performance resonated with a broader republican insistence on the primacy of the public sphere. These nongovernmental organizations, in other words, operated in a limited sphere of political engagement, their theatrical aid work circumscribed by the terms of public debate on immigrant integration.

References to self-government and autonomy in the context of such decidedly political theater projects may appear contradictory. Such terms call to mind a distinct yet also related set of debates on what Theodor Adorno has called committed art, a context wherein autonomy references the artwork's independence from political or social influences and engagements.[3] As Shannon Jackson has pointed out, in the context of both moral philosophy and aesthetic theory, autonomy refers to self-government, the ability of the human (or the artwork) to exert a degree of control over when and how its boundaries will be imposed upon by the demands of an outside world.[4] In Jackson's work, recognizing the limits of aesthetic autonomy involves a parallel acknowledgment of the necessity of social interdependency. Conversely, in RESF and La Cimade's theatrical theorizing, the moral and aesthetic versions of the autonomy/heteronomy divide can, at times, operate independently from one another. In other words, my interlocutors took the organizing principle of theatrical practice to be the mutual dependency of actor and spectator, as well as the co-presence of actor and actor. At certain moments, their understanding of theater even stressed the practice's ability to highlight more systemic dependencies, what Jackson has referred to as the "social infrastructure" that performance can bring into high relief.[5] Yet where theater as a practice of integration was concerned, moral autonomy and aesthetic autonomy also diverged at crucial moments that revealed the contradictions and limits of French discourses on autonomous individuality.

Where theatrical visions were concerned, RESF and La Cimade's references to aesthetic autonomy were mobilized from within a commitment to theater's technically efficacious dimensions, if not its phenomenological character. Like many of the organizations discussed in this book, RESF and La Cimade's understanding of the theater paired its signifying dimensions with its embodied situation, calling attention to its orientation from and rootedness within the body. Although the post-structuralist critique of phenomenology has cautioned against the underlying universality of references to a pure embodied experience, I will show that the undocumented actor's embodiment was always experienced in a particular idiom. Theatrical aid, in other words, was inhabited in ways that exceeded the expectations of aid workers, illustrating the diversity of bodily dispositions.

The two contexts in which I explore these dynamics share an interest in migratory flows, yet their daily work is relatively distinct. Founded in 2004 by a group of parents, educators, and human rights activists, RESF is largely composed of self-appointed, amateur aid workers, many of whom became involved with social action projects through personal encounters with *sans-papiers* youth educated in France. RESF's work focuses on minors whose ongoing education guarantees them residency in France, but whose undocumented parents are threatened with deportation to their countries of origin. Yet their work resonates with the human rights discourses of a range of aid organizations working with undocumented immigrants in France today, including Cimade. Unlike the recently formed RESF, Cimade has worked with displaced populations in France since the Second World War, a legacy that continues to figure in the organization's understanding of solidarity with migrant populations. Cimade's nationwide networks are composed of salaried workers as well as volunteers, and their public role exceeds the question of undocumented immigration to a broader consideration of reform in France's refugee and asylum policies.

Given the different degrees of historical expertise and different resources that structure the two organizations, their theater projects were likewise distinct. *La Plume sans papier* was a local effort that drew on minimal financial resources, often depending on contributions from RESF volunteers. Cimade's theater workshops, on the other hand, were made possible by an international partnership that drew on centralized European funding. In this chapter, the impact of these differences is evident in the practical dimensions of methodology. Whereas the RESF section is based on interviews, newspaper coverage, and the text of *La Plume sans papier,* the section on Cimade draws on the more established organization's extensive self-evaluations, manuals, and reports. Conversely, while I was able to speak to some of the participants of *La Plume sans papier,* Cimade's workshop participants were no longer residing in the vicinity when I began researching their theater activities a couple of years later, reflecting the lack of permanence that often characterizes the asylum process. In what follows, I begin by taking a closer look at *La Plume sans papier,* place this work in conversation with French debates on integration since the 1980s, and end with a focus on Cimade's theater workshops.

Réseau Education Sans Frontières and *La Plume sans papier*

In January 2007, when sixteen Essonne youth began the creative writing workshop that would eventually result in the performance of *La Plume sans papier,* RESF was one of a number of contexts in which immigration activism and public performance had begun to merge. In 2006 Cimade had published *Votre voisin n'a pas de papiers: Paroles d'étrangers* (*Your Neighbor Does Not Have Papers: The Words of Foreigners*), a volume of personal narratives from *sans-papiers* individuals interspersed with short historical and legal analyses of immigration laws.[6] A few months later, the organization collaborated with the acting school École Voie de l'Acteur to create a staged version of the work, a mobile spectacle of the same name that performed at over a hundred venues, from high schools and Cimade residences to Avignon Off.[7] In 2007 Cimade further established the first annual nationwide festival Migrant'Scène, which joined performances, debates, concerts, and films by activist-artists working on refuge, exile, and immigration. RESF's transformation from a humanitarian group to an agent of creative output, in other words, was not an exception.

Even so, RESF's unique profile as an aid organization working with *sans-papiers* students resulted in a unique theatrical approach to ideas of integration and moral autonomy. Indeed, while RESF members lauded the multimedia journey of *La Plume sans papier* as a successful extracurricular activity for the participating youth, my conversations about *La Plume sans papier* often revolved around less tangible outcomes. For RESF, theatrical performance had a dual function. On the one hand, the embodied, relational nature of theater practice could serve as a rehearsal for social relationality and incorporation. On the other, the administrative critique inherent to the youths' writing signaled their critical, self-affirming stance vis-à-vis the

French state. Often emphasized was theater's unique capacity to train the individual's proprioceptive abilities, the manner in which it allowed her to navigate her bodily presence in a shared world. Yet there was equal stress on the content of the youths' theatrical narratives, content that revealed social sharedness to be a distant ideal. These theatrical declarations of isolation were praised as evidence of the youths' ability to "reveal" their suffering, critique its source, and thus display their self-sufficiency.

When my RESF interlocutors spoke about theater, in other words, their comments were often premised on a key distinction between theater's formal contours, such as the display of a craft-acquired body and the collectivity implied by both rehearsal and performance, and its narrative content, such as the far-from-collectivist impact of undocumented status. Whereas references to form and content joined different kinds of autonomy (aesthetic and moral), I found over the course of my conversations that RESF's work often dissolved these binaries themselves.

Aid Work, Intimacy, and Integration

RESF's turn to theatrical practice is best understood in light of the organization's changing experience of aid work. During my conversations with RESF members from various Ile-de-France regions, I repeatedly heard that the organization's work was practical rather than conceptual. "What a militant does," one member told me, "is concrete." These "concrete" practices ranged from accompanying undocumented students on their trips to police stations to aiding families with (often self-taught) legal advice on their residency applications.[8] During the period of 2006–8, as immigration policies signaled a renewed focus on evidence of residency candidates' integration, RESF's emphasis on practical forms of aid structured their understanding of how this ideal was to be secured. For example, one member supported a *sans-papiers* couple from China who worked late-night shifts, and she had taken to caring for their two sons in her home. When I inquired as to how this practice related to her work as an RESF member, she replied: "If we really want these kids to become French, we have to open our doors; we can't just treat them administratively." Comments such as these revealed that while RESF members remained aware of the ambiguity of the process encapsulated by "becoming French," they were equally cognizant of the need to take such designations seriously, cultivating a series of everyday practices through which they sought to provide the elusive experience called integration. The reference to the opening of one's doors implied that the pragmatism of the "concrete" did not obscure its affective dimensions, the manner in which it overflowed into one's own sphere of intimacy and undid the binary positioning of the concrete and abstract.

A brief glance at the legal climate of these years demonstrates that RESF's focus on the integration of undocumented youth was not arbitrary. These comments were a direct response to legal windows generated by the French state, such as the Sarkozy Circulaire of June 13, 2006, on the regularization of foreign families with children being educated in the French school system. Authored by Minister of the Interior Nicolas Sarkozy, the Circulaire stated that if candidates met a set of criteria designed to determine both their practical circumstances and their "real will to integrate" (*réelle volonté d'intégration*), their family could be granted residency status through this "exceptional and humanitarian" category.[9] For the Circulaire, evidence of the will to integrate resided in the academic capacity and cultural aptness of undocumented teenagers; the legal framework took the French language in particular to be a sign of how enmeshed they were in their social milieu.[10] The history of French national education suggests that the Sarkozy Circulaire was not the first context to link academic success to the acquisition of cultural norms. As Trica Danielle Keaton has noted, cultivating a common culture has long been a key dimension of "acceptable progress in the school system."[11] Legal openings like the Sarkozy Circulaire simply reiterated these academic norms as an "exceptional" loophole, leaving aid workers with a specific vocabulary to negotiate, and aid recipients with a paradoxical, if not punitive, ideal to emulate.

The published version of *La Plume sans papier* illustrates the degree to which the republican framework of integration saturated the project, shaping its possibilities as well as delineating its limits. The text's concluding anecdote demonstrates the quality of social enmeshment sought by laws like the Sarkozy Circulaire, but also emphasizes self-sufficiency and moral autonomy:

> The final word will be that of a youth from the group who, without intending to, made us the most beautiful compliment that one can make to an adult: "You are useful, but you are not indispensable."
>
> Who would dare, after hearing this, to still doubt their good integration [*Qui oserait, après cela, douter encore de leur bonne intégration*]?[12]

In this excerpt, an integrated youth is one who can dispense with his systems of support, his adults. This scenario likens the relationship between RESF workers and the youth to kin relations of sustenance; where adulthood is concerned, aid and kinship serve as joint genitors whose product is a self-governing individual for whom adults *and* aid are dispensable. This framing underlines the significance of the interpersonal, but it is equally suggestive of the power differential that structures the relationship between aid worker and aid recipient. During my conversations, I found that RESF's twofold understanding of integration was an analogue to this vision of kinship: integration implied both dependence and independence. It referenced both the kind of social enmeshment that academic success was imagined to manifest *and* a degree of autonomy from environments that could nourish this success.

As a "concrete" practice, theater retained the ambiguities inherent in this hybrid model.

Sensory Training and Self-Revelation

Since *La Plume sans papier* began as a writing workshop, then resulted in a publication, and was finally refigured as a performance, the ever-increasing visibility of the youths' narratives led my RESF interlocutors to suggest that theater was first and foremost a vehicle of self-revelation. At the same time, theatrical storytelling signaled the revelation of more than one kind of truth, that of the story being told, as well as that of the body that had mastered the art of storytelling. In the words of RESF 91's Sofia:

> The writing workshop was a little like therapy, for the first time they wrote about what they were living through. They all cried, this did them good. With words, they can tell what happened to them but not with their bodies. The first rehearsal was difficult because these kids had never been on a stage, never sung, never done bodily exercises, been a part of a group or stood before others. They were afraid to do things that may come off as ridiculous. It is tough to show yourself to others, to pull the curtains back on your life, to reveal yourself.

In these comments, theater clearly retained the "therapeutic" function of the writing workshop. Both writing and theater were organized around the depiction of what one newspaper called "suffering and anguish."[13] Yet, equally clear were the differences structuring these two modes of self-revelation, since the stage entailed mastering a set of basic techniques. The daunting dimensions of theatrical self-expression included the cultivation of practical abilities like standing before others, telling a story with one's body, and doing so as a member of a group.

The basic stage conventions and bodily requirements of theatrical practice were a significant element of the *La Plume sans papier* rehearsals, further functioning as proof of the project's aesthetic ambitions. In the discourse surrounding the project, references to the autonomy of the artwork were premised on theater's embodied dimensions. Rachida Brakni, the well-known professional actor who worked with the youth, frequently commented on the need to generate "a real artistic project," rather than political mobilization for *sans-papiers* causes.[14] "I had to familiarize them with the theater, the space, the approach of the other," she told *Le Parisien*, indicating that aesthetic autonomy was contingent on theatrical proprioception.[15] This theme was visible in much of the coverage of the project. The *Le Parisien* reporter observed the group's rehearsals and quoted a choreographer addressing the youth: "Put all your sensors on alert! Learn to react as a group, be attentive to the gestures of others."[16] An article in *Le Républicain* added that becoming an actor "happens through a work that is ludic but also very serious, exacting. Thus, it is necessary to learn what exchange is, playing with the other, exiting from one's own reserve, agreeing to lower one's guard."[17] This constituted a "work on the body," as an RESF member referred to it, but also on the intellect, since acting implied the training of one's emotional imagination as well. The conceptual and corporeal worked together in rehearsal, as evidenced by Brakni's direction to the actors: "Imagine that you are in love, be languorous."[18]

Theatrical rehearsal, as these articles immediately reveal, had both practical and moral connotations. Onstage, one was responsible for "approaching" others in specific ways, employing one's sensory faculties to the fullest in order to stay aware of when and how one's motions within the group reflected on their physical composition as a whole. Brakni deemed these skills central to actorly dexterity and aesthetic achievement, but the embodied sensitivity of actor training also served as a physical structure through which to conceptualize membership in a collective, whether it be the rehearsing group or the social world more broadly. Theater trained the body, but also trained a specific kind of human person, underlining the suggestion that "exchange" with the "other" required a degree of both theatrical and social rehearsal. Yet, whereas theatrical rehearsal involved working toward what might be labeled an autonomous artistic ideal (a coherent, harmonious stage choreography that addressed the audience's aesthetic sensibilities as much as its social conscience), social rehearsal involved moral heteronomy, "playing with the other."

In the context of *La Plume sans papier*, then, aesthetic autonomy's connection to social heteronomy was contingent on a vision of theater that emphasized the lived experience of the body. In theater studies, this vision is often encapsulated in phenomenological approaches that, for Stanton Garner, "counter the signifying body in its dephysicalized readability with what we might call the 'embodied' body in its material resistance."[19] These approaches are often framed in opposition to a semiotic tendency that reads the body as a bearer of social meaning, and the staged body as but one element of a broader communicative medium. If the meaningful nature of undocumented theater reveals the rigidity of such a framing to be irrelevant, however, theatrical aid work is equally helpful in reframing challenges to phenomenology. As Garner shows, deconstructive critiques of phenomenology often underline the tendency to embrace a unified, Cartesian subject, organized around an intending consciousness made manifest at the level of the body. Yet the "embodied body" in theatrical aid work exists at a distance from an autonomous ideal, experiencing a phenomenal undocumentedness that rarely enjoys the luxury of self-presencing. Where the lived experience of undocumented immigration is concerned, in other words, neither self-revelation nor social exchange are predetermined givens. In what ways, then, did the youth engage with and inhabit this highly charged arena?

When I met with several of the actors involved with staging *La Plume sans papier,* their pride in Rachida Brakni's theatrical training was evident. At the same time, their experience of theatrical collectivity was mixed, both longed for and daunting. On the one hand, they noted the "pleasure" of appearing onstage and in the press. One participant noted that she wanted to hold onto "the gaze" (*le regard*) of the audience. Another laughed and shook his head as he remembered his earlier amusement: "They asked for our signatures! Look [mimicking an awestruck fan], they are *sans-papiers*!" The memory of this solicited signature was significant, for it allowed the youth to recognize their theatrical product by marking another surface with their presence, what Jacques Derrida might call their "nowness."[20] On the other hand, residues like this signature also identified them as the *source* of this transient event, which had an uncanny way of generating precarities in the weeks that followed. As the conversation turned to press coverage, several noted that pictures of their rehearsals were online, their faces often entirely visible. "There's a video too," a youth added, which caught another off guard: "What video?" His friend satisfied his curiosity and revealed that they were both prominently featured in a video fittingly titled "Youth without Papers," causing the group to burst into laughter. As we spoke, the distant sounds of police sirens reverberated in the secluded garden where we sat, further compounding their teenage merriment.

These bittersweet moments revealed that while they remembered theater fondly, the ubiquity of their theatrical signatures rarely confirmed the promise of embodied relationality. The warm gaze of the theatrical collective did not accompany the various other media through which they continued to experience exposure. For example, two of the youths recalled riding suburban train lines into Paris, when they found themselves seated next to commuters perusing newspapers that featured their story. Nervous, they changed cars. In fact, these references to public transit were significant. Paul Silverstein notes that the urban Métro and suburban RER train lines have long been "a space of harassment, racism and alienation" for the hyphenated residents of France,[21] its dangers only compounded for immigrants lacking documentation. In 2007, sharp increases in undocumented arrests in transit centers meant that *sans-papiers* individuals avoided public transportation. One of the anonymous voices of *La Plume sans papier* depicts a similar scene, underlining the fears and anxieties of phenomenal undocumentedness:

> Outside of my studies, I was fearful of going outside. One day, after finishing classes, I took the train to go back home. As usual, before entering the station, I checked to make sure there were no police. On this day, there wasn't anyone there but unfortunately, I wasn't done with surprises for the day. I was sitting with classmates who didn't know that I was "sans-papiers."

> All of a sudden, police officers opened the door; they approach our group, and pronounce one phrase, the phrase that kills: "identity check." My heart was beating so fast to the point where I thought that it was going to stop. All my friends passed through the controls but on this day, God was with me: they did not control me, I descended at my stop; my heart was still beating but my head told me, "It's good, it's over."[22]

In this scene, the undocumented youth's experience of sociality involves layers of alienation. Resonating with Frantz Fanon's oft-cited description of objecthood in *Black Skin, White Masks*, the youth's anticipated accusation reformulates Fanon's classic statement, revealing that "the [undocumented immigrant] suffers in his body quite differently from the white man."[23] In doing so, the youth's narrative designates the undocumented body as a space where signification and embodiment meet, where the abstractions of undocumented status congeal within the boundaries of an individual, racialized body.

These anecdotes underlined the complexity of *La Plume sans papier*'s theatrical vision, where theater was imagined to cultivate an embodied understanding of social presence. This understanding was both central to the training of the thespian (her ability to navigate the presence of her stage partners as well as that of her audience) and to the instilling of a slightly more intangible set of principles (considering oneself as a heteronomous being who is impressed by the movements of others, and in turn impresses her own bodily presence onto their consciousness). Yet theater's discursive dimensions were equally significant. As the above anecdote reveals, the *narrative content* for imagining oneself as spatially linked to a theatrical community was systematic isolation. And although these narratives of solitude could contradict the sharedness of theatrical embodiment, as well as prove damaging for having been "restored," in Richard Schechner's terms,[24] from a terrifying train ride, theatrical narration was nonetheless imagined to hold therapeutic potential. Theatrical aid work, in other words, struck a fragile balance in the terms of its engagement, risking the restoration of phenomenal suffering even as it sought to redress this pain.

Preparing for a Citizenship to Come

The text of *La Plume sans papier* further compounds the question of precisely what is enabled by theatrical aid work. The text is made up of several sections. It begins with acrostic poems that spell out the youths' countries of origin and continues with narratives constructed around the defensive phrase "get lost!" (*va t'en!*), before moving onto a collection of collectively assembled *cadavre exquis*. The text then follows with an assemblage of letters addressed to loved ones and ends with a set of freely written essays, all of them anonymous. Throughout, "La France" constitutes both the subject matter of the writing and its addressee. The youths reprimand the nation for betraying its republican principles, yet France's appearance in the text is almost always accompanied by the values it is meant to encapsulate. "Get lost, anxiety," one youth writes. "You who haunt the life of immigrants who live in France, country of liberty, equality and fraternity where blacks, Arabs and others live."[25] In excerpts like these, the anxiety of undocumented status disaggregates the republican motto from the cohabiting communities it is imagined to protect, but the possibility of a new republic remains vibrant: "If my heart were a book," another writes, "France would be written on every line."[26]

Other voices complicate this infatuation with reference to the colonial histories of contemporary immigration. Previous waves of migratory movement, whether in the form of the wartime recruitment of colonial infantries or postwar labor immigration, cast a shadow on the youths' own migratory trajectories. "France took my grandfather to fight the war on its side; she took my father to rebuild herself, so why doesn't she want me?"[27] asks one youth, laying bare a broader history of compromised citizenship for France's colonial and postcolonial populations. These individuals cannot be forgotten, yet they also cannot forget France, bound as they are in a relationship that swings between opposing and passionate extremes, as one youth states: "I hate France, I detest her, but I love her" (*Je hais la France, je la déteste, mais je l'aime*).[28] For some, these extremes result in a breakdown in social relationships and a desire to drift through everyday life unseen. For others, the outcome is a full-fledged battle, for as one youth states, "if regularization is war, I will be its blade."[29]

Neither present at *La Plume sans papier*'s performances, nor able to draw on recordings, my first experience of reading this text left me wondering how narratives of clandestine lives, thwarted educational opportunities, and social solitude signaled integration. Yet, I soon found that to ask such a question was to assume that theatrical practice functioned as the mere vehicle of a message, while I have endeavored to show that in RESF's theatrical aid work, its perceived capacities were far more ambitious in their reach. Indeed, *La Plume sans papier* revealed that critique itself was a valued category of self-expression, even when it contradicted the broader equation of integration-as-enmeshment. In fact, theatrical aid work derived its role precisely from these contradictions. Just as the relationship between the aid recipient and the aid network reached its desired conclusion via declarations of *dispensability*, the republic thus dismissed ("*va t'en!*") facilitated rather than inhibited the youths' emergence *as* self-sufficient, morally autonomous individuals. These theatrical figures could dismiss the aid collective only to forge a bond with an abstract community: republican citizens whose participation as national subjects materialized in the form of an inherently critical stance.

These tensions resonate with Gary Wilder's commentary on the literary and political practice of the Négritude poets. Commenting on republican traditions of civil society, Wilder notes that "republicanism and citizenship were defined not only by institutions but by a mental attitude and a type of behavior that is informed, critical, and participatory."[30] In French republicanism, "rights were a product of political association and participation, not the natural property of pre-political individuals."[31] Political participation, demands for reform, and critiques of the status quo, in other words, could serve as the practices through which rights were to be assumed. The Antillean, West African, and other colonial subjects who lived in continental France in the 1930s and who imagined the literary and cultural project of pan-African affirmation known as Négritude, articulated their share of demands for reform and accountability. Shaped by the paradoxical legacy of colonial assimilation, they critiqued the racial bias of French colonialism and did so precisely through the categories of public participation made available by the republican model. Wilder labels their literary and political practice "preparing for a citizenship to come":

> These colonial critics "practiced" citizenship in the imperial metropolis. Here practice has two connotations: behaving according to the protocols of republican citizenship and preparing for a citizenship to come. In both registers they were "acting" like citizens, doing what citizens are supposed to do, but also performing, pretending to be that which they could never fully be, not yet doing the real thing. Exercising civic virtue without enjoying full civil rights, they were at once part of the French cité and apart from it.[32]

The political status of the North, West, and sub-Saharan African youths who performed in *La Plume sans papier* were not unlike those of the Négritude group. Aimé Césaire, Léon Gontran Damas, and Léopold Sedar Senghor were not "illegal" presences in the metropole, but their claim to belonging was ruptured by the racial hierarchies of French colonialism, if not the contradictions of the republican principle of universal citizenship. The *La Plume sans papier* youths' exhortation that they are the first generation in their families to be refused entry into metropolitan French territory (following the recruitment of ancestors in combat and labor) underlined the ongoing contradictions of the relationship between French republicanism and immigration from former colonies. In *La Plume sans papier*, Wilder's theatrical metaphor morphed into a literal performance of the youths' simultaneous social enmeshment and their moral autonomy, exemplifying their readiness to do "the real thing" while displaying their objection to having been forced to "pretend."

Before turning to a broader consideration of autonomy and individuality in French debates on immigrant integration, it is important to highlight the challenge that undocumented theater might pose to canonical approaches to engaged and/or political art. When Wilder differentiates between the Négritude poets' "'acting' like citizens" and "perfoming, pretending to be that which they could never fully be," he unintentionally mirrors a Brechtian ideal: the alienated actor who "quotes" his character, delivering "the full substance of a human gesture even though it now represents a copy."[33] In other words, preparing for a citizenship to come is not unlike rehearsing Bertolt Brecht's alienation effect. In both cases, the actor's tendency to undertake a "total transformation" into character is interrupted by a detachment that rejects "the empathy operation."[34] This is a useful frame for considering *La Plume sans papier*'s negotiation of form and content: the theatrical display of suffering is imagined to signal social enmeshment, but the repeated references to "*va t'en*" invite audience members to recognize a detached autonomy. This is both the desired outcome of theatrical aid work and a recognition of the limits of the youths' total transformation into citizen-actors. Whereas the Brechtian model often ignites debates that square off autonomous art against political engagement, undocumented theater renders these antagonisms irrelevant, repurposing both ends of the divide.

Autonomy, Individuality, and Integration

RESF's emphasis on integration as a phenomenon of social belonging is relatively straightforward. Well beyond its usage in French immigration policy, the term *intégration*'s sociological definition underlines the processes by which the members of a collective come to articulate common awarenesses, sentiments, and goals. The aid network's interest in *autonomy* and *self-government*, however, references the term's uniquely French formulation. Indeed, moral autonomy and individual rationality have been central to French debates on immigrant integration; since the 1980s, questions regarding French integration policy have underlined a self-affirming and individualist notion of citizenship. This is often coupled with the insistence that the relationship between the individual and the state overrides the ties that individuals might have to particular religious, ethnic, or cultural groupings. Moral autonomy, in other words, has served less as an abstract ideal than as a perceived guard against the threat of communitarian tendencies.

This was not always the case, however. Prior to the 1980s, French integration policy was characterized by the term *insertion* and focused primarily on the welfare, housing, and labor conditions of immigrant populations. Adrian Favell notes that there were several interlinked phenomena that triggered the transition to a more symbolic debate.[35] The decentralizing tendencies of Socialist President François Mitterand rallied around the catchphrase *droit à la difference*, or the "right to difference," and were often characterized by the political Right as an affront to the centralized tradition of the French state. In practice, *droit à la difference* largely referenced changes in cultural policy to ensure the democratization of cultural access.[36] Yet such efforts were often perceived as a celebration of ethnic (and particularly *North African immigrant* ethnic) difference.[37] Coupled with the turn to a supranational,

European framework for the consideration of welfare, Favell notes that decentralization was considered by many to be a threat to France's centralized political and cultural unity. The electoral rise of Jean-Marie Le Pen and the anti-immigrant rhetoric of his far-right political party Front National only contributed to the perceived link between immigration, difference, and social disintegration.[38]

In 1987 President Jacques Chirac announced the launch of a commission to debate the rewriting of French nationality laws, the Code de la Nationalité. Composed largely of Parisian academics, the commission consulted with a variety of political and civic actors and produced a report entitled *Être Français aujourd'hui et demain* (*To Be French Today and Tomorrow*) in which they underlined "the self-constituting and self-conscious individualist idea of French nationality."[39] This emphasis on self-election was reflected in the commission's proposed changes to the nationality code. While maintaining the code's long-standing commitment to *droit du sol* or citizenship by birth, the report asked that second-generation children declare their willingness to adhere to the French nation between the ages of 16 and 20. These proposals were met with criticism in 1988, but they would be signed into law in 1993 by Minister of the Interior Charles Pasqua, along with a series of amendments to the nation's immigration laws. Meanwhile, a Haut Conseil à l'Intégration was founded in 1990 to further elaborate upon the particularities of the French model of integration. This was the first political body to put forward the notion of a Contrat d'Accueil et d'Intégration (CAI), a literal contract signed between the French state and the migrant individual. The CAI would spell out this individual's rights on French soil as well as determine their duties vis-à-vis their incorporation into French social life. During the following decade, this proposal was revisited and became law in 2007.

Throughout this period, French integration policy was often portrayed as a direct inheritor of the values of the Revolution.[40] The framework supplied by Dominique Schnapper, Pascale Krief, and Emmanuel Peignard is an excellent example:

> National belonging is thought to be the result of cultural belonging and the individual's political will: this is the major source of the elective ideology of the nation which has dominated the French concept. Through its universal and abstract ambitions, the Revolution implied that all those who adhered to the nation's values, in particular human rights, could all become its members.[41]

Encapsulated here are some of the major tropes of French republicanism. The French model's "universal and abstract ambitions" guard against an emphasis on particular characteristics that belong in the sphere of private life. The abstract individual is not marked by race, ethnicity, gender, or religious affiliation, thus incarnating the common good and universality of national citizenship. Unlike the German model of nationality, membership in the French nation does not require a particular linguistic or racial makeup, relying instead on the force of individuals' willingness to submit to a *cultural* unity.[42] This "elective ideology" is often credited to Jean-Jacques Rousseau, whose vision of political order emphasized the nation as "a moral and collective body, composed of as many members as the assembly has voices, and which receives from this same act its unity, its common self, its life and its will."[43] Eventually termed "the general will of the people," this "common self" could exercise sovereignty, author laws, and become the framework through which individuals could exercise their freedom.

Theoretical as this framework was, it nonetheless served as a reference point for the polarized integration debates of the 1980s and 1990s. Schnapper distinguishes two camps: the "integrationists" and the "multiculturalists."[44] As can be surmised, the first group is composed of intellectuals who warn that the public recognition of particular rights and characteristics could lead to communitarianism:

> The first [risk] is that of contradicting the liberty of individuals. Affirming the existence of particular rights risks shutting individuals away in their particularism, of assigning them to a group, against their personal liberty and their possibility of exchange with others . . . The second risk concerns social integration. The public recognition of particular groups would risk consecrating and crystallizing these particularisms at the expense of what unifies citizens, organizing the withdrawal of individuals into their communities of origin in place of giving them the means to exceed and enter into relations with others.[45]

As this excerpt makes clear, the "integrationist" viewpoint institutes a strong separation between local, ethnic, or religious communities and the national community, implying that belonging to the former might jeopardize belonging to the latter. Conversely, the "multiculturalists" suggest that abstract citizenship can generate its own exclusions. "Moderate multiculturalists," however, are aware of the risks of communitarianism and impose a certain number of conditions:

> The first is that individuals shouldn't be authoritatively assigned to take part in a particular group. They ought to be free to enter and exit. The second condition is that one should recognize only those cultures that do not carry traits that are incompatible with human rights. One should not admit, in the name of an absolute cultural relativism as do some thinkers of extreme multiculturalism, that a traditional culture should be invoked to justify the statutory inequality of men and women, the circumcision of little girls or the rights of husbands to beat their wives.[46]

"Moderate multiculturalists," in other words, reject the suggestion that cultural unity is a condition for social equality. Their celebration of cultural plurality, however, takes place within a series of limits set by French republican law, here equated with universal human rights.

What Schnapper's binary reveals is the broader framework within which both camps position their definitions of individuality and citizenship. For both the integrationists and the multiculturalists, individuals are imagined to stand at a distance from their "culture," whether this particular grouping is religious, ethnic, or cultural in nature. Despite having been formed, as individuals, in accordance with the norms of that particular grouping, their "entry" and "exit" are imagined to function as relatively *autonomous*, self-willed phenomena. The Haut Conseil à l'Intégration has underlined this autonomy while stressing the French republic's commitment to *laïcité*, suggesting that religious affiliations in particular are best exercised through public associations and "an official engagement in the public space."[47] And as Favell makes clear, this formula carries an attendant *moral* configuration:

> Only the individual who chooses to act within the political structure offered can be moral, since acting outside of it is by definition to act in a selfish, particularistic or anti-national way; to fail to do so is to fail to be truly French.[48]

The term "integration," in other words, harbors a variety of connotations, both practical and moral. Schnapper's definition of the "moderate multiculturalist" position allows a glimpse of the kinds of activities that have, since the 1980s, been perceived as brakes on immigrants' moral autonomy and social integration: inequality between men and women, female circumcision, and domestic violence. Indeed, when the incommensurable tendencies of immigrant populations have garnered public attention, in cases ranging from televised discoveries of basement mosques in immigrant neighborhoods to polygamous family arrangements, female circumcisions, and the headscarf, these events have been positioned as evidence of *nonnational* moral commitments, deriving from responsibilities toward sources other than the French nation-state.

What is equally significant about this list is that its focus has been on *bodily practices*, corporeal traditions that are perceived as rupturing French bodily behavior. While moral autonomy is the category through which the ideal of the abstract individual is sought, embodied life is one of the key domains in which moral autonomy is imagined to manifest itself. I had illustrated this dynamic in the context of the headscarf debates in the introduction to this book. Here, I am more interested in how the links between moral autonomy, integration, and bodily life emerge in the activities of nongovernmental organizations that work on immigration and theater. How do organizations like RESF and Cimade translate these public discourses? How do they espouse or alter the official definitions of "autonomy" and "integration"? I have suggested that RESF's *La Plume sans papier* provided the participating youth with an embodied domain through which to rehearse their participation in French social life, a project that illustrates the possibilities as well as the limitations of theater as a practice of integration. Cimade offers a parallel example that further interrogates the relationship between theater, embodiment, and collective living.

La Cimade's Theater Workshops

While RESF is a relatively recent formation, La Cimade was founded in Bièvres in 1939 as a response to the refugee crisis that followed the evacuation of the German-occupied Alsace and Lorraine territories. With strong ties to Protestant unions and student associations, Cimade's work was defined at the time as "both evangelical and social,"[49] a spiritual orientation that has since given way to a secular enterprise yet is nonetheless present in the organization's commitment to *témoignage*, or "witnessing" the experience of the aided individual. Indeed, Cimade's humanitarian presence in German internment camps figures largely in the organization's narrative of its origins. Publications on their contemporary theatrical ventures often conclude with reference to the theatrical activities that Cimade participated in at Gurs, an internment camp. Today, Cimade's public profile is built in large part around migratory flows and the juridical aid that they provide to refugees and asylum seekers in France, often as the only nongovernmental organization allowed into retention centers and prisons. The organization's vast network of nationwide salaried workers and volunteers provides a range of services, including social activities designed to accompany asylum seekers during the evaluation of their request for refugee status.

Theater is one such accompaniment action. The annual theater workshops that Cimade conducted with asylum seekers from 2003 to 2007 were coordinated by Service Formation, the branch of the organization dedicated to education and training, and funded by an Exchanges Partnership[50] between French, Hungarian, and British aid organizations promoting the "social and vocational integration of asylum seekers."[51] Cimade's focus was on language training, a service that they had provided previously and in the context of which they had experimented with theatrical techniques. In 2003 the Service Formation partnered with the actor and director Hélène Cinque, the head of the theater company L'Instant d'une Résonance, who directed the theater workshops as well as their public performances. Each year, the theater workshops lasted six months and included anywhere from 25 to 50 participants whose national origins ranged from North and sub-Saharan Africa to the Middle East, the Balkans, Russia, and the Caucasus. Each year's influx reflected the dominant patterns of the period's migratory flows, and the 2006 and 2007 workshops in particular included large groups of Chechen men and women,[52] partly as a result of the ongoing conflict in Chechnya and partly as the fruit of a collaboration between Cimade and the Franco-Chechen Cultural Center.[53]

Although the Exchanges Partnership generated a variety of social and vocational projects, the key term that spanned all of the activities was "empowerment," defined by the partners as a strategy that included the beneficiaries in the development of the aid project. Cimade's brochure conceded that in French, "no word in itself embodies all the meanings the word 'empowerment' has in English," but added that "in French, process and output, autonomy and confidence, opportunity and capacity are complementary words needed to approach the full meaning of empowerment."[54] Not coincidentally, these French-language approximations of "empowerment" revealed as much about Cimade's approach to French integration debates as they did about the complexities of translation. During my conversations with the theater projects' planners, it became clear that much like RESF, Cimade practiced theater in a context where nongovernmental sponsorship of creativity inadvertently retained a conversation with a larger semantic field. As a language-learning tool, theater allowed workshop participants to practice one of the key dimensions of language acquisition: learning to accommodate the bodily repertoire attached to the French language and culture. This gestural vocabulary was viewed as a significant dimension of a refugee or asylum seeker's experience of autonomy and self-confidence. At the same time, mounting a performance was understood as an exercise in interculturalism and *vivre ensemble* or living together. As a collective practice, theater fostered a sense of interdependence through participants' experience of the rehearsal process as well as their eventual ownership of the performance output. On both embodied and collective levels, in other words, Cimade positioned theater as a practice of integration. A closer look indicates how larger public debates on moral autonomy and bodily life impacted Cimade workers' understanding of this positioning, even as they sought to address the paradoxes of French discourses on autonomous individuality.

Asylum, Accompaniment, and Integration

Cimade's translation of "empowerment" into a clear set of objectives reflected broader administrative changes, including the emergence of accompaniment as a nongovernmental intervention. Indeed, Cimade's decision to engage asylum seekers in theatrical activity was a direct result of policy changes lengthening the evaluation of asylum applications. Historically, an individual seeking asylum in France would have their application assessed by the Office Français de Protection des Réfugiés et Apatrides (OFPRA), during which time they would be offered a temporary authorization of residency, an authorization that made them eligible to receive temporary housing or financial allocations yet denied them the right to work.[55] OFPRA was originally attached to the Ministry of Foreign Affairs, thus keeping asylum applications distinct from the Ministry of the Interior's evaluation of larger migratory flows. A series of legal changes in 2003 and 2006 ended OFPRA's status as a "consulate for the stateless,"[56] joining the evaluation of asylum demands to all categories of immigration. The elongated waiting period that resulted from this shift left individuals without the right to work, living in temporary (or nonexistent) housing conditions and in vague administrative categories for years at a time. The Cimade worker Liliana referred to these individuals as "subjects without rights" (*des sujets de non-droit*), immobilized by the ambiguous temporality of the evaluation process. Cimade's six-month theater workshop thus signaled the organization's need to transition accompaniment from a durational to an *ongoing* service. Theatrical spectatorship, I was told, reversed the dynamics of *l'attente* or "the wait";[57] instead of waiting for news, the participant-actors would find that they were *waited for*, the source of others' anticipation.

If Cimade's theatrical interlude sought to respond to asylum's unique temporality, however, Cimade workers were equally aware that these theatrical activities could trigger administrative recognition. In a context where immigration policies increasingly insisted on evidence of residency candidates' adequate integration, theater appeared to function as a practice capable of cultivating this status. During our conversation, Liliana differentiated between adult asylum seekers and their children, noting that French law guaranteed every child of school age access to education: "So the children are at school, they learn French, and they are on their path to integration [*sur leur chemin d'intégration*] while the parents are in a hotel room or a residence hall where nothing is happening for them." With these comments, Liliana referenced the well-worn trope of the republican school as the "paradigm of integration,"[58] the universal institution charged with generating cultural unity. At the same time, she identified access to French language instruction as the cornerstone of this experience, contrasting the classroom and the temporary residence hall. As she continued, it became clear that nongovernmental organizations working on immigration performed a similar task vis-à-vis the adults, generating activities that could function as proof of adult asylum seekers' acculturation. Moreover, the numbers seemed to suggest that their efforts paid off more often than not. Shaking her head, Liliana noted:

> When individuals are taken care of in the context of a project like this [the theater workshops], asylum seekers have a greater chance at obtaining refugee status, which isn't normal. When others mobilize for someone's application to be evaluated, it works better. Do you see? This is terrible, because it shows that there is a certain arbitrariness to the system in France.

Whereas "accompaniment" was designed to alleviate the incapacitation that the French state's asylum policies induced, Cimade workers realized that it could equally serve as a vehicle of administrative recognition, with a higher chance of reward. Put differently, aid strategies that developed in response to changing immigration policies inadvertently created openings within the same bureaucracies. Alison Jeffers's notion of refugees' "bureaucratic performance" best captures the ambivalent role that theater thus played in the symbiotic relationship between nongovernmental organizations and the French state: although Cimade framed theatrical practice as a vehicle of autonomous self-expression and empowerment, theater's meanings were equally shaped by the bureaucracies against which these practices were positioned.[59] Liliana's reference to the "arbitrariness" faced by Cimade also echoes the state-civil society partnerships studied by Aihwa Ong, which led the anthropologist to ask: "Can NGOs, in their actual representations of excluded populations, operate independently of relationships to the nation-state and to the market?"[60] During my conversations, I found that theater functioned as part of a broader dynamic wherein the work of caring for the displaced was increasingly subcontracted to nongovernmental entities, creating a space for different models of autonomy and different strategies for administrative recognition.[61]

Cimade's translation of "empowerment" into the goals of theatrical language training is a good example of the dependence of which Ong speaks. For Cimade, the workshops' goals range from providing a "symbolic and physical space for asylum seekers" to developing "a public policy of welcome and accompaniment," and from guidance "on the path to integration in the host country" to fostering "an intercultural 'living together' in our society."[62] These items contain a great degree of intertextuality. The "symbolic and physical" space that the organization seeks to install is a direct reaction to the precariousness of elongated waiting periods. In turn, references to "a public policy of welcome" and "an intercultural 'living together' " reveal that the theater workshops are both the product of Cimade's own unique vision of French society and part of a larger public discourse on social accompaniment and hospitality, a point to which I will return. Meanwhile, "the path to integration" is differentiated from an earlier item referencing "insertion" into professional markets, a nod to the political separation of questions of employment and welfare from a more abstract process of acculturation. Over the course of my conversations, I found that the theater workshops themselves were greatly intertextual, both working with and altering the official understanding of integration.

Gestural Competence and New Desires

Cimade workers gravitated toward theater for a number of reasons, one of which was the well-documented link between theater exercises and language learning. When articulating theater's role as a practice of integration,

Cimade's booklets noted that both domains shared an emphasis on bodily life. In *Théâtre et apprentissage du français* (*Theater and Learning French*), an extensive booklet evaluating Cimade's experience with theatrical language training, the organization's rationale for using theater is clear:

> The legitimation of work on gesture and on the body in didactic situations has to do with the fact that the learner must not simply assimilate the verbal signs and sounds of a language but must also be capable of understanding the gestures of a society, of producing them, of knowing what is implicated by them, of seizing the adequate ones in such or such a situation.[63]

For Cimade, communication between the members of a society involved both verbal output and the ability to participate in a repertoire of gestures, thereby implicating corporeality in the verbal act. Cimade noted that this "work on gesture and on the body" was necessary because assimilation took place via both linguistic and corporeal registers, acknowledging the significance of what Paul Connerton has called "incorporating practice."[64] In his work on the embodied dimensions of collective memory, Connerton has noted that "culturally specific postural performances provide us with a mnemonics of the body,"[65] allowing individuals entry into collectively acknowledged habit memories as well as the social stratifications to which these habits are inevitably attached. Where gesture's social and ideological work was concerned, Cimade's booklet was quick to note that their goal was not to generate a series of imitated, perfected gestures. Instead, the organization's goal was identified as the development of a broader "gestural competence" that could aid individuals in communicating their thoughts.[66]

This connection between thoughts and gestures (or actions) seemed straightforward enough, yet my conversation with Hélène Cinque revealed a more complicated understanding. For Cinque, gestures were more than the bodily manifestation of intentional acts of communication. Gestures could themselves generate new intentions, emotions, and even sensibilities. Cinque elaborated this dynamic by linking the rehearsal of a physical gesture of rejection to the ability to occupy a dismissive stance in everyday life:

> [Cinque scrunched her shoulders for me and shook her head from side to side, mimicking the gesture she had shown her students.] "I don't want to! I'm tired! I hate this, I am sick of it!" This [indicating the gesture] will come back to them, in the moment, and they will be able to say to someone, "You don't have the right to speak to me this way, I won't take it!" I especially provoked things like this.

In instances such as these, the physical gesture of defiance that Cinque asked her students to rehearse was less an exercise in perfected imitation than an instance of *bodily* learning. Yet the muscular work at its base also held out the possibility of an *ideological* transformation: a readiness to act with cognition of one's rights and the rights of others. Theatrical language learning, in other words, taught more than one kind of competence. It sought to instill a sense of the relationship between bodily life and linguistic familiarity, and it emphasized the kinds of moral and ideological principles that were imagined to compose an individual's "path to integration."

On the one hand, we might attribute Cinque's emphasis on physicality to her theatrical background. As a young actor, Cinque had trained at the Théâtre du Soleil, a theater company with a distinct emphasis on bodily work and discipline. Théâtre du Soleil's focus on their actors' corporeal training ranges from mastering the gestural repertoire of highly codified performance forms like Kathakali dance to producing the Western classics in a distinctly athleticized fashion. My conversation with Cinque revealed the traces of a theatrical apprenticeship that emphasized the physical, outer contours of theatrical character over its inner life. She noted: "The work of the actor that I learned, and that I practice, has to do with the body, and with emotions of course, but first with a body that is moving this way or that, with lips, with eyes moving left or right. It is a microscopic work, scientific even, the work of a researcher." Lest such an emphasis obscure the workshop's focus on language and articulation exercises, Cinque was quick to note that she did not bypass the discursive dimensions of language learning.[67] However, her theatrical training had pushed her to emphasize the gestural life of social communication, as well as the potential that corporeal practice held for altering an individual's broader world.

On the other hand, Cinque's as well as Cimade's approach to theatrical physicality underlined the opacities and contradictions of theater as a practice of integration. Indeed, Cinque's view that gestural competence could produce certain moral sensibilities was a commitment that was shared by the larger organization. For example, Cimade's booklet noted that participants would "acquire a better understanding of their desires, of their objectives, of the reality of the path that must be traveled to prepare serenely and to succeed with their professional insertion and individual integration."[68] Statements such as these revealed the ambiguities of bodily training. Exercises like Cinque's defensive shoulder scrunch were significant in that their bodily components could encapsulate a conceptual principle: the notion that individuals are endowed with rights and that such endowedness is an essential element of "the reality of the path that must be traveled" in France. At the same time, this stipulation could seem at odds with an emphasis on participants' own "desires" and "objectives," which might or might not have subscribed to that "reality." In many ways, the particular brand of ideological-corporeal acculturation at stake in Cimade's references to gestural competence resonated with Connerton's comments on habitually observed rituals of social propriety. The scholar notes that such habits are "'forgotten' as maxims only when they have been well remembered as habits."[69] In Cimade's theatrical theorizing, gestural competence encapsulated the passage from maxim to habit, with all of the attendant ambiguities and forms of control that permeated this path.

One way of negotiating this conundrum might be to understand Cimade's approach to theatrical practice as a cultivating, rather than inculcating, process.[70] Approached from this framework, gestural competence implied that participants would translate their desires and objectives *through* this new bodily repertoire. In other words, they would formulate defiant responses *because* they would come to conceive of themselves as rights-bearing individuals. At stake in Cimade's rehearsals, then, was a process of translation whereby, through the vehicle of theatrical acting, the workshop participants' sense of themselves and their future was transformed into a new language.

Given the complexity that underwrote this approach to bodily practice, Cinque's theatrical exercises might appear slightly abstracted from the goal of accompaniment. In fact, the majority of the improvisational exercises designed by Cinque and Service Formation addressed the concrete situations that asylum seekers faced, such as interviews in various government offices or managing their bills in residence halls. Despite the workshop's emphasis on the practical, however, in my conversations, the intangibility of "empowerment" often mirrored the ephemerality of "integration." This process was often depicted through the metaphor of a path, route, or road. When I asked Liliana what counted as successful integration, she smiled, noting that integration was a matter of personal effort and day-to-day self-fashioning. She added: "For me, integration is a personal path [*un chemin personel*], it is a process undertaken by a person on a path, on his/her own path, as a person relative to others. Integration is always an exchange, an ebb and tide between one person and another person." Much like empowerment, in other words, integration was difficult to quantify or approximate, a difficulty captured by the fact that Liliana prefaced her reply through reference to her own subject position, acknowledging the impossibility of an authoritative description. In her definition, integration encapsulated a set of qualities that were implicitly deemed central to social life in the host country; similar to the balance between autonomy and interdependence suggested by *La Plume sans papier*, Cimade's integrated individual displayed both self-sufficiency (indicated by the image of the personal path) and relationality (the exchange implied by the ebb and tide of human contact).

An Intercultural Living Together

If gestural competence was one dimension of the relationship between theater and integration, the promotion of an "intercultural 'living together' [*vivre ensemble*]" was the other. The phrase *vivre ensemble* is widely used in Cimade's publications to suggest a kind of social cohesion that is more affirmative than the terminology of organizations like the Haut Conseil à l'Intégration, highlighting cohabitation over historically loaded terms like "assimilation." The phrase's origins can be found in the kinds of multicultural sensibilities that emerged during the promotion of *droit à la différence,* but Cimade's usage pointed at a more contemporary mix of reference points as well. References to "living together" as well as statements regarding "a public policy of welcome and accompaniment" partook of what Mireille Rosello has called "a widespread, diverse and multicultural debate about hospitality" in France in the late 1990s and early 2000s.[71]

Rosello notes that whereas the 1980s landscape was marked by the activism of immigrants' associations, "the involvement of cultural agents, intellectuals, artists, and social scientists who [were] taking strong and visible positions"[72] transformed the politicization of immigration in the 1990s. One outcome of this process was the emergence of a discourse of hospitality that became an idiom for critiquing immigration policy. Tahar Ben Jelloun's 1984 *Hospitalité Française* was republished in 1998, along with Jacques Derrida's *De l'hospitalité* and Alain Montandon's edited volume *Le Livre de l'hospitalité,* which, not surprisingly, called hospitality "a manner of living together" (*une manière de vivre ensemble*).[73] In these works, personal hospitality was often framed in opposition to administrative inhospitality and political xenophobia. As Rosello notes, however, simple dichotomies between an inhospitable state and hospitable citizens hinged on the ambiguity of a vaguely defined hospitality ethic, linking immigration to "apparently private notions of generosity and goodwill."[74] For Cimade, *vivre ensemble* was a way of capturing the interdependence that theater could generate. Yet the phrase retained the complexities of this larger debate, indicating the changeable role that "private notions" could play in the maintenance of experiments in living together.

Liliana's references to *vivre ensemble* paired this phrase with the term "intercultural" to differentiate Cimade's usage from "multicultural," but her reasons for rejecting the term differed from the integrationist position of the 1980s and 1990s. During these decades, debates around immigration had counterposed integration and multiculturalism, with the latter position likened to American-style communitarianism and perceived ghettoization. The backlash against multiculturalism took the form of a particularly rigid, universalist understanding of citizenship that Liliana clearly condemned. During our conversation, she referenced the linguistic and cultural homogenization of the French countryside, a process most closely associated with the nation-building project of the Third Republic. "France has been assimilationist for a long time, it is part of the history of the republic," she told me, "my Breton grandmother knew this well." Yet Liliana rejected the term "multiculturalism," noting that it generated a logic of tolerant inclusion that she found unacceptable. She added instead:

> Living interculturally means every individual finds their place with all the cultural aspects that compose them. Me for example, I am French,

> I can also say that I am English, Breton, Catholic, Protestant, there are plenty of things that compose the person that I am, each person is a kaleidoscope.

Liliana's idea of human beings as kaleidoscopes or fragmented compositions paralleled Cimade's understanding of *vivre ensemble*. Key to this understanding was the fact that references to kaleidoscopic beings were often evoked in a manner that was continuous with Cimade's emphasis on autonomy and individuality. For example, *Théâtre et apprentissage du français* praised the Théâtre du Soleil's understanding of theater, which entailed "accepting the other in his/her individuality, which is recognizing them above all as a unique person and not as a national of this or that country, originating in this ethnicity or that community."[75] Recalling earlier debates between "integrationists" and "multiculturalists," excerpts like these framed individuality as the counterpoint to collectivity, rendering the recognition of individual uniqueness contingent on that individual's insulation from collective formations. Put otherwise, the image of the kaleidoscope suggested that an individual's "cultural aspects" might make demands on their sense of self and community, yet these cultural aspects did not preclude recognizing this person as an autonomous individual.

What did such continuities entail for an experiment in theatrical "living together"? During my conversations, the theater workshop's decision to mount a concluding public performance was repeatedly identified as the ultimate exercise in living together. Indeed, *Théâtre et apprentissage du français* writes that "a particularly telling example of the equilibrium between a group and an individual and the construction of a work was experienced by participants by way of the responsibilities of the management of the stage."[76] The creation of a public performance afforded the participants with what the Service Formation considered a community of need and responsibility. Cinque related to me that "When someone said, 'I can't do this, I can't,' we would say 'But we need you [*on a besoin de toi*], the collective needs you.'" Workshop participants, in other words, were responsible for acting on stage, clearing the stage between scenes, setting up costumes, and being accountable for the smooth run of their collective product. They were, for Cinque, entirely dependent on functioning as a collective:

> The collective is made of individuals, there are no individuals without a collective and there is no collective without individuality. This has nothing to do with being a mass. Each individual creates something individual in a collective form. This is the same vision I have for my own theater company.

Lingering in Cinque's comment were residues of the Théâtre du Soleil's emphasis on collectivity, an emphasis which has famously led the company to prioritize the ensemble over individual actors and mandate equal pay for all those involved with theatrical production. At the same time, what Cinque identified as a philosophy of the theater resonated with a far more rooted republican tradition of collectivity, one that positioned the pursuit of individual creativity as the vehicle for adhering to a collective form. Thus, much like RESF, Cimade workers positioned theater as a mechanical structure through which individuals could conceptualize their membership in a broader collective, both theatrical and social. In turn, conceptualizing this theatrical-social collective as one composed of individuals from a variety of backgrounds meant encountering the complications that structure "intercultural" polities. In fact, the different models of personhood suggested by "the kaleidoscopic individual" and "the unique individual" generated complicated situations that joined the question of autonomous individuality to that of artistic autonomy.

Rethinking Autonomy: Process versus Product

The annual performances that resulted from Cimade's four consecutive theater workshops (2003–7) were composed of a variety of different vignettes. For example, one year included participants reading poems by the French poet Jacques Prévert, another featured an a capella Edith Piaf song. In a more abstract vignette, the entire cast of one workshop stood downstage, staring at a terrifying and imagined object hovering over the audience and eventually crashing down on them like a wave, accompanied by an alarm-inducing musical score.[77] Short, repeated vignettes underscored the basic injustices that asylum seekers face on a regular basis. For example, throughout the 2007 performance, one actor asked another if he was human, and upon receiving an affirmative answer, responded: "Are you sure?"[78] At the same time, final performances often emphasized participants' personal narratives, an emphasis that influenced the rehearsal process as well. Scenes based on participants' experiences of harassment in hostels, stores, and bureaucratic encounters were plentiful, as were scenes depicting the kindness of strangers. And every once in a while, a performance would depict a scene from a country of origin, such as a 2005 piece that showed the violence experienced by a participant in Taliban-ruled Kabul.[79]

In *Théâtre et apprentissage du français*, the turn to personal narrative is depicted as a slow and steady development that was nonetheless hastened by the demands of a final product.[80] During our conversation, Cinque told me that the revelation of personal experience was difficult for the participants, an exercise rendered even more trying when conducted in French. She had therefore asked them to recount painful memories and narratives in their native languages, an exercise that facilitated participants' delivery and maintained the bodily and vocal "authenticity"[81] of the narrative recounted. Cinque noted that her role as director was to retain and re-create this authenticity:

> I understood nothing except that I have the advantage in my expertise of observing, of listening, of memorizing and recording. [In their narratives] there was emotion, music, emotionality, and musicality, so even if I didn't understand, I could see what they had gone through, what they had experienced.

Cinque's goal as a director was to re-create the emotionality and musicality of these narratives when translated into French, thus retaining the authenticity of the original deliveries in a form that would facilitate the comprehension of the performance's French audience. Cinque's decision to balance linguistic familiarity with authenticity of delivery complicated the workshops' emphasis on integrating participants to a new gestural (and thus emotional) competence: what was revealed was the difference between a rehearsal process dependent on engendering new bodily repertoires and a performance product dependent on displaying the "authentic" foreign origins of the bodies that were undertaking this training.

We might interpret such complications as evidence of the vexed relationship between moral autonomy and the autonomy of art. On one level, the workshop's goal was to have participants undergo transformative experiences in the theater. On another, having them remain "other" for the duration of that transformation could result in a theatrically compelling display of narrative and emotionality. The workshop could transition between models of kaleidoscopic and unique individuality, in other words, based on where it felt the project's aesthetic ambitions lay. At the same time, these differences took place at a slightly more conceptual level, revealing two different visions of theatrical performance. First, participation in the theater was a cultivating process. More than a mere representation of the social reality that lay beyond its walls, theater held the potential to engender new sensibilities, both corporeal and intellectual. Second, theater was a signifying event, demanding "a constant flow of hermeneutic processes of understanding"[82] that emphasized the representational force of the person, action, or object on stage. It would be a mistake to suggest that these two understandings were necessarily at odds with one another; the point is that they resulted in performance *products* whose needs were different from those mandated by the performance *process*.

The varied requirements of process and product had implications for the broader ideological principles that the workshop mobilized. For Cimade, theatrical aid work could not be divorced from a broader political context in which aid organizations geared their cultural activism toward fulfilling bureaucratic needs. Indeed, they considered theatrical practice to be a space in which artistic emphases on bodily awareness or collective coordination could generate certain social sensibilities: namely, a sense of collectivity premised on unique individuality. At the same time, the organization's desire to produce an evocative, authentically delivered public performance resulted in rehearsal strategies that relied on evoking the presence of kaleidoscopic individualities, attached to different bodily repertoires. This simultaneous emphasis on sameness and difference could result in a paradoxical project. The demands of aesthetic ideals (or autonomous art) triggered strategies that revealed that these different models of individuality (unique vs. kaleidoscopic) were not so easy to parse, and that bodily life was linked to moral autonomy in complicated ways.

Conclusion

During my conversations with the Service Formation, I found that the relationship between moral autonomy, bodily life, and social integration did not translate into clear-cut rehearsal strategies. For example, organizers noted that some of the participants were unwilling to participate in exercises of a bodily nature. Such moments of reluctance pushed Cimade workers to question their own assumptions as to whether embodied life could be taken as a space where signs of autonomy manifested themselves. At times, they responded to these participants in ways that underlined the pragmatic challenges of these embodied vocabularies, seeking a middle ground that could accommodate participants' hesitations even as they challenged the limits of their comfort zones. At others, Cimade workers responded to reluctant participants with ideological principles, relating these bodily exercises to abstract ideals of rights-bearing and emancipation, as Cinque had with her shoulder scrunch.

These conversations soon revealed, however, that theater's "liberty" and "collectivity" were not predetermined givens. Instead, they were relationships and attitudes cultivated over long periods of time and practice. During our conversation, Liliana told me that the theater workshops had challenged her own limits as to the flexibility of theatrical "living together." When theater demanded unique individuality, its public performance lacked the desired aesthetic authenticity. When theatrical practice was positioned as requiring morally autonomous bodies, the presence of kaleidoscopic individuality revealed the limits of theater's autonomy from its political and social context. In many ways, Liliana's recognition of the limits of theater as a practice of integration displayed the contradictions of a political context that identified moral autonomy *from* cultural or religious affiliations as the requirement for citizenship.

At the same time, it is equally important to remember that in the context of RESF and Cimade's work, the moral and the aesthetic versions of the autonomy/heteronomy divide operated independently of one another. References to theater's ability to signal the moral autonomy of the individual speaking on stage were never divorced from an expectation that theatrical events were themselves inherently heteronomous. The autonomy of *La Plume sans papier*'s narrative content never negated the enmeshment of theater, while Cimade's empowering of an individual to proceed down their personal path to integration was imagined to take place in a literal relationship of theatrical *accompaniment*. The references to autonomy, self-government, and self-sufficiency that are scattered throughout these pages thus arise in contexts that are already cognizant of their philosophical and aesthetic openness to critique. I have suggested that theater *as a practice of integration* may challenge us to think about the limits of republican discourses of autonomous individuality. But it is equally vital to recognize that for nongovernmental contexts that aim to strike a fragile balance in the terms of their aesthetic and ethical engagement, these limits are always visible. Put differently, theatrical immigration activism makes clear the fact that *others* need to prepare the groundwork for one's exercise of aesthetic autonomy. Thus it follows that these contexts' political-moral understandings of self-government are equally influenced by the rendering visible of the event's collectively maintained theatrical infrastructure. In a way, this chapter has been about how theatrically inclined social workers negotiate the insights that result from this exposure.

Chapter 4

✦

Rethinking Community and Culture

In the fall of 2005, a series of violent protests of unprecedented size and duration occurred in a number of metropolitan suburbs across France. Variously labeled the protests, *émeutes* (riots), or *révoltes* (revolts) of 2005, the events drew a range of reactions from across the political spectrum. Initial commentators identified a religious motivation and interpreted the unrest as evidence of a broader, transnational network of Islamic uprisings. Others bemoaned the breakdown of republican ideals of citizenship, and underlined the anger of racialized, seemingly unintegrated youth. To these commentators the events seemed to signal a deep-seated violence against the very idea of France itself. Meanwhile, yet others situated the protests against a lengthier history of confrontation in the French *banlieue*. Arguing that the unrest was a product of structural conditions, these commentators noted that economic impoverishment, racial discrimination, and increased police violence in urban peripheries had reached a breaking point. In the weeks and months that followed, these interpretations vied for attention in the public imagination, even as most agreed that France was witnessing the collective expression of an economic and social frustration felt by residents in mostly immigrant housing projects.

In the Paris suburb of Blanc-Mesnil, the protests led to the creation of a women's collective, Quelques unes d'entre nous (A few from among us), one of whose first activities was a writing workshop where members shared their reactions to the violence. This project soon resulted in a theatrical performance, *Le Bruit du monde m'est rentré dans l'oreille* (*The Sounds of the Crowd Entered My Ear*), which chronicled the women's reactions to the unrest while negotiating the addressee toward whom such a chronicle would direct its grievances. Indeed, *Le Bruit du monde* featured a series of rhetorical questions that lacked definitive addressees, such as Charlotte's plaintive query: "What does it mean to be French? They wear us out with this identity thing, is the question of identity specific to Arabs?" This question was meant to be delivered in a sarcastic tone, underlining the elusiveness of the very notion it sought, yet it was borrowed from the entirely tangible lexicon of public debate: what, indeed, was and is French identity? Both before and after the events of 2005, references to Frenchness were ubiquitous, from televised debates to policy documents, and the term itself often crystallized around the legacy of French republican universalism, positing citizenship as the manifestation of individual attachment to the national community. Republicanism's counterpoint was cultural communitarianism, the privileging of ethnic, cultural, or religious identity categories over participation in national institutions. And as Charlotte made abundantly clear, this phenomenon was uniquely associated with communities of Arab descent.

As ubiquitous as Charlotte's question was, *Le Bruit du monde*'s answer did not follow the pattern that I had come to identify in the work of artists of immigrant descent. Charlotte and her compatriots did not call for a counter-valorization of difference, nor did they seek to underline the significance of community formations. Despite Charlotte's reference to an elusively gathered "us," the play's politics exceeded a conceptual framework that opposed republican individuality and cultural community. Upon meeting the group and attending several rehearsals in 2008, I was further surprised to note that terms like "culture" or "community" were altogether absent from my conversations. Versed in the conceptual categories of North American theater and performance scholarship, I was puzzled: Quelques unes d'entre nous's work resonates with the rubric of community-based theater, a designation that seeks to identify politically progressive theater practices in which *community* operates as a structuring ideal. As a group that formed through women's workshops held at the Maison des Tilleuls, a social center located in a disadvantaged neighborhood of Blanc-Mesnil, Quelques unes d'entre nous invites the question of communal affiliation. As a group composed of first-generation North African, Middle Eastern, and sub-Saharan African women in the final quarter of their lives and younger, second-generation women of equally diverse origins, its work is also likely to be identified as an instance of intercultural experimentation, revealing the interactions of "cultures and cultural forms."[1] Where the combination of these rubrics is concerned, *Le Bruit du monde* is semingly tailor-made for consideration beneath the category of cross-cultural theater praxis that Jacqueline Lo and Helen Gilbert call "multicultural community theater": as a domain that "generally incorporates a range of languages and cultural resources, including performing traditions, drawn from the community," multicultural community theater encapsulates a form of social activism premised on cultural plurality, if not equality.[2] Whereas such touchstones are decidedly relevant to understanding the forms of sociability that characterize Quelques unes d'entre nous, my goal in this chapter is to underline the challenges of applying terms like "culture" and "community" to characterize the political, social, and aesthetic background against which Quelques unes d'entre nous produces theater. These rubrics are indeed relevant, yet this relevance stems less from community's status as a universally available emancipatory project and more so from the fraught history of community and communalism in the French national context.

Over the course of my conversations with theater practitioners in Paris, I rarely encountered the term "community" or *la communauté*. Yet I often spoke with individuals and organizations that were either deeply rooted within specific geographic locales or took themselves to be representative of a collective ethnic or political identity. Why, I wondered, is a term that is so readily available in the self-conceptions of grassroots theaters in the United States so markedly absent from their French counterparts? This absence is particularly intriguing in a national context that is often labeled the inheritor of an unchanged, centralized *patrimoine* or cultural heritage. As Herman Lebovics has argued, French anxieties over national artistic traditions have remained constant across the twentieth century, from the final years of the Third Republic to the recent emergence of supranational formations like the European Union.[3] Yet French cultural heritage discourses are distinctive in that the manner in which they have underlined the heritage of specific territories or communities has inevitably also reinforced a common *national* tradition. Put differently, communal affiliation has been positioned in tension with national culture.

This tendency is due in part to a political inheritance that has overlapped cultural unity with political unity, rooting citizenship in political participation and assimilation via national institutions rather than an ethno-cultural identity. As Mark Ingram has noted, the French state has been "an important voice promoting 'republican universalism' by treating culture as a medium for transcending the particular interests of specific groups."[4] French national belonging, in other words, has had an aesthetic dimension. As a result, the political formations and artistic products of immigrants in postwar France have avoided vigorous evocations of cultural or communal difference. Even in the aftermath of the Socialist reforms of the early 1980s, when the government of François Mitterrand lifted the ban on immigrants' right of association and cautiously celebrated cultural and ethnic mobilization, the terms of the celebration would dictate that the principles of associationalism remain national in scope. Today, immigrant artists negotiate an evolving landscape where demands for political recognition employ a variety of rationales, both underlining and negating difference. In such a context, terms like "community," "collectivity," and "culture" cannot be taken to reference predefined collective groupings, much less utopian aspirations. Instead, such terms are political gestures with which artists of immigrant descent point at ambiguities in the role that republican universalism continues to play in cultural activism.

Performance in particular reveals the complexities of the French republican model of citizenship in the everyday lives of immigrants. In this chapter, I argue that *Le Bruit du monde*'s aesthetic-political vision is shaped by collective members' geographic context. Whereas scholarship on community-based theater often links sharedness to the primacy of the local, in the twenty-first-century French *banlieue*, it is precisely the local context that troubles the attempt to imagine community formations. Blanc-Mesnil is a small township located in Seine-Saint-Denis, a department that is closely associated with the contemporary image of the French *banlieue*. A shifty term that has come to carry a complex of negative associations, *banlieue* refers to the suburbs that surround metropolitan centers. Michel Kokoreff and Didier Lapeyronnie suggest, however, that the term's connotations exceed the geographic unit itself, operating as shorthand for the forms of civic unrest that have emerged in response to several decades of neoliberal urban planning, security-minded segregation, and economic deprivation. The scholars note that whereas this period has witnessed the degradation of both physical structures and social relationships in suburban housing projects, it has also resulted in *banlieue* residents' inability to impact their own representations.[5] Whereas *Le Bruit du monde* is just such an effort, it is forced to negotiate the difficulties of ascribing community or cultural homogeneity to a deeply fragmented, heterogeneous geography. Thus, one of the ways that *Le Bruit du monde* maintains a vision of belonging is by disaggregating the political institutions and social realities of republican France from the ideal of a universalist republic itself, expressing desire for a republican community to come, while negotiating their frustration with a political landscape that has rendered community undesirable. In what follows, I begin with a brief glance at notions of community and culture in theater and performance scholarship, link these theoretical musings to the history of immigrant associationalism in postwar France, and end with a closer look at Quelques unes d'entre nous and *Le Bruit du monde m'est rentré dans l'oreille.*

Understanding Community-Based Theater

When is a theatrical project "community-based"? The phrase refers to the products of theatrical collaboration between artists and the members of a specific community or communities. For Jan Cohen-Cruz, the "community" in question can emerge as "a shared primary identity based in place, ethnicity, class, race, sexual preference, profession, circumstances or political orientation."[6] Conversely, artists can dismiss the claim to sharedness, locating the development of this mutuality within the performance process rather than designating it as the criterion for participation. In the United States, community-based theater is often identified as "a cultural expression of identity politics,"[7] but a secondary strand has also emphasized the dimensions of the practice that draw on *locality*. Representations of the local (often via oral history and personal storytelling) have been a key element of grassroots and community theater in the American context.[8] Tobin Nellhaus and Susan Haedicke note that the intersection of "community" questions and "local" concerns emerges with particular force in *urban* contexts: "current concerns about community," they write, "often revolve around the dynamics of city life: the city offers both anonymity and alienation, freedom and confinement."[9]

Framing urban spaces through reference to "alienation" and "anonymity" is a familiar move, central to what Miranda Joseph terms "a Romantic narrative of community."[10] For Joseph, this narrative participates in "locating community in a long-lost past for which we yearn nostalgically from our current fallen state of alienation, bureaucratization, rationality."[11] If city life is emblematic of alienation and anonymity, then its "long-lost past" of relationality and known-ness is also a long-lost pastoral: an idyllic rural setting marked by human recognition and commonality. Not coincidentally, scholarship on community-based theater has challenged the binary in which community serves as the counterpoint to modernity, producing a series of probing questions. If the turn to community-based arts derives from a yearning for this "long-lost past," in what ways are theater and performance imagined to meet this need? Is theater only meaningful when intended for and targeting a community? If notions of community are so closely bound with *rural* geographies, are urban and nonurban performance practices beholden to generating and valorizing, respectively, these notions?

Indeed, the ambiguous nature of theatrical community mirrors concerns from contemporary Continental philosophy on the relationship between "community" and alterity. In *The Inoperative Community,* for example, Jean-Luc Nancy is critical of the tradition of Western thought (from Jean-Jacques Rousseau to the German Romantics) that posits an original human community as the antecedent of modern society, a tradition that references "a lost age in which community was woven of tight, harmonious, and infrangible bonds and in which above all it played back to itself, through its institutions, its rituals, and its symbols, the representation, indeed the living offering, of its own immanent unity, intimacy, and autonomy."[12] Nancy notes that this (belated) longing has served as the seed of violent conflict, most notably in the fascist production of community and more recently in the renewed nationalisms of the late twentieth century. Recent discussions on the limits of identity political movements to address social inequality have posed parallel questions that are equally relevant in the sphere of community-based theater. If the sharing of the cultural, emotional, and even financial resources of the theater will be contingent on the theatrical collective being defined according to a set of universalizing norms, how will difference become morally relevant? In his work on Canadian political theater, for example, Alan Filewod critiques a Romantic discourse of community that obscures economic disparity. "The sentimental quest to rediscover a sense of community, allegedly lost in the alienated world of postindustrial transnational capital," he writes, "has framed much of the political theater work of the past two decades, particularly in North America, where *community* frequently erases *class* in popular discourse."[13] Filewod's commentary mirrors critics of identity political movements, suggesting that when community is the central idiom for theatrical radicalism, it erases the need for a radical materialist critique.

If community and (transnational) capital cannot be pried apart, Joseph further notes that the idealization of community as an unprompted and voluntary group formation obscures the political circumstances that would render such a formation desirable. Joseph's analysis of the discourse of voluntarism in the formation of nonprofits and nongovernmental organizations in the contemporary United States is particularly relevant to community-based theater. Her contention is that while participation in voluntary associations is often taken as the outward sign of "an authentic expression of real 'grassroots' communities and their interests,"[14] the nonprofit is one of a number of sites where the willingness to participate that is emblematic of the figure of the liberal individual is in fact *produced.* Far from a preformed, static notion, "community" is an experience that is cultivated, and often ambivalently, in the process of its promotion.

Community as a Social Strategy

Joseph's understanding of community is a resonant starting point for scholars of community-based theater. After all, a theatrical performance is only the most publicly available dimension of a rehearsal process that painstakingly *cultivates* that performance. Process, in other words, is hardly an afterthought when it comes to displaying "authentic expression" in the theater. Yet community-based theater scholarship often retains an investment in what Joseph terms "the rhetoric of voluntarism,"[15] the notion that the desire to promote, celebrate, or maintain a shared culture is what drives participation in the theater. To be clear, my suggestion is not that theatrical formations can never be voluntary. Rather, following Joseph, I wish to understand the specifics of a historical moment that would make such voluntarism appealing or even intelligible. *Le Bruit du monde* is in fact animated by perceptions of a shared identity, a commonality centered on the geographic form of the peri-urban *banlieue*. Yet positing community as a *social strategy* that emerges in particular geographies and historical moments (rather than an ahistorical group formation) invites us to consider this sharedness as a situated strategy entirely cognizant of its limits (rather than a yearning for an original entity that transcends history and geography).

Put simply, the term "community" has specific connotations in contemporary France, hence my desire to refer to it as a *problematic* rather than a given. Beyond site-specificity, however, equally at stake here is a broader concern with the analytic frames through which community has emerged as the central idiom and highest stake for political theater. As Jacques Rancière has stated, "it is high time we examine this idea that the theater is, in and of itself, a community site."[16] For Rancière, emancipation in the theater is premised on "the capacity of anonymous people, the capacity that makes everyone equal to everyone else."[17] Audiences are composed of "individuals plotting their own paths in the forest of things, acts and signs that confront or surround them."[18] Like Nancy, Rancière traces the modern Western association of theater and community (or theater "as a form of aesthetic constitution . . . of the community")[19] to German Romanticism, a decisive moment since which all theater philosophy, from the distance-instituting Bertolt Brecht to the distance-abolishing Antonin Artaud, have sought to restore an ideal theatrical collective, routinely denouncing theater's mimetic illusionism along the way. Where intervening in a genealogy of the communal in performance is concerned, a broader historical or disciplinary lens might include the cleansed community of Aristotelian tragedy or "the spontaneous moments of ego-dissolution that bind performers to audiences and audience members to one another," in Judith Hamera's reading of *communitas*.[20] Whereas these visions of mutuality beckon questions regarding coherence or consistency, negating "the potentially world-making power of performance" seems hardly the point. Rather, I wish to stay attuned to moments where theoretical approaches to theatrical community risk overwhelming the discursive world of theater's lived experience, particularly when that world is attached to a unique cultural space whose own imaginings belay different political priorities.

Where the question of politics is concerned, Rancière distinguishes between an approach that attributes political potential to the mere proximity of human bodies and one that locates political change in "the transformation of the sensory fabric of 'being together.'"[21] For the philosopher, this distinction is central to identifying communal emancipation in the theater. Rancière's critique, however, aligns community with *audience*, with individuals *facing* a "forest of things, acts and signs," whereas community-based theater's reference for the communal includes the forest itself, the unique sensory fabric involved in the theatrical act. After all, the "community" in community-based theater has a dual referent: the audience gathered before the theatrical event is one group formation, and the participants (actors, writers, designers, directors) who produce that event are another. Rancière's skepticism regarding theater's communal potential is relevant to both forms of human proximity. In contemporary theater and performance scholarship, references to the "shared primary identity" of this secondary group formation inevitably evoke the literature on interculturalism. In what follows, I clarify where the critique of theatrical community stands in relation to that domain.

The "Culture" in Interculturalism

While the question of "community" is not of central concern to scholars of intercultural performance, a notion of commonality nonetheless often pervades the principles by which performance projects are identified as animating "intercultural" concerns. Ric Knowles characterizes interculturalism as a rubric for understanding "how cultures and cultural forms interact and negotiate their differences through performative exchange."[22] Referencing a list that extends from cross-cultural to transcultural, Knowles singles out the term "intercultural" to capture both the "contested, unsettling, and often unequal spaces *between* cultures" and the sheer "multiplicity of cultural positionings" that any performance encounter may bring into high relief.[23] Thus positioned, the term "intercultural" serves as a lens for studying historical traditions of theatrical intermixing (whose genealogy commonly covers interwar European primitivism and its later century resonances) as well as for considering a broader set of performance products that employ multiple "cultures" or "cultural forms." An intriguing element of the list, however, is that while the qualifying term (inter, intra, cross, trans, multi, etc.) shoulders the burden of generating an ever more precise analytic, the qualified term "culture" remains relatively untouched. Yet, as Raymond Williams reminds us, the term "culture" is in fact "one of the two or three most complicated terms in the English language."[24] Its earlier associations with cultivation and civilization are part and parcel of its present-day circulation, and the "particular way of life" it is commonly taken to denote can encompass the material, intellectual, aesthetic, spiritual, and practical dimensions of human life.[25]

The ambiguity of the "culture" in interculturalism has consequences for the "community" in community-based theater. When the referent of interculturalism is broadened from the mixing of multiple "cultural forms" to any theater that involves more than one readily identifiable "culture," then the human bodies through which that theatrical practice manifests itself are already identified as the vessels of a particular shared reality: a relatively coherent, containable, transparent set of qualities that are imagined to serve as the national, geographic, ethno-racial, or folkloric grounding of the individuals in question. The question remains, however, as to what constitutes culture and how we know when we are in its presence. What meanings need to be affirmed by and attached to particular human acts in order for them to be deemed "cultural," both reflective and constitutive of a set of values, beliefs, and practices? Often, such recognition takes place when performance practices that involve particular ways of moving and speaking by particular bodies are understood to be and are construed as affirming the preexistence of that practice and its "cultural" sphere, made manifest in acts that are taken to function as signs of themselves. Indeed, Daphne Lei notes that these moments of "quick recognition" are contingent on forms of "tokenization" that have survived well into the seemingly boundaryless age of globalization.[26]

"Culture," in other words, plays a role in the maintenance of the kinds of transnational performance marketplaces described by Lei. Yet it is also an inevitable rubric when considering performative exchange; in James Clifford's words, "culture is a deeply compromised idea I cannot yet do without."[27] Thus, a humbler conclusion might be to recognize that denoting the culture(s) of a staged event, like denoting its community, asks of the performers that they implicate themselves in a specific way in the theatrical formation at hand. My question is whether an insistence on qualifying a performance as primarily communal or cultural is commensurable with the analysis of theater practices, experiences, and products whose organizing principle is neither the negotiation of a communal identity, nor an engagement with cultural traditions. If we begin with the premise that *community* and *culture* do not compose the limits of their aesthetic, political, and ethical imaginaries, what alternative analytics arise?

Of course, in posing this question, I run the risk of "privileging content specificity."[28] Lo and Gilbert note that where analyses of specific cross-cultural theater practices are concerned, a "reluctance to engage with the 'big picture'" can overlook the operations of broader institutional contexts or (global) political systems. The scholars' revision of Patrice Pavis's hourglass model of intercultural exchange is premised on reading these systems back into the unidirectional image of distillation encapsulated by the hourglass. While cognizant of the fact that site-specificity has its limits, my goal is to place local particularity in continuity with the bigger institutional and political picture, allowing us to pose the particular as an instance of a broader theoretical concern. My question is thus both site-specific and conceptual: references to community formation and cultural difference have been rare in the artistic products of immigrant communities in postwar France. This is due in no small part to the fact that terms like *communauté* or *culture* have been anything but neutral reference points in the development of immigrant associations. Understanding their absence in the arts requires a brief glance at their contrasting proliferation in politics.

Immigrant Associations and Universalism

The emergence and activity of immigrants' associations have posed a number of dilemmas for political institutions in France. On the one hand, the proliferation of associations formed by second- and third-generation immigrants has served as evidence that immigrants have conformed to the forms of collective political expression characterizing their host country.[29] On the other hand, immigrant political associations have had to negotiate a national context where models of citizenship have traditionally been unconcerned with collective categories and identities. The challenges facing the associational work of immigrants, in other words, are related to the role that the republican tradition has accorded associational life. As Catherine Wihtol de Wenden and Rémy Leveau have noted, the 1901 Law on Associations continues to regulate the activities of voluntary associations in France.[30] This law states that an *association* (often translated into English as an association, but basically referring to nonprofit organizations or charities) is based on a contract that allows two or more persons to come together in the pursuit of a nonprofit end. Notably, the 1901 law includes religious congregations within its reach, provided their activities do not focus exclusively on worship. This anticlerical impulse is visible in its most significant form in the 1905 law on the separation of church and state, the legislation that continues to serve as the basis for the uniquely French form of secularism, *laïcité*. According to the 1905 law, the French republic assures the liberty of conscience of all citizens and offers no recognition (or subsidy) to any particular religion or *culte*. On a slightly more conceptual register, the law has generated a political culture opposed to clericalism, rendering the political order *responsible* for protecting individuals from religious bodies.

The figure of the *abstract individual*, however, an autonomous individual shorn of racial, regional, or religious identity markers, is not a product of the Third Republic's legal reforms. As we have seen in previous chapters, the figure of the abstract individual is central to Jean-Jacques Rousseau's vision of a universalist political order, where the appropriate channel through which individuals seek affiliation and self-expression is the national community. Dominique Schnapper has noted that for Rousseau, "citizenship was, like the nation, an indivisible totality, it had to be organized and guaranteed by a centralized state, itself an expression of the general will, and the generator of society."[31] Indeed, Rousseau posited the general will as the only structure through which individuals could exercise their freedom, whereas "intermediary bodies between the individual-citizen and the state prevented man from being free [*libre*] and had to be destroyed."[32] Concretely, this has meant that republican political culture has been wary of the mobilization of communal or group identities. As Joan Scott summarizes, "in theory there is no possibility of a hyphenated ethnic/national identity—one belongs either to a group or to the nation."[33]

As a group formation, voluntary associations have thus occupied a peculiar position, one that is particularly visible in the case of immigrants' associations. The individual-citizen's autonomy and self-government are central to the French tradition of political participation, but the collective actions that might result from autonomous political wills and focus on a particular identity grouping have historically not been encouraged. Jocelyne Cesari notes that

> in the French model, accessing citizenship means taking a pledge to do politics within the framework of groups that are offered by the French political system, meaning special interest groups or universalist groups who present themselves as the incarnation of public interest and whose grouping is not legitimately and officially founded on belonging to a group with a prescribed status.[34]

Cesari distinguishes between "universalist" groups and "prescribed" groups, later noting that in recent years, associations formed to valorize particular collectives have increasingly been encouraged to imagine services functioning on *individual* scales rather than collective ones. Immigrants' associations, in other words, have been asked to direct their energies toward the support and rehabilitation of individuals *as* individuals, rather than as the members of an ethnic, cultural, or religious collective. This formula has a lengthy history in France, but its more recent manifestation can be traced to October 1981, when a 1939 decree limiting foreigners' right of association was lifted by the newly elected Socialist government. First- and second-generation immigrants had been involved in social mobilization for decades prior to the Socialists' reforms,[35] but scholarship often identifies a "generational" switch from the 1970s to the 1980s, as immigrant mobilization transitioned from a focus on labor militancy to the struggle for cultural recognition now called *le mouvement Beur.*[36] The emergence of Beur identity is an excellent site for examining how French politics have transformed associationalism to manage a multicultural polity.

The Beur Movement

The term "Beur" is an inversion of the word *Arabe* (Arab), perhaps the best-known instance of the urban slang referred to as *verlan.* The fact that the term "Beur" has now been reinverted to become "Rebeu" underlines the specificity of the historical moment that witnessed Beur activism. "The Beur movement," Paul Silverstein notes, "in its various actions and productions throughout the 1980s, emphasized the 'second generation' of North African immigrants as a particular multicultural political subject."[37] The term "Beur" typically identified North African youth who had been born into first generation working-class immigrant families, grown up in public housing projects on the peripheries of urban conglomerations, and came of age during a time when mainstream perceptions of immigration (particularly from North Africa) continued to be nourished by colonial stereotypes. The Beur movement's initial goals were to deconstruct the oft-pronounced link between immigrant youth and delinquency and to lobby for the recognition of Maghrebi identity as an essential component of French society. Yet Beur activism formed at a time when a number of developments converged to reframe their insistence on a particular identity. An important shift was the emergence of what Yasemin Nuhoğlu Soysal has called "human rights as a world-level organizing principle,"[38] the notion that the basis and authority of rights can be derived from principles that exceed the boundaries of the nation-state. Throughout the 1980s, the identity practices associated with the Beur movement underlined the participants' statuses as ethnic minorities in France, but activists also began to incorporate vocabularies that rendered them supranational, universal agents.

Compounding the growing prevalence of human rights vocabulary was the French state's own "individual-universalist" logic, which resulted in an emphasis on *antiracism* as a common *moral* goal that immigrants' associations were encouraged to privilege over ethnic communalism.[39] During the

1980s, the Beur movement negotiated an activist terrain where the political demands of immigrants were reformulated as part of the larger and *centralized* struggle of "human beings who reject racism."[40] This discursive shift was symbolized by organizations like SOS Racisme and France Plus, whose work replaced references to ethnic identities with new themes like "anti-racism, cultural diversity and plural citizenship."[41] In the early 1980s, such developments held the potential for rethinking the republican paradigm through the rubric of cultural diversity. However, many of the civic activists with whom I spoke viewed the institutionalization of the Beur movement as a dispersal of its political aims. They conceded that the numerous associations that flourished during the decade had served key administrative functions on local levels: groups founded by Beur activists provided educational support, literacy programs, and general social aid networks in numerous immigrant neighborhoods. Yet the financial support that these organizations received through the Fonds d'Action Sociale was coupled with the expectation that their work would promote individual success stories, rather than valorize local and collective identities. As the 1980s drew to a close, the keyword that captured this expectation was *intégration*, a phenomenon for which immigrants' associations would rapidly become responsible.

In fact, the history of the Beur movement is closely associated with the relationship between state-sponsored ideals of integration and projects of urban reform. As Beth Epstein has shown, one of the outcomes of prefect Baron Haussman's notorious reconstruction of Paris in the 1850s and 1860s was a city starkly segregated along class lines. In turn, this spatial reality resulted in a search for models of urban organization that would improve social integration, a theme that prevailed well into the period following the Second World War. The postwar construction of *grands ensembles,* or large-scale public housing complexes, "would house a balance of the poor and the middle classes, workers and families, in new mid-to-high density districts that were also to include commercial and recreational activity."[42] The construction of these *cités* or housing projects intensified during and after the Algerian War, targeting North African immigrant workers and their families. Later waves of migratory movement added to the *cités*' racial and cultural mixity, resulting in multicultural populations for whom the promise of social uplift rarely materialized. Paul Silverstein notes that the dilapidated and lifeless *grands ensembles* that dot the twenty-first-century urban landscape display how public housing has produced exclusion rather than integration.[43] And whereas grassroots civic activism has been central to creating community life in the *cités*, the Beur movement itself has transformed in relation to this changing urban landscape.

The emergence of the term *Beurgeoisie* is an excellent indicator of the ambivalence that many immigrant activists have felt toward the Beur movement.[44] A clear play on the term *bourgeoisie*, which designates the culturally conformist dimensions of middle-class French society, the *Beurgeoisie* designated Beur elites whose participation in the movement eventually served as a springboard toward careers in politics and business. More importantly, as Alec Hargreaves has shown, their adoption of the republican model of integration signaled their willingness to dismiss ethnic communalism and espouse the principles of *laïcité*.[45] Silverstein notes that

> as Beur activists strayed further and further from the housing projects in which they were born and moved to professional careers in business and academics, the *cités* themselves transformed in their absence. While the physical and economic degradation of the housing projects—including the increase in drug abuse and gang violence—continued apace, very few community development associations arose to take the place of those established during the Beur movement.[46]

Writing in 2013, Kokoreff and Lapeyronnie further note that in the twenty-first-century *banlieue,* "community" itself has become an irrelevant category. In direct contrast with models of emancipation premised on class struggle, "[social difficulties] are understood through personal particularities and biographic trajectories, problems of distance and of obstacles."[47] That is not to say, of course, that collective struggles are nonexistent; rather, the heyday of immigrant associationalism has resulted in a terrain where the communal is a complicated idiom.

"Cultural" Theater

Now, to state that the fraught history of the immigrant associational movement has erased any reference to communal expression and cultural difference in French theater would be mistaken. Where community theater is concerned, Bérénice Hamidi-Kim's detailed work on the Lyon-based Théâtre du Grabuge has explored the possibilities as well as limitations of a twenty-first-century "*communauté théâtrale*."[48] Scholars of interculturalism might further note that Patrice Pavis's seminal *Theatre at the Crossroads of Culture* sought one of the first theoretical models for analyzing intercultural transfer, and drew its examples squarely from the hexagon: "France between 1968 and 1988, with some geographic forays."[49] Yet Pavis himself was quick to note that for artists like Eugenio Barba, Peter Brook, and Ariane Mnouchkine, "culture" often referenced "both a quest for foreign sensuality and for coded abstraction."[50] The emphasis on the "foreign" is equally visible in one of the very few English-language monographs on cultural pluralism in French theater. David Bradby and Maria M. Delgado's *The Paris Jigsaw: Internationalism and the City's Stages* clearly seeks to argue for the multicultural dimensions of what is often celebrated as a national heritage, yet does so by cementing multiculturalism as an *international* affair. Whereas the scholars rightly argue that the migration of individual artists (like Peter Brook or August Boal) has left an indelible mark on the theatrical life of Paris, their emphasis on "Paris' emergence as a major center for European theatre"[51] risks enlarging pluralism's scale to the point where *local* difference is rendered invisible.

Conversely, where *immigrant* cultural expression is concerned, "culture" is neither a matter of foreign influence, nor the abstraction embodied by tokenized performance forms. Resolutely political, references to culture have been fraught with concrete effects. During the 1980s, as immigrant initiatives drew on centralized support, they gravitated away from political vocabularies and toward mainstream (and increasingly professionalized) aesthetic forms.[52] Militancy and community, in other words, were very much conjoined. Whereas it would be a mistake to posit a direct continuity between the early years of the immigrant associational movement and the first decade of the twenty-first century, it is nonetheless necessary to underline the continued presence of these dynamics in contemporary cultural activism: community and communalism remain fraught terms in French public discourse. At the same time, however, the binary of militancy and professionalism is no longer as rigid; militancy does not automatically connote community, and vice versa. *Le Bruit du monde* is exemplary of these transformations. The play *is* in fact animated by an idea of collectivity, and a desire to generate novel forms of social relationships, but community and collectivity are not framed as the counterpoints of republican universalism. This is partly because recent developments in the *banlieues* have revealed the broader limits of urban belonging in twenty-first-century France, yet it is also because a commitment to community is not the play's primary idiom for political resistance.

Theater in Blanc-Mesnil: Quelques Unes d'Entre Nous

Le Bruit du monde m'est rentré dans l'oreille was created by the collective Quelques unes d'entre nous, a women's group that formed from the regular gatherings that were held at the social center Maison des Tilleuls (MDT) in 2002. The MDT is situated squarely in the heart of Blanc-Mesnil, a small, industrialized township in the department of Seine-Saint-Denis, which forms a ring around the northeastern corner of Paris. While relatively small in surface area, Seine-Saint-Denis has loomed large in the urban imagination, from its historical identity as a traditionally communist-voting *banlieue rouge* to its central role in the representation of Paris's northern suburbs as zones of conflict between immigrant youth and the French state. The reality of Blanc-Mesnil is more complex. As late as 2008, MDT reported that only about 28 percent of the township (then numbering slightly more than 14,000) was foreign-born.[53] Blanc Mesnil's broader population, much like that of its neighboring towns, is highly mixed, comprised of older generations of working classes, as well as recent waves of immigration from North, West, and sub-Saharan Africa and the Middle East. The image of unemployment that is generally attached to immigrant youth is a reality that is shared by many of the township's inhabitants; the ongoing deindustrialization of urban centers throughout France has contributed to an economic stagnation that cuts across national, racial, or ethnic barriers, rendering social ascent difficult for most *banlieue* residents.[54] The services that MDT has provided for the Tilleul neighborhood of Blanc-Mesnil have reflected the organization's efforts to generate and valorize "civic participation."[55] These have ranged from housing a variety of associations, educational resources, and cultural activities to providing access to public services such as juridical aid and social security allocations. During the highly publicized events of 2005, the mixed inhabitants of the Tilleul experienced symbolic disputes over the ownership of this public space, an experience that galvanized Quelques unes d'entre nous and pushed the collective toward generating a public, and eventually theatrical, dimension to their activities.

Although most MDT documents trace the origins of Quelques unes d'entre nous to the autumn of 2005, the collective's seeds had in fact been sown several years earlier by the social worker Samia. In 2002 Samia had arranged cooking workshops to bring together the Maghrebi, Turkish, West African, and European women who frequented the center. During our conversation, Samia's comments mirrored a strategy that I encountered often during my time in Paris, as many social workers noted that civic projects had to be premised on how individuals inhabited their everyday activities and skills. "What interested me," Samia told me, "was using the competences that they already had." The following year, the cooking workshops transformed into a *salon de thé* (tea salon) centered on conversation and the women soon began to participate in local debates. In 2004 they created a photography exhibition in collaboration with a professional photographer and exchanged photos and messages with two women's groups, one in Afghanistan and one in a Palestinian refugee camp in Lebanon. Whereas these axes of engagement mirrored the broader transnational tendencies of civic activism in Paris in the early 2000s, the events of 2005 focused the women's attention on their neighborhood or *quartier*, a turn that coincided with their burgeoning interest in theater. While touring their exhibition at the Festival des Libértés in Brussels, the members of Quelques unes d'entre nous saw a performance by the French actress Rachida Khalil. This triggered an interest in the stage and, with Samia's guidance and connections, paved the way for a series of writing and staging workshops. The eventual performance was stitched together by Philip Boulay, a director involved in theatrical activism in Blanc-Mesnil, and Elsa Solal, a writer who synthesized the women's writings and oral narratives to produce *Le Bruit du monde*.[56] When I met with the collective in 2008, they had performed at the Forum Sociale des Quartiers Populaires in Blanc-Mesnil, the Festival des Libértés, the Théâtre Fontenay-sous-Bois, and the prestigious Parisian institution Théâtre du Rond Point. They were about to pack their suitcases for a performance in Portugal.[57]

Although my conversations with the group referenced their turn to theater as an event that happened to coincide with their focus on local politics, it is important to note that the cooking workshops' transformation into a *narrative* workshop mirrors a genealogy of theatrical activism that includes personal narrative within the broader sphere of personal "competences." Echoing a terminology that invokes Al Assifa's ruminations in Barbès if not AGO's struggles with professionalization, Samia's projects resonate with a broad array of theater practices in which personal narrative performance emerges as the theatrical correlate of *personal skills*, endowing participants with an agency as transformative as it is fragile. Where oral history and personal storytelling are concerned, the resonance with frameworks like community-based and intercultural theater is once again difficult to ignore: *Le Bruit du monde* is not only based on the women's life experiences, but a large number of collective members are first-generation immigrant women or young adults born in France to parents of foreign origin. References to colonial war, exile, and immigration permeate the play. Yet the absence of terms like "community" or "culture" is more than a testament to the geographic limits of theater and performance scholarship. Rather, this absence is evidence of the fragility of the relationship between personal narrative, theatrical agency, and "a shared primary identity" in the early twenty-first-century *banlieue*.

A French Intifada?

The events of 2005 refer to the succession of violence and unrest that erupted in a number of French towns in October of that year. Responding in part to the deaths of teenagers Zyed Benna and Bouna Traoré while being chased by police in the Seine-Saint-Denis township of Clichy-sous-Bois, the public unrest that began in the town quickly spread to surrounding municipalities and urban centers throughout France. Cars were stolen and burned, recalling patterns of unrest dating back to the early 1980s and reigniting the long-standing perception of violent immigrant *cités*. By the time a state of emergency was officially declared on November 8, both national and international media coverage had racialized the images of violence, with *Newsweek* writer Christopher Dickey announcing that "like a Middle Eastern intifada, the violence is stripping away whatever comfortable assumptions existed about the authorities' ability to cope."[58] Dickey was not the first to establish a discursive link between the protest actions of *banlieue* youth and political conflict in the Middle East; the implicit understanding that these instances constituted two different ends of an imagined, unified network of international terrorism was common in the right-leaning French media in the era following 9/11.[59] Dickey's criticism did touch on the French state's withdrawal from its housing projects, yet the journalist insistently identified the violence as a religious issue, referencing "Muslim Arab and African" communities plagued by "a sort of chronic intifada" the following week.[60] While press coverage insisted on identifying deep-seated resentment of an ethno-religious character, Interior Minister Nicolas Sarkozy focused on the seeming youthfulness of the protests, identifying protesters as "*racaille*" (scum), later adding that they needed to be cleaned with an industrial pressure washer.

Sarkozy's characterization of the protests through an age-based lens pointed to a transformation in perceptions of immigrant activism. Earlier hierarchies between the upwardly mobile *beurgeois* and the militant *banlieue* activist were effectively adapted to new categories of youth: the nonviolent and docile teenager vs. the unintegrated and racialized *racaille*.[61] In the aftermath of the events, academics and social workers sought to explain how such a binary obscured the widespread unemployment, economic precariousness, and social isolation experienced by *banlieue* residents. Patrick Braouezze noted that the literal targets of the protest violence (cars and public buildings) were revelatory:

> On the one hand, the car, the consumer good par excellence that is most "advertised," synonymous with luxury and power; and on the other, public equipment associated with institutions and particularly with schools that are considered (rightly or wrongly) as the first space of failure, of inequality, of injustice.[62]

In fact, cars as symbols of social privilege and the school as the signature institution of the republic had been at the core of *banlieue* protests since the early 1980s. They are featured prominently in Mehdi Charef's groundbreaking 1983 novel *Le Thé au harem d'Archi Ahmed*. Charef portrays Majid and his multiracial friends, growing up yet stagnating in the fictional Cité des Fleurs, nestled in an imaginary corner of the northern *banlieues* of Paris.[63] Charef himself wrote in the wake of the so-called *rodéos* of 1981, when inhabitants in three of Lyon's immigration-saturated suburbs responded to police violence by stealing and burning hundreds of residents' cars, cementing the perception of immigrant *cités* as zones of violence.

These continuities notwithstanding, scholars have noted that what *has* intensified since the early 1980s and is specific to the contemporary experience of *cité* life is the routine identity controls and police harassment experienced by dark-skinned (perceived) immigrant bodies, evidence of how the global "war on terror" has permeated *banlieue* life. Although the public perception of immigrant *cités* is as "lawless zones" (*zones de non-droit*), immigrant youth in fact find themselves encountering the law on a regular basis,[64] often asked to produce their identifying documents multiple times over the course of a single day. Benna and Traoré had been electrocuted in a power station while hiding from the police, and it was precisely the tragically ordinary nature of this desperate act that sparked the outrage and violence that lasted well into the following month.

Fear and Dread in Blanc-Mesnil

Blanc-Mesnil was not untouched by the protests, and during the period of unrest that soon engulfed the town, the MDT was set on fire. Although physical damage to the building was limited, the event drew a wide range of ambivalent reactions. Stephane Beaud and Sabrina Hamache's chronicle of MDT women's reactions for *Vu d'Ici,* the center's quarterly periodical, revealed these ambivalences in detail. The authors wrote: "What remains in their memory, the 'strong images' as today's media call them, are primarily and before all else these burning cars, these buildings in their immediate environment that disappear beneath flames, this state of physical and moral desolation left after the battle."[65] Images of conflagration and questions of personal safety were visible in the testimonials that accompanied the article. For example, Fatiha noted that her grandchildren were "traumatized about their commute from the city center to come to the Tilleuls because there were trucks burning in the streets."[66] As Fatiha underlined the immediacy of the need to protect one's own, Nadia's "desolation" referenced the environment itself, adding that "it is difficult to see one's town, one's streets, one's neighborhood closed off by the police."[67] While the women were deeply critical of the violence that flooded their neighborhoods during the protests, the anger they felt was directed largely toward Minister of the Interior Nicolas Sarkozy. When I visited rehearsals for *Le Bruit du monde* in April 2008, for example, I noted that the protests had left the women with a grammar for theatrical action, if not political resistance. The original group's composition had changed and director Philip Boulay had returned to the MDT to re-choreograph the piece and refresh his actors' muscle memories for an upcoming performance. In between side conversations, laughter, and sips of mint tea, the women were nodding at Boulay's instructions, ready to settle into an afternoon of friendly conversation. At moments like this, the director galvanized his reluctant actors by exhorting them to "think about the reality! Think of Sarkozy! You are warriors!" His references pointed at a collective history of political resentment.

If daily safety concerns and anger at the political establishment were some of the more expected reactions to the events, however, Beaud and Hamache's chronicle revealed another layer of dread, "more durable, more insidious, and certainly more essential"[68] than the trepidation of watching a vehicle burn. In Beaud and Hamache's account, this fear emerges in two specific forms. First, it is articulated as the dual need to both chastise and protect the "youth" as a collective category. Indeed, when the women opposed the series of violent actions that threatened to tear at the fabric of the Tilleuls neighborhood, they were aware that such a critique inevitably positioned the French state as the only force strong enough to quell the widespread aggression. As long-term residents of Seine-Saint-Denis, however, these women were equally aware of the decades-long withdrawal of the state from its *banlieues* and housing projects, leaving behind a generation of youth whose experience of daily life was one of "de facto urban apartheid" and whose relationship to the French state had been composed from a largely securitarian and punitive angle.[69] These ambivalent impulses were visible in Nadia's comments: "Me, I see this as an aggression because the youth, they are not bad [*méchants*], if they are left in peace, if we let them be, they are not bad, I don't see why they do all of this nonsense . . . in fact they were hurt, they were hurt."[70] Nadia's comments illustrated the complicated emotional response outlined by Beaud and Hamache. Although the MDT had been central to the women's ability to enter the social and associational fabric of their town, this entry also introduced them to the despair with which others experienced their *quartier*. How were they to recognize this anguish while nonetheless chastising the destruction of physical structures?

The second form of dread which Beaud and Hamache identified was motivated by concern that the women felt for their *own* future. "For them," the authors noted, "these riots foreshadow a relatively terrible fear: that of having to leave once again, admit defeat [*baisser pavillon*], escape once again from poverty and misery, lose one's resources and this close protection that the neighborhood offers."[71] Upon first glance, this "terrible fear" may come across as generalized dismay at the possibility of descending the social ladder. Rather, it is a fear that is deeply intertwined with the urban history of postwar immigration. Indeed, the descent into "poverty and misery" that Beaud and Hamache chronicle is a reference to the living conditions of the majority of women immigrants who arrived in France during the 1960s and early 1970s. For many of the North African immigrant workers who migrated to France before and during the Algerian War of Independence, their residences were transitory, often in dormitories hastily built around factories. Familial reunification policies slowly rectified this gender imbalance, and growing, multigenerational immigrant communities moved into *bidonvilles* or shantytowns that were built on abandoned fields and often with discarded construction materials. Azouz Begag's *Le Gone de Chaâba* is the best-known literary representation of the *bidonville* and reveals the extent to which these shantytowns became self-sustaining and complexly organized communities.[72]

As this population grew into the thousands, however, its inhabitants were regularly moved, first to transitional *cités de transit* and finally to the *grands ensembles* that had been built explicitly to house a mix of social classes, a cornerstone of the French state's territorialized integration policy, aimed at entering shantytown residents "into the currents of mainstream French life."[73] While welcomed by many who wished to partake of modern amenities like running water and tiled floors, the desertion (and later destruction) of the *bidonvilles* also symbolized the dissolution of neighborly networks and the embryonic forms of solidarity that had made urban life bearable for the displaced. The "close protection" that Beaud and Hamache attributed to the Tilleuls neighborhood was thus a magnified version of earlier forms of urban belonging. In turn, the "terrible fear" they identified was a reference to how changeable and precarious these affiliations had been.

Theater as a Space of Close Protection

Le Bruit du monde replicated this dynamic of "close protection" in the space of the theatrical spectacle. It served a metonymic function vis-à-vis the larger world in which the MDT women lived, and it allowed them to explore their political engagement with this world. At the same time, the project was equally indicative of the limits of theater's ability to provide the "close protection" of an aesthetically maintained community. The text of *Le Bruit du monde* was written by the professional playwright Elsa Solal and based on the MDT women's own textual output in the writing workshop that Samia had organized. "My only condition," Samia told me, "was that they must do the writing for the piece, the text. They won't play someone else's text." Yet whereas the characters that populated *Le Bruit du monde* were based on the members of the collective, they were renamed, fictionalized by Solal, and randomly cast from among the group. Underlining the women's desire to avoid coinciding actors with roles, Samia noted that "this is to protect them from the gaze of others," adding, "because they are not narrating easy stories, we make sure that the speaker is never delivering a narrative that she herself has contributed." Roles, in other words, were not meant to implicate specific actors, nor expose them to the potential harm that public speech could entail. Thus, the oral immediacy of the theatrical space nonetheless avoided the display of what Kristin Langellier and Eric Peterson have called "identity's body," personal revelations embodied onstage by their author.[74] Close protection, in other words, had less to do with the assumption that theater provided the groundwork for an actor-spectator communion and more to do with theatrical strategies that developed out of the precariousness of such an exchange.

In the context of the women's rehearsal process, these strategies resulted in specific practices and challenges. On an embodied level, the disjointed relationship between actor and character meant that the women were required to enact emotions and gestures that their emotional or embodied repertoires may not have harbored. Acting posed the challenge of merging oneself, publicly, with an attitude and its accompanying actions. At the few rehearsals that I visited in April 2008, part of Philip Boulay's directorial work was dedicated to finding the correct verbal triggers (including "Sarkozy!") with which to tap into an attitude like anger or resentment. This effort was often met with both determination and nervous laughter on the part of the women. Learning to slip into the words and gestures of a character whose world did not coincide with one's own was coupled with the basic choreography of stage action which Boulay outlined: arranging oneself in relation to other individuals onstage and listening and responding to their speech. Additionally, a number of the MDT women had limited literacy, meaning that their experience of the creative process happened through an engagement that was largely oral: they narrated their stories and once Solal had transcribed and reworked their testimonials, they re-memorized these adapted versions during rehearsals. As a result, the theatrical language that they eventually performed had transformed from a personal testimonial into the material of a relatively disciplined practice long before the women arrived onstage.

A short chronicle of the women's reactions revealed the development of actorly sensibilities. "I was a little anxious when we read it," Arlette noted, "but as I learned my text, I understood what Philip asked of me: how to forget about myself and invent a character."[75] Likewise, Yamina distinguished between the staged reading of texts and theatrical acting: "I had already done staged readings—it was difficult, I was sweating—but theater is even more different. You have to bring together gestures and words."[76] Samia also acknowledged the attainment of skills, stating "we are no longer a group but a troupe."[77] Meanwhile, these acknowledgments were interspersed with joyful declarations, like that of Taous, who recalled her five grown daughters' wish that she perform again. "I would love to play every day!" she noted.[78]

During my conversations with several of the women involved with the project, their contentment was evident. Equally clear was the fact that this enjoyment was often maintained by a radical separation between what Yamina had called "gestures and words"; whereas they grew to enjoy the physical demands of theatrical practice, the content of the stories remained fragile, even when relegated to another speaker. At the same time, they were cognizant of the fact that gestures and words were bound together in an unbroken *act*. One participant smiled as she told me that her awareness of the embodied novelty of the theatrical experience had been most acute in a moment when she had delivered an angry line accompanied by physical gestures of irritation. The display of public anger served as a moment of heightened reflexivity regarding both her bodily limits and her changing relationship to the audience. If theatrical rehearsal served as a space where human bodies could be asked to explore the limits of their political-emotional capacity, in other words, theatrical performance was where pleasure could spring from such an exercise, however momentary and intangible.

Despite the women's overwhelmingly positive feedback, Samia noted that she regularly reminded the participants that they could halt their activities. "Each time," she added, "the decision to come back was *their* decision." The women's agency vis-à-vis their theatrical work was visible in the ways in which they spoke of the different venues where they had performed, and the different publics with whom they had come into contact. I will return to the question of audiences in the conclusion to this chapter, but it is worth mentioning here that their local, Blanc-Mesnil-based performances stood out for the women, underlining the degree to which they understood theater to be governed by an ethics of neighborly sociability. Indeed, in my conversations with several of the women who had performed in *Le Bruit du monde*, as well as with Samia, they noted that their work referenced ancient Greek theater. For them, *Le Bruit du monde* functioned as a modern agora, calling to mind the central marketplace of ancient Greek city-states. The agora served as a gathering space for commercial and political interests and continues to be referenced as the urban form most allied with the emergence of democracy.

Not surprisingly, this reference parallels what Nicholas Ridout has called theater scholars' and practitioners' tendency to locate the connection between theater and community "'after' Athens," in reference to an imagined antiquity during which theatrical spectators were coincident with the community of citizens.[79] Ridout rightly notes that such references to ancient Greece have less to do with the historical realities of the classical world and more so with the ambivalence with which contemporary theater-makers "point to a future horizon at which such a coincidence might reappear."[80] Quelques unes d'entre nous members' references to a Blanc-Mesnil agora did similar work: they underlined the uncertainties that surrounded the notion of community in contemporary Blanc-Mesnil by displacing this possibility onto an imagined past, itself refashioned in anticipation of a future ideal. These dynamics were replicated throughout *Le Bruit du monde*, where the model for "community" was at once local and the far larger collective category of the French nation.

Rethinking the Republic

The opening scene of *Le Bruit du monde* takes place at the entrance to the National Assembly, where the women have traveled within the context of an MDT-sponsored citizenship activity. They will eventually find their way inside, marveling at the enormousness of the architectural shape and the miniscule, mostly male bodies that populate it. A large portion of the scene, however, takes place around the building's threshold, where the paraphernalia of official bureaucracy highlights the inaccessibility of French nationality. Aicha, for example, is wearing a headscarf, which the women soon realize she will have to remove if she is to enter this public building. Aicha refuses, adding "it is my personal relationship with God."[81] Soon, the women with headscarves make their way in, while a number of others are stalled at the metal detector. Their arms are adorned with gold bracelets, some of which they cannot remove. Eventually, the women find their way inside a hall where Ekram balks, unable to look at a Delacroix painting showing seminude human bodies. She launches into a short monologue that declares her incredulity, adding:

> I've never seen this in my life. All my life, I haven't seen something like this. I was born in Thoras, and I've been here since '63, all my life has passed without seeing the National Assembly. I haven't seen anything in my life . . . this reminds me of the war, my village which they bombarded, destroyed, and then, nothing. I know, they came

> to Algeria to look for men to fight in the war. They left the women and children crying. I remember, this lasted 7 years, 6 months and 18 days, from '54 to '62.[82]

In the lines that follow, the women's exchanges are more jocular, as they comment on their surroundings and find themselves in awe of the ornate rooms and libraries of parliament. Yet Ekram's brief comment signals a transition that emerges throughout the following pages. The threshold of the National Assembly presents a number of barriers to the nonnative French, ranging from physical obstacles that demand a shift in one's bodily comportment to those that command familiarity with a set of cultural and aesthetic codes. Yet what lies beyond these barriers, the promise of representative democracy, is both visually and conceptually troubled by memories of French colonialism. For Ekram, the "unseen" National Assembly is a reminder of a "seen" war, the Algerian War that launches the independent Algerian nation-state and Ekram's migratory journey toward the former colonial center. If the National Assembly has not yet been seen by Ekram, its effects have been felt, and all the more so because she is of Algerian origin.

The unique relationship between the host country and immigrants from formerly colonized territories emerges as a theme throughout the rest of the play, complicating a simple separation between native and nonnative, citizen and foreigner. "We were French before we were immigrants,"[83] Rahma declares at one point, reversing the traditional temporality of the accession from migrant to citizen. The impenetrability of French identity is thus depicted in both spatial and temporal terms. The women's physical entry into the National Assembly is clumsy, and their accession to French citizenship reverses their colonial past, mapping that historical experience onto an indefinite future where the promise of belonging is continuously deferred. In Rahma's words, "How many generations are necessary to be able to say, legitimately: I am French . . ."[84]

The MDT women's paradoxical relationship to French citizenship is particularly visible in moments where they distinguish between the institutions of the French state (such as the National Assembly) and the republican ideals these institutions are meant to embody.[85] The tension between institutions and ideals results in dialogues that reveal the difficulties of disaggregating the history of colonialism from that of the republic. For example, when Khadija asks, "Really, what does it mean to be French? A sort of diploma?"[86] the women respond to this meritocratic logic by referencing beauty contests and singing competitions: "Star Academy?" one asks jokingly, while another adds, "Miss France?" Soon, Shahinez interrupts this banter:

> SHAHINEZ: French . . . You see . . . It's the spirit of the Enlightenment . . . Tolerance . . . Humanity . . . Philosophy . . . We had a revolution!

> ANISSA: You know that women didn't even have the right to vote with your revolution.
> SHAHINEZ: And so?
> EKRAM: So "women" weren't French.
> KAHINA: Without rights, you get it? A bit like "immigrants." Worse than Arab.[87]

As Shahinez defines French identity through the legacy of the French Revolution, Anissa's critique of revolutionary history references women's absence from the political field, an absence that Kahina soon links to the hierarchies generated by colonialism. Republican history, in other words, is critiqued for having generated multiple and overlapping avenues of exclusion from citizenship. What *Le Bruit du monde* ultimately makes clear, however, is the fact that whereas republicanism's exclusions are the target of the women's critique, the universal ideals of the republic still serve as a horizon of political possibility. In the exhortation that ends the play, Rahma rallies her stage partners in a final cry:

> Yes, perfectly, changing the world! One dreams, but one does it! Eh girls? One is going to do it. Damn, let her live, this Republic. [*Bordel mais qu'elle vive cette République.*] Let her exist finally! [*Qu'elle existe enfin!*][88]

The play thus ends on what would seem a definitive note, but the final two phrases emphasize the grammatical ambiguity of the subjunctive. The republic to come is both a *wish* and a *commandment*; both a yearning for the continuation (*qu'elle vive*) of what has never been more than an unrealized model, and the desire for an imagined community still to come (*qu'elle existe enfin*). The republic is thus the target of *Le Bruit du monde*'s social critique but also the ideal undergirding its model of deliverance. This dynamic is not unlike what Emile Chabal has called the transformative narrative of republicanism, a narrative that "underlines republicanism's normative ambition and rests on a specific narrative of French history that stresses its revolutionary origins and its trans-historical potential."[89] Chabal further notes that whereas this narrative has historically been the preserve of the French Left, since the 1980s its reach has multiplied, providing a variety of political actors with a language of protest. Where Rahma's references to a republic to come are concerned, *Le Bruit du monde* clearly joins this aspirational narrative tendency. Yet the collective's treatment of this legacy also critiques the very "revolutionary origins" in question, revealing the women's simultaneous attachment to and skepticism of republicanism's transformational potential.

If *Le Bruit du monde*'s vision of republican universalism negotiates the tension between an idealized model and its realization via exclusionary institutions, a closer look at the performance's infrastructure reveals that the women's relationship to institutions themselves is not foreclosed. Here again, the associational structure (the Maison des Tilleuls) proves a complicated reference point. On the one hand, as we have seen, the history of the Beur movement shows how immigrant associationalism can reproduce state-sponsored ideals of integration, even as it works to change them. On the other hand, the civic architecture of Blanc-Mesnil, which literally houses the women's rehearsal process, can produce cultural forms (like theater) that ultimately express the need to protect these public institutions. In Blanc-Mesnil, this was especially clear when these institutions become the target of *public* conflagrations. For Quelques unes d'entre nous, associationalism, like the republican ideals to which it is so deeply connected, remains a source of citizenly possibility.

Ultimately, *Le Bruit du monde*'s use of the language of republicanism imagines collectivity at a scale that is too large to render references to shared primary identities relevant. Only at the play's conclusion do we see the contours of a "community" emerge. Rahma's final call is to a multigenerational group of "girls" (*les filles*):

> The other day, the sounds of the world entered my ear, perfectly! It wouldn't stop speaking to me, it told me this: go liberate your country Rahma, go! Go my girl! A little bit like that other one who ended up as a shish-kebab, poor thing . . . That young nut, Jeanne, what courage! She battled to liberate her country, and they roasted her!
>
> The voice in my ear, it won't stop speaking to me, it bothers me.
>
> . . .
>
> —[The voice speaks] I am your intelligence, I am your political conscience! . . . I am the past, the present, the future of your children, of the planet.[90]

In the lines that follow, Rahma details how this voice tells her to stir her lazy husband awake. As she does so, Rahma has not yet shaken the reference to the medieval folk heroine Jeanne d'Arc, and the alternating lines that she addresses to her husband (and to the invisible voice) contain different layers of reference: Jeanne's body is burned at the stake, and Rahma herself lives in a neighborhood where war rages and buildings burn. The voice echoes themes that emerge earlier in the play, pushing Rahma to admonish her husband, find her "sisters," and let them know that they too can become religious and cultural leaders in their communities. As she turns to the audience for the final section of her monologue, Rahma adds:

> And that's how the voice, she [gendered female, *la voix*] entered my ear, and she convinced me that I was responsible for the world, not just the great chef in the kitchen and of logistics but in the exterior world too. So I met other women like me, that the voice had visited,

> and we did things together . . . During the revolts we were outside, every evening, we made tea and spoke to people. We created an exhibition that toured in Europe. We even did . . . theater. Incidentally it is rehearsal time, with the director, and for that matter I am rehearsing here with you, I am working at the moment, yes . . . I am an actress![91]

As this lengthy and technically demanding monologue switches from embodying various voices (Rahma, the voice, and the husband) to a direct address to the audience, it becomes clear that the grouping of those who have been visited by this voice is the grouping of women that audience members can see standing around the stage. Theater, in Rahma's formulation, is not conceptualized as the cultural expression of an identity political stance. Rather, theater is a vehicle for communicating to the audience that which the "voice" has communicated to oneself. In other words, it is a fleeting, temporary collective arrangement that responds to a temporally and spatially situated need for a form of public expression. Community might be central to making this expression powerful, but it is not theater's definitive mandate.

Conclusion

Although I have outlined the complicated forms of belonging that *Le Bruit du monde* sought to narrate, it is equally important to note that there remained an inevitable distance between the interior logic of the theatrical text and the audiences' experience of its three-dimensional unfolding. Post-show debates in particular revealed a variety of engagements with the play. The audience of the Forum Social des Quartiers Populaires in Blanc-Mesnil, for example, was arguably more familiar with the locality *Le Bruit du monde* portrayed. Furthermore, they were quite literally connected to the piece through friends and family members who performed in the play. In contrast, audiences at the prestigious Parisian institution Théâtre du Rond Point, situated right off the Champs-Élysées, responded differently. When I inquired as to the experience of performing at this venue, one actor said quietly and tersely: "Culture isn't the same in Paris and the *banlieues*." Upon hearing her comment, I assumed that her reference to "culture" encompassed the term's wide range of associations in French, from the class connotations that often positioned Parisian high art in opposition to the *banlieue*'s *culture populaire* to the specific content of Quelques unes d'entre nous's artistic project. I wondered, in other words, if her comment referred to an experience where their aesthetic credentials had been cross-examined. When I inquired further as to the meaning of this enigmatic sentence, however, I was told that during the post-show debate, an audience member had asked whether the women's husbands were allowing them to do theater. During our conversation, Samia recalled the same incident, as well as the frustration that it had evoked. Shaking her head, she asked: "Does one direct this question to someone who is blond?" Her reaction underlined the question's "tokenization," its mapping of perceived ethno-racial difference onto an imagined complex of cultural differences. Samia, in other words, had dismissed the question as thinly veiled racism.

In retrospect, the *Le Bruit du monde* actor's earlier comment encapsulated a broader frustration regarding the changeability of audiences. In effect, this actor had recognized that there were a vast array of performance contexts and "cultural" categorizations through which audiences could understand themselves *and* performers as belonging to certain kinds of communities. Although their bodies and voices, their costumes and acting style and their staging choices could influence which contexts and categorizations became relevant, they in fact exercised little control over whether they were perceived as "immigrant women" or "Blanc-Mesnilois citizens" or "amateur performers." Collective members were acutely aware of the indeterminacy of notions like culture, aware that they acquired altered forms depending on an audience member's angle of vision. In other words, they experienced the methodological limitations of rubrics like intercultural or community-based theater through direct experience with what Richard Bauman would term the "interpretive frame" of their performance.[92]

Recognizing the limits of these scholarly rubrics, however, is not tantamount to suggesting that they are never apt or even efficacious. Rather, my point has been that such rubrics are best employed when we recognize where they stand in relation to the political, ethical, and aesthetic imaginary that surrounds theater's lived experience. In the context of *Le Bruit du monde*, references to "community" and "culture" have to confront the complexities of a suburban geography that has borne witness to decades of social fragmentation, as well as a republican political tradition that has historically disaggregated "culture" from group identities. At the same time, however, *Le Bruit du monde* is evidence of the resilience of republican ideals, of how they continue to be repurposed for both communal and cultural ends.

Chapter 5

✦

Theater without Borders?

In 2008 I attended a fund-raiser that Réseau Education Sans Frontières (RESF) held in an eastern suburb of Paris. Organized around short information sessions on recent developments in Parisian retention centers for immigrants, the event included a community potluck and arts and crafts activities for children. Midway through this fast-paced evening was a performance that had been written and directed by Natalie and adapted from narratives the artist had collected from undocumented immigrant women. Natalie's performance began with the story of Aminata. An actress who had left her West African home for performance engagements in Switzerland in 2003, Aminata had found that she was unable to return when political violence engulfed her city. Her thoughts with the only son that she had left behind, Aminata had entered France illegally, where she had held clandestine jobs, lodged in hotels filled with refugees, and was ultimately rendered homeless. When the lights initially flooded the stage, there was a black woman sitting downstage and to the left, accompanied by a white French woman who stood in the center, narrating Aminata's story in the first person. Barely moving from her designated spot yet talented at maintaining momentum, the actress often glanced at her stage partner in a reciprocal gaze that was later revealed to have been the signal identifying the black woman as Aminata herself. Soon the two Aminatas, real and rehearsed, were joined by an actress narrating the story of Fatma, a refugee from the Middle East whose narrative centered on the child for whom she had decided to leave the miserable home of her father-in-law. She was then joined by an actress delivering the narrative of Mariama, also from West Africa, who had left her country of origin in order to provide her daughter with a better education. All three were finally joined by an actress representing Amira, from North Africa, who had arrived with her family to join her sister-in-law in France only to find that familial hospitality was short-lived. Not long after Amira's narrative was introduced, approximately sixty women flooded the small stage from the sidelines and stood distributed, as motionless as the Aminatas but swiftly breaking into the parts of the four stories they wished to contribute to. As the performance drew to a close and the lights faded, they lingered on the only black woman on stage, the real Aminata, who had remained speechless throughout.

Natalie's performance constituted my first, fleeting exposure to theatrical immigration activism in Paris, alerting me to the multiple ways that theater was used to address the relationship between immigration, citizenship, and national identity. Yet Natalie's work also encapsulated a number of principles that were unique to a subgenre of this theatrical activity: a broad array of commercial and noncommercial works that portrayed narratives of exile, displacement, and suffering from undocumented immigrants, refugees, and asylum seekers. This subgenre was permeated by the term *témoignage* (witnessing). Referring to the oral accounts of the individuals whose narratives formed the backbone of the performances, *témoignage* captured the act of witnessing that characterized the relationship between event and narrator as well as that between narrator and listener. The underlying principles of this emergent subgenre borrowed from medical humanitarianism, legal aid, and immigrant social movements, the larger contexts within which an ever-growing number of theatrical works on migration were taking place. The values, ideals, and representative practices of these domains were increasingly influencing both how Parisian artists articulated the capacities they attributed to political art, and the explanatory principles they put to use to position themselves in relation to the suffering they wished to portray.

In this chapter, I suggest that these imagined capacities and explanatory principles resulted in a *humanitarian theater* premised on two recurring characteristics, both of which were readily visible in Natalie's performance. Although the artist drew on the testimonial connotations of *témoignage* to highlight the truthfulness of the narratives on which her work was based, our conversations soon revealed that her use of the term *témoignage* involved a subtle negotiation between the subjective and the objective: Natalie's narrative focus had prioritized poignant anecdotes and moments of emotional appeal, glossing over the dimensions of her interlocutors' accounts that endowed them with political personhood. These narrative choices prioritized moments of heightened sentiment on the part of her narrators, and as such, they resonated with what scholars like Julie Salverson and James Thompson have identified as a deliberate emphasis on testimonies of injury in community-based and activist theater practices.[1] Humanitarian theater like Natalie's, however, avoided direct voyeurism because other actors delivered the narratives themselves, even as Animata herself figured in the performance in ways that both authorized and authenticated the work of the professionals. The narrating women who flooded the stage served as the anonymous public that witnessed Aminata's story, yet Aminata's presence also corroborated the sincerity of their words, thus joining the biological origin of these narratives with their expert conduits, imitating newly constructed systems of reporting from the global information economy.

The critical literature on refugee theater has approached such representational strategies with caution. Responding to the emergence of what Caroline Wake has called a "growing global genre" of verbatim, testimonial, and documentary performance practices,[2] these critiques often recognize the wholesome intentions of the activists producing them, but hasten to underline the distance between intentions and end products. Introducing a special issue on "Theatre and Statelessness" for example, Azadeh Sharifi and S. E. Wilmer note that "in the majority of projects with, for, and about refugees, there is a gap between what is intended and what will be the outcome, namely an unintended reproduction of racism and (colonial) stereotypes."[3] The authors note that this dynamic plagues any number of cultural institutions, adding that what is often missing is a question of "insight and expertise" with regard to refugee participants' ongoing situations.

Sharifi and Wilmer are correct, of course. As exemplified by Natalie's performance, humanitarian theater is rife with the racial and gendered tropes that often accompany the depiction of spectacular suffering, particularly where postcolonial geographies are concerned. In studying the relationship between humanitarianism and theater, however, my goal is to take the gap between intention and outcome as a *given*, rather than an unexpected by-product of artistic processes. Moreover, I hope to show that intentions and outcomes rarely exist in binary opposition and that the day-to-day production of theater involves the *translation* of humanitarian ideals into the flawed experience of humanitarian practice. To be clear, however, my point is not to excuse the reproduction of racist genre conventions derived from colonialism. Instead, I consider the production of such conventions from within their particular national contexts and moral universes. The example of French humanitarianism will show that expert insight and intervention are not guarantees of ethical aesthetic conduct, as expertise itself is a form of knowledge production with multiple and often problematic investments.

In what follows, I illustrate these dynamics through a gradually widening scale. Natalie's project, my first example, is indicative of the kind of theatrical work that circulated in the small-scale and mostly neighborhood-based platforms of aid networks like RESF in the early twenty-first century. These theatrical performances supplemented aid workers' broader efforts to keep their audiences informed of the kinds of legal and political developments that characterized French immigration policy. Natalie's play debuted in 2008 and continued to be performed during the years that followed, largely along a suburban Parisian circuit, drawing audiences that numbered around 80–100 on each occasion. My next example is a performance project that was developed by the artistic director Michel at a midsized and prestigious arts center in downtown Paris a few years earlier. Given its geographic location, the piece drew on the center's regular subscribers while mobilizing a larger urban audience, permeated once again by members of the broad array of aid associations with whom the arts center collaborated during the development of the performance. In my analysis of Natalie and Michel's work, I focus on narratives of everyday interactions and intimate encounters to illustrate the logic of humanitarian theater. To do so, I draw on my interviews as well as other performance documents. Conversely, my final example draws on the broader body of material that characterizes the self-historicizing tendencies of a long-lasting and leading theater company: drawing on the transnational work of the Paris-based Théâtre du Soleil, I end by focusing on the company's much-traveled 2003 production *Le Dernier Caravansérail* (*The Last Caravansary*).

The representative strategies that unify these artists' theatrical output have been in conversation with a number of political, legislative, and humanitarian shifts. The emphasis on affect and emotionality mentioned earlier is related to a political context that has increasingly positioned immigration policies as a set of *compassionate* measures that reward those in true need. In turn, the specific representational strategies by which this compassion is culled is best considered in light of the tradition of witnessing or *témoignage* that has been key to the medical humanitarian movements that have emerged in France since the Second World War. Finally, the media practices of the undocumented immigrants' movement reveal the ubiquity and force of the kind of representations that have framed immigration and refuge. Indeed, the question of *sans-papiers* rights has occupied a key position in both political and public discourse in France since the early 1990s, when the immigration laws authored by then Minister of the Interior Charles Pasqua rendered formerly legal categories of migratory movement unlawful and severely restricted access to residency permits for nonnationals already dwelling in France.[4] As these policies went into effect, undocumented laborers and families joined forces with aid organizations to stage a series of public occupations. These events served as the origin of what has since been labeled *le mouvement des sans-papiers*, referring to undocumented immigrants' ongoing struggle to achieve both juridical recognition *and* a social identity based on juridical status, rather than the murky image of criminality signified by earlier media labels like *les clandestins*.[5] Whereas I argue that these broader representational struggles have a direct impact on emergent aesthetic forms like humanitarian theater, I also endeavor to show how such forms can serve as the basis for new practices of exchange, communication, and intimacy, however fraught they might be.

The Humanitarianization of Theater

When I met with Natalie in the weeks following the RESF fund-raiser, it was clear that her theatrical reference points were multiple, nourished as they were by the wide community of politically engaged artists with whom she often worked and collaborated. At the same time, it was clear that her work on immigration borrowed a series of strategies from the larger world of humanitarian aid, even as theater's unique embodiedness and flexibility altered the predictable representations that such borrowing could produce.

Natalie had decided to create a performance piece based on *sans-papiers* narratives in 2007, when she met Aminata through friends who were active in the aid world and was subsequently introduced to the other three women portrayed in her work. When I inquired into the experience of working with these women, her reply was revelatory of her understanding of the term *témoignage*. For Natalie, *témoignage* was both *personal* speech that carried a documentary connotation and a decidedly *public* output, performed for an audience:

> When I met with these women, they trusted me because they knew who I was; I explained why I was doing this. Aminata came to my home. I met Fatma at a friend's place and Amira at her home. I had a recorder. We drank tea and coffee, we had some cake. Amira was very factual. Mariama also, she only talked about her daughter. But Aminata and Fatma, they gave me so much material, they cried, that's where the emotion was. One of my qualities is that I am really capable of listening. And then I just let things flow out . . . This was the first time that they were talking to people about these things and they played [*jouer*] with absolute sincerity. What's true and what's false, that is not important. I actually know that some of what they told me was false. Memory deforms things, some things you can't say. I just want to hear what can be said, not search for the truth. Theater is like this though, it's not like TV, and it's a place where we can say false things as though they were true.

Throughout my conversation with Natalie, the director distinguished between the veracity of her interlocutors' claims and the embodied forms that characterized their moment of utterance. In a move that would be familiar to both oral historians and ethnographers, she privileged form over content, a choice that was paralleled by her insistence on describing the particulars of her own scene of ethnographic research. For Natalie, the tea and the cake, the comforted tears and her physical presence were not the marginalia of a scene of oral transmission but its very vehicles. Natalie's dismissal of these narratives' veracity or internal consistency was less a question of recognizing the changeability or diversity of human experience than it was a result of her interest in the *performance of sincerity*. As is clear from the comments above, Natalie sought evidence of "emotions" rather than "facts," the outward manifestation of sentiments rather than the communication of evidence. She labeled this emotional outpouring both *sincere* and an instance of *play*, underlining its mediated nature.

These dynamics are well captured by *témoignage*, a term that both references and exceeds the judiciary encounter. The figure of the *témoin* can appear in a range of scenes, from the groomsman approving the legitimacy of a marital union to a passerby who can legitimate the facts of a past event.

The *témoin* thus initiates a set of social, physical, and legal relationships premised on what Paul Ricoeur has called "credit granted to the word of others."[6] What was significant about the use of *témoignage* in my conversations with artists was that although they relied on the fact that the term's quotidian usage "preserves," in Ricoeur's words, "those essential features of the fact of testifying,"[7] they were uninterested in relaying the broader actuality that had produced the testimony in question. Natalie was not alone in privileging emotions over facts. Whereas the term *témoignage* evoked a range of references associated with the legitimating functions of institutionalized speech acts, the vast majority of my interlocutors repeated the refrain that nobody wanted to hear about laws, rights discourses, or, as one simply put it, "politics." Although the personal emotionality of Aminata, Fatma, Mariama, and Amira's narratives was a direct result of legal and political developments, presenting their precariousness required abandoning juridical or political particulars.

My conversations with artists working on migration thus paralleled a tendency that Liisa Malkki has called "deshistoricizing universalism,"[8] referencing how the representational practices surrounding humanitarian intervention often void refugees of their specific political, historical, and cultural worlds, presenting them as instances of universal humanity caught in a moment of life-altering distress. This was clearly the case in Natalie's work, yet the parallels did not end there. Much like the humanitarian workers discussed by Malkki, who spoke on behalf of refugees as their "expert voice,"[9] Aminata was joined on stage by the conduit of her narrative. During our conversation, Natalie related that this had been a tough decision:

> With Aminata it was difficult. She took great pleasure from performing. All of a sudden, she had a place for herself on a stage. But it was difficult as well. There are limits. She is always on the verge of falling apart [*craquer*]. I didn't want her to speak. She shouldn't speak.

In linking stage speech to the performer's psychology, Natalie expressed a concern that haunted a number of my interlocutors, many of whom worked with personal narratives of a traumatic nature. This concern was premised on the assumption that the public revelation of traumatic memory risked altering the speaker's relationality to the world as well as their relationship to the memory itself. Natalie's decision to place Aminata on stage but to do so without including her verbal output, revealed a sharp distinction between visual revelation (or the display of the traumatized body) and verbal revelation (or the spoken delivery of traumatic narrative). Whereas the first was linked to having "a place for herself on a stage," the second was linked to psychic "limits" and was transferred to a conduit.

In instances such as these, audience recognition or validation was expected to arise from within a visual relationship, what James Thompson has identified as an emphasis on physiognomy that asks audience members to "diagnose a history, a need or vulnerability from the wrinkles of a forehead, from the depth of a frown or the crease of a smile."[10] Thompson refers here to applied theater practices in zones of violence where the presence of a performer's face functions less as a Levinasian summons to responsibility and more so as physiognomic "evidence of some inner condition." To chastise Natalie's work for occupying the physiognomic end of this scale seems unfair, and Thompson himself is well aware that "a popular hermeneutic response within the arts cannot be simply switched off."[11] More important to note, perhaps, is the fact that this hermeneutic response is not activated in the same way everywhere. Hermeneutic practices in the theater are far from standardized and they are often shaped by a set of associated viewing practices.

The presence of the body as evidence of traumatic experience in humanitarian theater is inevitably in conversation with a broader trend characterizing the relationship between asylum seekers and immigrant aid organizations catering specifically to psychiatric needs in France. Didier Fassin and Richard Rechtman have noted that the French state's increasingly strict asylum policies have influenced nongovernmental strategies for working with asylum applicants. Agents of care often find that in order for applicants to be granted asylum on humanitarian grounds, they have to offer proof of psychiatric suffering. "Clinical psychological truth"[12] often involves a negotiation between the physical evidence of scars (related to cases of political violence and torture) and the less visible evidence of trauma. What Fassin and Rechtman call "the evidence of the body" is coproduced by the French state, aid organizations, and asylum seekers themselves.[13] Theatrical spectatorship, in other words, is one among a number of viewing practices that have repurposed the visuality of the body for humanitarian activism.

To be clear, my suggestion is not that Natalie was working with a self-consciously humanitarian agenda that sought to silence Aminata. To the contrary, Natalie was concerned that Aminata experience the familiar sensation of stage recognition but do so without damaging her sense of dignity and day-to-day functionality. My point is that regardless of her ethical commitments, Natalie's aesthetic choices participated in a world of shifting representational practices. Whereas Aminata was safeguarded from the potentially harmful consequences of public speech, her *biological* presence served as the fleshly evidence authorizing the speech of her stage partner. This bodily exchange was premised on both the notion that speech is the domain of self-expression that is most compromised by traumatic experience *and* that the body is what enhances the legibility and veracity of that speech once it is transferred to a more "able" speaker. Indeed, however universalizing Aminata's dehistoricization had been, her body's affective appeal was nonetheless directly tied to her racial and gender identity.

These parallels between humanitarian and theatrical representation reveal how both domains negotiate questions of authenticity. At the same time, these resonances run the risk of simplifying the unique processes and codes of theatrical spectatorship. I was reminded of this when Natalie related the audience's perception of the performance:

> There were people who didn't imagine that she [the speechless black woman on stage] was Aminata. They told me that there was too much violence for her to be the real person that was being talked about. There were many people who did not imagine that it was her.

Natalie's audience, in other words, had been unable to identify Aminata as herself, unable to connect her to the narrative spoken by her rehearsed version and unable finally to recognize the glance between the two actresses as a sign of their mutual recognition.

This error in theatrical communication is telling. On the one hand, the audience's confusion resonates with the politics of hope that Emma Cox identifies in the reception of theatricalized refugee narratives. Cox argues that the trauma associated with migration is often "made comprehensible and *meaningful* to the extent that it generates hope in/for spectators."[14] In other words, the presentation of trauma legitimates its moral quest through reference to a hopeful ending. The identification of the speechless stage presence as Aminata breaks such an expectation because it illustrates the ongoing vicissitudes of her precarious status in France, forcing audience members into a different moral relation to her suffering. On the other hand, the fact that Aminata's presence on stage could not be registered within the audience's imaginary of migrant trauma reveals the extent to which the representational strategies of humanitarianism alter the traditional hermeneutic response associated with theatrical representations of exile, displacement, or violence. Although global audiences are habituated to disaggregating narratives of violence from the person of the humanitarian aid worker relating it, such a viewing habit cannot be taken for granted in the theater, where the staging either displays the suffering individual or replaces her with an actress assuming her role. Instead, Natalie had *bundled* the two together to produce a new kind of theatrical truth: one where the biological source of the specific *témoignage* was joined by its narrative performer.

Compassion and Witnessing

Why have the representational strategies of humanitarian aid movements emerged in artistic domains? The answer to this question lies in concurrent shifts in the political life of immigration. Indeed, scholarship on the management of immigration in France has noted that the early years of the new millennium witnessed the growing "humanitarianisation" of immigration policy,[15] a reference to the fact that although increasingly restrictive legislation was forcing borders to close, the language of security and border control was infused with references to compassion. In a 2007 presidential campaign speech in Toulouse, Minister of the Interior Nicolas Sarkozy exemplified this shift as he reformulated an oft-quoted statement from Michel Rocard, the Socialist prime minister (1988–91): "One cannot welcome all the misery of the world" (*On ne peut pas accueillir toute la misère du monde*). In Sarkozy's version, France's inability to play host to all those who desired escape from misery was reformulated as a concern for the immigrants' self-respect, a concern that seemingly escaped his political opponents. "The Left," Sarkozy noted, "does not want to see the impossibility of welcoming all the misery of the world with dignity."[16] In statements such as these, the management of immigration carried a decidedly apolitical dimension, centered on references to universally recognizable thresholds of human dignity.

Over the course of the 2000s, the *moral* legitimacy attributed to security measures resulted in what Miriam Ticktin has called "exceptional 'apolitical' humanitarian clauses"[17] that replaced long-standing legal promises to honor familial reunification and political asylum with emergency measures designed to end perceived human suffering.[18] Of course, the theme of misery and suffering had already entered French political discourse during the previous decade, guiding decisions from the allocation of emergency unemployment benefits to instituting support centers for psychic ills. Didier Fassin notes that "the semantic configuration" of the 1990s privileged empathic reactions to social inequality,[19] creating an environment where those who wished to benefit from state aid would have to *demonstrate* their need in terms that would be recognizable to those allocating it. By the early twenty-first century, both the logic of compassion and its performance imperative had entered the domain of immigration politics.

Yet what did it mean to have humanitarianism do political work? As the moral imperative to eradicate human suffering universally, humanitarianism's history is often traced through religious traditions of charity and their respective ideals of salvation.[20] Christiane Vollaire notes that what remains constant in humanitarianism's later career as a *secular* phenomenon is its "unifying intention,"[21] one that is premised on the existence of a universal humanity. Humanitarianism's nineteenth-century institutionalization and its emergence in international law (through the founding of the Red Cross and the signing of the Geneva Convention, respectively) are premised on the idea that the right to humane treatment transcends citizenship, responding to universal, "species-level needs and health."[22] Whereas humanitarianism's various historical lineages alternately avow and disavow the moral and political dimensions of the phenomenon, what Fassin calls humanitarianism's "second age"[23] has been indelibly political.

"The second age" or "new humanitarianism" refers to the activities of the emergency medical care movements that were established during the 1970s and 1980s, chief among them Médecins Sans Frontières (MSF) or Doctors Without Borders. Founded in 1971 by a medical collective that returned to

France after working in Nigeria during the Biafra-Nigeria War, MSF's vision of universalism had a uniquely humanitarian orientation, one which modified the anticolonial solidarity movements of the 1968 generation into a concern for the human rights and dignity of Third World victims.[24] Unlike their intellectual predecessor, the Swiss-originated Red Cross, MSF's commitment to neutrality was partial. In Peter Redfield's words:

> The greater ethic of impartiality would find its sharpest definition through medical care. Operational neutrality, by contrast, must always allow for moral duty and its potential politics. To describe this delicate balance in the precise terms of its engagement, MSF gradually adopted the term *témoignage* to imply an active sense of witnessing, as motivated by humanitarian concern for suffering.[25]

The term *témoignage*, in other words, levied MSF's political neutrality as agents of intervention against their moral partiality as agents of reportage. In 1978 disagreements over the role of *témoignage* resulted in a separate organization, Médecins du Monde (MDM) or Doctors of the World, whose leader, Bernard Kouchner, would eventually became synonymous with *le devoir d'ingérence* (the duty to intervene) and the broader militarization of humanitarian sentiment as the millennium drew to a close. Although MSF's later leadership reoriented the organization toward medical intervention, the politics of witnessing and the moral duties of the "neutral" aid worker have left an indelible mark on the second age of French humanitarianism.[26]

Redfield notes that medical humanitarian workers' ability to function as moral agents is premised on how their vision of medical aid ("without borders") signals both the purported universality of the sentiments they bring to bear on the spaces of suffering in which they work *and* the specific credibility they can claim by way of their expertise. Redfield calls "this positioned assemblage of fact and value 'motivated truth' to highlight the overt combination of reason and sentiment that it represents."[27] The figure of the expert witness has since appeared at the crossroads of political and moral systems, as scholars have noted how the nongovernmental arena has been called upon to serve specific bureaucratic needs or even justify international humanitarian interventions undertaken by armed military personnel.[28]

Given the ubiquity with which the term *témoignage* now appears in nongovernmental politics in France, it was perhaps only a matter of time before it entered the "semantic configuration" of theatrical representations of exile, displacement, and immigration. Over the course of my conversations with theater artists working on migration, however, I found that their use of terms like *témoignage* exceeded theater and humanitarianism's shared commitment to compassionate social action. Theater, much like medicine in the words of Bernard Kouchner, "presented the advantage of having a utility without borders, and being in the interest of a universal ethic."[29] Just as medicine could address physical illness, the key manifestation of our common humanity, theater could address the universal need for self-expression. And whereas medical humanitarian expertise and theatrical expertise signaled different levels of urgency, both entailed combinations of reason and sentiment, of motivated truths.

Representational Strategies

If my conversations in the worlds of theatrical practice and humanitarian aid revealed a joint interest in the representation of suffering, I also repeatedly came across shared concerns as to the efficacy of this representation. Two themes were particularly visible. Both theater artists and humanitarian aid workers expressed concern over whether they should privilege collective representations of suffering or focus on individualized portraits of distress. And whereas such concerns were motivated by larger questions regarding strategies for evoking universal ethics and human bonds, they were equally revelatory of how both sets of individuals thought about expertise.

Insofar as organizations like the MSF and MDM are driven, as Renée Fox notes, by "a global vision of a 'new world order' governed by the principles of the UDHR,"[30] it has become imperative to recognize the patterns through which the public representatives of "motivated truths" often originate in the First World, whereas those they aid hail from beyond. The relationship between the aid provider and the aid recipient is thus an important site of power, one that renders compassion a deeply unequal sentiment, lacking in mutuality. Liisa Malkki has shown how the representational strategies of humanitarian movements often reveal these power dynamics through their tendency to dehistoricize the figure of the refugee, rendering her into an instance of universal humanity that is devoid of political or social context yet in need of expert interpretation. For Malkki, the visual corollary of the refugee as a universal human being is mass scenes of displaced bodies, composing an unidentifiable throng functioning as a "sea of humanity."[31] Whereas Malkki goes on to note how less crowded representations draw on equally conventionalized tropes of victimhood (such as the depiction of women and children), her disapproval of *collective* representations of suffering belongs to a longer tradition of critique with regard to political movements and committed artworks. In *On Revolution*, her classic study of the eighteenth century's revolutionary upheavals, Hannah Arendt distinguished between compassion's ability to respond to individual suffering and to collective angst:

> Compassion, by its very nature, cannot be touched off by the sufferings of a whole class or a people, or, least of all, mankind as a whole. It cannot reach out farther than what is suffered by one person and still remain what it is supposed to be, co-suffering. Its strength hinges on the strength of passion itself, which, in contrast to reason, can

> comprehend only the particular, but has no notion of the general and no capacity for generalization.[32]

Today Arendt's discussion has a slightly different ring, as the relationship between compassion and individual suffering resonates with the contemporary American politics of "compassionate conservatism" critiqued by Lauren Berlant,[33] a politics that displaces the target of social compassion from structural inequality to individual economic need. Arendt draws on a different set of reference points, however, occupying herself primarily with the limits of "passion" and individual emotional capacity. I reference her comments here, for Arendt's distinction would have been familiar to the artists with whom I spoke. These were individuals who were critical of the (global) neoliberal turn outlined by Berlant, yet who nonetheless felt that particularity was the only antidote to immigration policies that wed various categories of migration to one another and the phenomenon as a whole to criminality. For these artists, a seemingly accessible body held greater potential for identification than an unwieldy mass. Over the course of my research, I found that this aesthetic tendency mirrored the changing representational strategies of the undocumented immigrants' movement.

Ironically, it was precisely when *le mouvement de sans-papiers* was negotiating the question of communal survival that its aesthetic representations began to shift toward individualized portraits and specific stories. In 1996 a group of undocumented immigrants occupied the St. Bernard Church in the 18th arrondissement of Paris. Both during and after the occupation of St. Bernard (now synonymous with the term *sans-papiers*), the group was supported by artists, filmmakers, and public figures. Shortly after the movement was evacuated from St. Bernard following an exhaustive police operation, the Théâtre du Soleil moved the approximately 300 evacuees to the Cartoucherie, the group's extensive rehearsal and performance space in the eastern Parisian suburb of Vincennes. As the *sans-papiers* activists, the Théâtre du Soleil, and the various associations involved with the movement struggled to handle the group's day-to-day needs, they found themselves facing the challenge of transitioning from the fast-paced momentum of occupation to the maintenance of a long-term existence that few architectural spaces and few human rights organizations could support. Meanwhile, a group of supportive filmmakers had created *Nous, sans-papiers de France*, a short film that showed one of the movement's representatives, Madjiguène Cissé, standing against a dark background and reading the *sans-papiers* manifesto that had appeared in the newspaper *Libération*. For a few weeks, the short preceded movie showings in countless theaters, making Cissé into the most visible face and the undeniable spokesperson of the *sans-papiers* struggle. When I spoke to Jacques, a high-profile aid worker associated with the movement, he confirmed that a shift had taken place in 1997:

> For the first time in the history of France, practically every evening the French saw on their TVs *sans-papiers* narrating their stories. In the past, the *sans-papiers*' image was that of someone who is not respectable . . . Here, we have all of the ingredients of melodrama, we have someone who is honest, who is pursued as if in a tragedy, who is trying to escape this thing. And as in a tragedy, there is fortune. This no longer belongs to the world of men but of Gods. And everyone knows that the French state is in the role of the state. And the *sans-papiers* is perceived as a heroic actor. In my opinion, this is a new kind of reflection from performing arts people [*les gens du spectacle*]. We have a character who is a fiction but who is also real. I promise you that if Racine, if he were a contemporary of the *sans-papiers*, he would have written a tragedy about Madjiguène Cissé. Maybe Iphigenia would have been Madjiguène Cissé.

Jacques's comments are revelatory of a number of the tendencies that accompanied the individuation of *sans-papiers* representations. Whereas Jacques began with a reference to a *sans-papiers* individual's narrative of their experience, his emphasis was less on the factual content of this narrative than on the interpretive frame through which the French television viewer experienced it. The elevated moral stakes of tragedy and melodrama characterized the reception of this narrative, a narrative in which the *sans-papiers* individual was subject to the winds of fate and fortune rather than a person negotiating changing residency requirements. And as the caricaturized struggle between good and evil (the *sans-papiers* and the French state) developed, the ungendered *sans-papiers* individual morphed into the gendered Madjiguène Cissé, whose historical counterpart was the hapless Iphigenia, sacrificed to the gods for the safety of a sea voyage.

What was significant about Jacques's take on the movement's changing representations was the role that "performing arts people" played in this transformation. In other words, if the "motivated truth" that characterized aesthetic representations of singular figures positioned the *sans-papiers* individual as the last in a long line of sacrificial heroes, this truth was replete with *the expertise of performing artists*. This formulation is important, for it was one that I encountered often: the potential contribution that artists could make to a larger project of social justice was articulated less through a language of citizenly activism and much more so through references to the specific kinds of credibility that performing arts expertise could bring to bear on the representation of suffering. Whereas it would be a mistake to consider such discursive moves only in the light of medical humanitarian discourses, it is equally impossible to avoid these parallel turns to expertise, a theme to which I will return.

The relationship between humanitarianism and theater was also not unidirectional, however, as aesthetic representations influenced the strategies of humanitarian aid workers. This influence was well captured by an RESF worker who told me that as immigration policies increasingly favored case-by-case evaluations of residency applications, RESF increasingly focused on sensationalizing individual applications. For example, the organization worked with a *sans-papiers* youth who had, during the period of the evaluation of his residency application, coincidentally saved an elderly woman from a fire. RESF had used every media outlet possible to render what she termed a "heroic" story impossible to ignore. During our conversation, the RESF worker smiled wearily, noting that finding an affective angle to every application was getting to be exhausting. Nonetheless, the "heroic" youth, whose chances at residency had previously been labeled quite low, had been awarded a ten-year residency permit. "Heroism" functioned as both an interpretive frame and an advocacy strategy, and often interchangeably, blurring the lines between aesthetic and political strategies.

Aesthetic Constraints and Humanitarian Politics

During my stay in Paris, Natalie's emphasis on the relationship between immigration, *témoignage*, and the performance of sincerity was a recurring theme. These connections reemerged during my conversation with Michel, who, several years earlier, had paired Paris-based refugees with professional actors to present a panoramic representation of experiences of refuge, exile, and immigration in France. The artistic director of a well-known and prestigious arts center in Paris, Michel began by differentiating between the exilic movements of the first half of the twentieth century (characterized for him by a southern European and South American influx and responding to a variety of fascisms) and those that followed the 1960s, when both the geographic origins of and the motivations behind human displacement expanded exponentially. Michel began by contacting prominent aid associations such as Cimade, GISTI, and La Ligue des Droits de l'Homme, visiting Parisian residence halls for immigrant workers and attending municipal meetings on immigration-related issues to recruit, in his words, "thirty refugees." He then contacted a highly prestigious theatrical association, composed of the graduates of the national conservatories, for ten volunteer actors. Once Michel had gathered his participants, each actor was paired with two to three refugees, the goal being to create thirty-minute presentations on the narratives of each individual. The actors met with the refugees, whose origins ranged from Morocco to Argentina, throughout a six-month period. They exchanged stories, discussed different staging alternatives, and prepared for the final presentation. Eventually, Michel and his artistic team laced each thirty-minute episode together into a day-long performance that played once in its entirety, and otherwise as rotating sets of three to four narratives.

During our conversation, it became clear that Michel's project, much like Natalie's, was not structured around a self-consciously humanitarian ideal. In fact, as I will soon detail, Michel explicitly critiqued approaches that assigned theater a healing role. What was significant about the explanatory principles motivating Michel's aesthetic choices was how these principles paralleled the logic of humanitarian representation even as he refused theater's capacity to function as or compel *moral action*. The artistic director connected his choices to staging imperatives that were related to audience satisfaction and affective appeal, yet over the course of our conversations, I couldn't help but note how closely such imperatives paralleled the perceived information economy negotiated by the humanitarian aid worker. These dynamics are well captured by two of what Michel called the performance's "constraints," one narrative, the other choreographic. In designing this performance, Michel had asked his actors to focus on their interlocutors' voyages, rather than their lives in their countries of origin, or their experiences since coming to France. Additionally, although professional actors would deliver the refugees' narratives, Michel had asked that the refugee be present on stage at one point during the performance. Taken together, these choices mirrored the representational strategies of humanitarianism. By abstracting the experience of displacement from its specific historical and political context, the performance underlined its moral weight as a universal human experience. By pairing biological sources of *truth* to expert conduits of *facts*, it bundled them together to generate a *motivated* performance.

Constraints for Actors

Michel's first constraint was that the actors' narrative focus should be the refugees' voyages. In a comment that resembled Natalie's emphasis on the irrelevance of truth, Michel explained the rationale for this choice:

> The first condition is to narrate the voyage. Why the voyage? Because the voyage is not moral . . . The theater is not a place where one recounts the truth, sometimes it is the truth, sometimes it is whatever I want it to be, wouldn't you say? So, I want the stories to be only about voyages, why is that? Because, it is not because Sarkozy says that immigrants smell bad that the theater is obliged to say the opposite. That they smell good. This is not the role of theater. So, it is important to exit from the moral posture that consists of saying, the government mistreats immigrants, so we are going to say that they are in fact good people. No. Maybe these aren't good people, but they have gone on voyages. And this is the story that we are going to tell.

These comments illustrate the complicated aesthetic value that Michel ascribed to the voyage. On the one hand, the voyage was the tangible action resulting in an individual's arrival on French soil. It thus functioned as a mere plot detail, emptied of *moral* value. On the other hand, the voyage (the experience of geographic displacement, willed or forced) served as a universalizing principle uniting "good" immigrants to those who were not. Despite Michel's insistence that the voyage itself could not exercise a moral claim on the spectator's imagination, in other words, the positioning of the voyage as a neutered or in Giorgio Agamben's terms, "bare"[34] dimension of human life beckoned the moral necessity to recognize this experience's fundamental universality.

In many ways, Michel's simultaneous rejection of and appeal to moral sentiments was itself a reaction to the terms of public discourse on immigration and refuge. Whereas the "Sarkozy" speaking in Michel's comments is clearly a caricaturized version of the politician, the comment on the "smells" of immigrants references an oft-quoted statement by former President Jacques Chirac, in which the politician spoke of the "noises and smells [*le bruit et l'odeur*]" of immigrants.[35] Michel's desire to have theater fulfill a role beyond that of chastising political rhetoric (i.e., retorting that immigrants smell good and thus recycling the terms of debate) referred to a broader question central to then-President Nicolas Sarkozy's immigration policies: although restrictions on immigration had grown increasingly strict during Sarkozy's tenure, there was equal emphasis on France's image as a land of asylum. This meant, however, that political rhetoric routinely distinguished economic migrants from asylum seekers, even as policy changes wedded their evaluation procedures to one another. With the notion of "good" and "bad" immigrants, in other words, Michel drew attention to the discourse of legitimacy that surrounded the idea of refuge. In many ways, his comments resonate with what Peter Nyers has identified as the expectation of apolitical subjectivity associated with the traditional category of the refugee. As noncitizens and recipients of humanitarian aid, Nyers notes, refugees are expected to be passive agents with little access to the realm of politics; therefore those refugee communities actively involved in political movements or even violent struggles constitute "a misnomer, a category mistake."[36] When Michel scoffed at the notion that refugees were categorically good people with upright pasts, his refusal in a sense reconfigured "the relationship between refugees and the political," imbuing their experience of displacement with a political context.

Michel's insistence that voyages were worthy of narration regardless of whether they enshrined an apolitical human being at their core was itself a fundamentally moral and political stance. What was significant about this stance's translation into an *aesthetic* vocabulary was that it nonetheless resulted in narrative choices that fundamentally dehistoricized and depoliticized the voyages themselves. Thus, when actors complained to Michel that their refugees were enthusiastically relating the political circumstances of their countries of origin, he asked them to focus strictly on the refugees' voyages, abstracting them from their broader context. Political circumstances, in other words, became irrelevant in a project premised on the human universality of displacement.

Meanwhile, Michel's second constraint was that the person whose story was being told would be present on stage at one point in the performance. When I inquired as to why this was, Michel replied: "Because we live in a world where there is a question of the gaze [*le regard*] and there is also a question of witnessing [*témoignage*]." Much like Natalie, in other words, Michel felt that a theatrical documentation of refuge held the potential to endow the individual involved with the recognition of the spectators. Testimony's need for what Ricoeur has called an "echo response"[37] informed his sense that theater could provide this temporary hospitality, this makeshift echo. Importantly, however, Michel distinguished between *le regard* and theater's perceived therapeutic dimensions, dismissing the title *humanitaire*:

> I was invited to a conference. There were psychiatrists who had worked with victims of war, refugees who had been tortured, individuals who had suffered enormously. Their first comment to me was: "Sir, I am a psychiatrist, I try to do good for the refugees. What do you do for refugees in your work?" I replied that I don't try to do good for the refugees; I try to do good for the audience. This is my work [*travail*]. Make them laugh, make them cry, this is my work. This doesn't mean that I harm the refugees, of course, but that we are going to create a show. And a show is emotion, laughter, tears, magic.

Michel's comments show that although his decision to have the refugees participate relied on the potential impact of stage recognition, the primary emotional work of performance involved the spectators. These comments are equally revelatory of the complexity of audience roles in what has broadly been called "refugee performance."[38] Alison Jeffers notes that these audiences are generally categorized into two positions. Those occupying the first are "in need of education" with regard to the myriad difficulties faced by refugees, asylum seekers, and undocumented immigrants. The second position implies "a more knowing audience who attend refugee theater events in a spirit of solidarity, in sympathy with the 'plight' of refugees."[39] Jeffers argues that such dichotomies obscure the complex ways that audiences negotiate the relationship between "seeing and understanding." Here Michel's comments imply his awareness of a different order of audience experience altogether, one where viewership is less oriented toward connecting stage data to the political, social, and economic complexities of migration, and more so toward activating the emotional and aesthetic expectations of other viewing experiences and genre conventions.

What was equally significant about the comment above was the weight that Michel placed on his "work," recalling aid worker Jacques's reference to the contributions and capacities of "performing arts people." Indeed, Michel dismissed the suggestion that his theater was "humanitarian," thus entailing an active betterment of the individual involved. Yet when he spoke of what theater could contribute to the *enjeu* or the stakes of immigration debates, the language of performing arts expertise was a significant component. The familiar representational formula that paired the refugee (the owner of the narrative) with the actor (that narrative's performer) was addressed as a question of professionalism and expertise:

> I didn't want poor [*pauvre*] actors to depict poor stories. I wanted the best actors to depict poor stories. [Referencing refugees who wanted to have greater control over their piece or act themselves:] If you want to tell your own story, then you have to come meet with me every morning, and you have to do this: ba, be, bi, bo, bu. Then again. Then again . . . Of course, there is always the desire to serve a humanitarian purpose, but it [the show] won't serve a humanitarian purpose if it is mediocre.

These comments were rhetorically striking for the manner in which they connected the "poverty" of an amateur stage presence to the "poverty" of a story of displacement. In the first case, poverty referred to a lack of training that would diminish (render "mediocre") the artistic merit of the project. In the other case, it referred to the suffering that refugees' narratives encapsulated. Michel's parallel usage was intentional, meant to underline the challenges of producing this project in a theatrical venue that (as alternative as its vision could be) nonetheless depended on mainstream middle-class revenues. In instances such as these, Michel's comments also revealed that "humanitarianism" encapsulated more than the provision of relief to those in pain. Rather, humanitarianism was a reference to representational practices infused with expertise. Whereas the credibility of the reports of humanitarian aid workers rested on their medical expertise, the efficaciousness of theatrical humanitarianism was premised on theatrical proficiencies such as articulation and the presence of a professional articulator, the actor.

Michel's comments join a global turn to expert discourse, a shift that scholars often take to be indicative of the changing relationship between neoliberal states, global markets, and nongovernmental organizations. In recent ethnographies of humanitarian practices in particular, the representational coupling of aid provider and aid recipient is often premised on the notion that corporeal wounds *require* expert interpretation, sidelining the narrative of the refugee. "So, in a sense," Malkki notes, "they [in this case, refugees in Tanzania] had to be cared for and understood obliquely, *despite themselves*."[40] Similarly, Michel's emphasis on theatrical professionalism resulted in disagreements over what form *theatrical care* should take. Smiling, Michel remembered that on the first day of performances, a Kurdish man from Turkey had shown up wearing a fancy suit and sunglasses and smoking a cigar.

Michel had admonished him, adding that he was a Kurdish refugee, "not a Mafioso." In relating this anecdote to me, Michel was well aware that he was asking this man to know his (theatrical) place in the world, participating in what Silvija Jestrovic has called the "paradoxes of hyper-authenticity."[41] Jestrovic refers here to performances of exile where authenticity is a mediated phenomenon, determined less by the performing individual and more so "through the gaze of the beholder."[42] We might further note that the implicit message given to this man was that in order to elicit the desired outcome (i.e., interest and compassion) from his audience, he had to manifest a readiness with *the forms of self-presentation expected of him*. He was expected, in other words, to participate in the management of his own affective resonances, with an emphasis on a specific kind of (nonthreatening) masculinity. In my conversations, however, such complexities were often subsumed beneath the broader imperative to avoid a mediocre performance, to entertain an audience through expert displays of theatrical skill.

Another Approach

As stated in the introduction, my aim here is neither to calibrate the distance between Michel's stated ideals and his actual practice, nor to critique theater practitioners' to-be-expected awareness of audience experience. Rather, my goal has been to understand the ways in which artists have adopted and responded to shifting representational modes and the larger moral economy in which these modes participate. However, such an approach has the potential to generate its own blind spots. In placing Natalie and Michel's choices in conversation with the recent humanitarianization of immigration policy, I risk positioning aesthetic trends as the mere side effects of political change. A different conceptual move might be to ask what transformations may take place *as a result of* Michel's aesthetic choices. Michel felt that if his project held the potential to provide any "good" for the refugees, this would take place in the context of the performance itself, where they could potentially sense the way that their story would resonate with audience members and experience a moment of fleeting recognition. Yet a brief conversation with one of the actors involved with the project showed me that the rehearsal period offered a different kind of identification between narrator and listener, far more complicated yet perhaps more intimate as well.

From the many rehearsal anecdotes that Michel shared with me, it was clear that the six-month rehearsal period that preceded the performance had been long, alternately conflict-ridden and tedious, and ultimately draining for all involved. When I met with Anne, one of the actors who had been involved with the project, she recalled how concerned she had been with the question of form: "What bothered me most," she remembered, "was what form one ought choose to stage these narratives." Her discomfort with speaking on behalf of her interlocutors had been a constant throughout the rehearsal period. One of the refugees with whom she worked did not speak French and she feared that her translator was not as sensitive to nuance as she would have wished. What was interesting about Anne's comments on the *formal* contours of her staging (i.e., what image to place in the background of the stage action, how to choreograph a key moment of exchange between herself and one of the refugees) was that her recollections revolved around memories of her interlocutors' bodily lives: "One person in particular was a large man, very stocky [*costaud*] and a great sense of propriety [*pudeur*]. When you translate, this propriety was lost; somehow it all became very factual." Anne's memory of this individual's lost propriety, and the "factual" transcription to which it gave rise recalls Natalie's similar preference for shows of emotionality over her interlocutors' factual narratives. My tendency has been to interpret this preference as indicative of a broader trend in the representational strategies of humanitarianism, emphasizing individuals' suffering over their political or historical memories. Yet Anne's frustrations remind us that the day-to-day intimacies of theatrical practice resulted in unexpected moral configurations. As previous chapters have shown, immigrant aid contexts can position foreign bodily repertoires as brakes on integration, in need of adaptation and acculturation. In Anne's case, the line of mimicry was reversed. Her interlocutor's bodily life became the physical ideal she sought to retain in his narratives and then re-create and embody on stage.

It would be naive to suggest that these fleeting moments of bodily identification held the potential to alter the power dynamics of Michel's project. It is equally impossible to assess whether Anne's anxieties and awareness as a trained actor were even legible as meaningful actions to her "refugee" interlocutors. After all, the day-to-day concerns of these men and women ranged from visa applications and housing restrictions to the broader precariousness of displacement. My point is simply that such details might invite us to rethink an understanding of aesthetics as the by-product of politics, and instead focus our attention on the kinds of social and political experiences that can be made possible *by* aesthetic practices.[43]

Théâtre du Soleil: Ethnography, Representation, and Expertise

My final example of theatrical humanitarianism is also the most widely circulated one. When it comes to the question of migration, the Théâtre du Soleil's epic 2003 production *Le Dernier Caravansérail* (*The Last Caravansary*) has dominated the global theatrical imagination. The production's renown is due in no small part to its role in the Théâtre du Soleil's own history, coinciding as it did with the celebrated company's fortieth anniversary and its widely recognized status as one of the leading theater companies in the world and "the most heavily subsidized private theatre company in France."[44] Founded in 1964 as a cooperative by Ariane Mnouchkine and a host of collaborators then studying at the Sorbonne, the company's early work thrived on the atmosphere of labor unrest, bourgeois critique, and artistic experimentation that characterized the years leading up to the general strikes of May 1968. In the aftermath of these events, the group cemented a number of ideological and aesthetic tendencies that have since become their calling cards in the French cultural imagination: equal salaries to all those involved in production work, and the collective creation and authorship of performance products. Soon the troupe was hailed as the latest in a long and rich tradition of French *théâtre populaire* and Mnouchkine emerged as a progressive public voice that has since grown ever more prominent.[45] Despite the director's individual fame, however, the company's early commitment to collective discipline has remained a constant, from their signature 1970 production *1789*, a collective narrative of the French Revolution as told by eighteenth-century fairground players, to *Caravansérail,* a collective creation based on stories that company members collected from migrants in detention centers and refugee camps around the world.

When placed in conversation with Natalie and Michel's work, my decision to include the Théâtre du Soleil within this chapter's fold may seem somewhat counterintuitive. Natalie and Michel's work, like many of the theatrical projects discussed in this book, circulate widely but do so within largely associational and nongovernmental networks, benefiting from close connections to humanitarian groups and civic alliances. In contrast, the Théâtre du Soleil is the most visible face of left-leaning French theater, a company whose sustainability has few parallels in postwar western Europe. Yet in many ways, Soleil's relationship to migration, French humanitarianism, and personal narrative parallels the dynamics structuring these smaller ventures. In what follows, I examine not only the familiar ways in which the representational strategies of humanitarianism have emerged in the company's recent theatrical work, but also the unique ways in which these strategies function in relation to the company's established politics and aesthetics in *Le Dernier Caravansérail.*

Ethnography in Théâtre du Soleil Practice

One of the persistent questions characterizing scholarship on the Théâtre du Soleil has been that of collective creation. More specifically, scholars have queried how this ideological principle has filtered into the company's rehearsal process, structuring the everyday decisions that result in the final artistic product. Historically, Soleil's rehearsal process has been built around improvisations that are animated by the actors but guided by Mnouchkine. Judith Miller notes that whereas Mnouchkine and her assistant memorized these improvisations during the company's early years, their practices have since been impacted by changing technologies: improvisations are digitally recorded and the resulting data is combed through, kept, or discarded by

Mnouchkine at the end of every rehearsal day.[46] Although I am less interested in the company's internal data-gathering practices than in their fieldwork, this merger of collective improvisation and individual selection is a useful frame to understand the company's approach toward their *external* sources as well.

Le Dernier Caravansérail was built from improvisations whose bases were the narratives that company members had been collecting from migrants, refugees, and asylum seekers since 2001. Their fieldwork had taken them from the controversial Sangatte Refugee Camp outside Calais to the Villawood detention center in Australia, including several locations in Indonesia and New Zealand. *Caravansérail*'s improvisations were thus constructed from the narratives that company members chose to keep; others were discarded along the way.[47] During my conversation with one of the actors who had participated in the fieldwork and later performed in the show, I inquired as to the principles behind these selections. The actor's response mirrored the kinds of preferences expressed by Natalie and Michel: narratives manifesting emotional attachments to people and places were encouraged over political memories. "[We were interested in] their daily lives, their daughters, their homes, their gardens," this actor told me, adding: "these were the treasures that they really gave us." In statements such as these, examples of *evocative* personal experience had a distinctly gendered dimension as intimate spaces (homes), or spaces that were labored over (gardens) were linked to *daughters*. Young women, in other words, emerged as the embodiment of painful experience. Whereas the gender dynamics of moments such as these may be linked to "the visual prominence of women and children as embodiments of refugeeness"[48] in the previous decade, the larger predilection for stories that somehow exist *beyond* politics can be traced as far back as the company's early years.

In the years leading up to *L'Âge d'or* (*The Age of Gold*), the 1975 production featuring the Algerian construction worker Abdallah, Théâtre du Soleil members were performing sketches in factories and interviewing their audience on their work-related grievances. *L'Âge d'or*, like many of Théâtre du Soleil's later productions, drew on the highly stylized performance vocabulary of the commedia dell'arte and Chinese opera. But unlike many subsequent performances, it drew equally on the lived experience of factory workers and strikers. In a 1974 interview with Denis Bablet, Mnouchkine recalled the experience of interviewing workers and political militants in factories and articulated a principle of selection that was mirrored in my conversations three decades later:

> We have chosen to talk about people rather than great events. And in order to do so, we have tried to get groups of workers from particular factories, groups of nurses or soldiers to come tell us not what we already know about them—in other words, what one reads in any of the left-wing newspapers—but what we don't know. And that's

> what's most difficult to get them to express. . . . Listening to them is a bit like reading passages from *Libération, Politique-Hebdo, L'Huma*. So after a while we say: Yes, we know that, we read the papers. But what we want to know is the other side of all of this. Repression with a capital R doesn't exist; what does exist is one person repressing another. How does that happen? How is it manifested? And also how is it betrayed, how can you fight against it?[49]

As is clear in this commentary, Mnouchkine's distinction privileged personal experience over political opinion. In 1974, such a distinction would have been nourished by the post-1968 surveying or *enquête* tradition and its emphasis on "collective authorship 'from below.' "[50] Likewise, the distinction between (R)epression and (r)epression was premised on the changing notions of power with which the early 1970s French intellectual circuit experimented: power, in Michel Foucault's seminal formulation, was not characterized by the domination of an all-encompassing force but was rather productive of the relationships between individuals. In retrospect, what is significant about this brief excerpt is that whereas its interest in hearing "what's most difficult to get them [the workers] to express" parallels the more recent emphasis on emotional life and attachments, the end goal of the interview process is to identify the contours of a "fight" rather than to document the experience of victimhood.

In contrast, the framing of *Le Dernier Caravansérail*'s ethnographic dimensions emphasizes trauma and the aesthetic principles that need to be mobilized to represent this trauma's incommunicability. In an article on the ethical deliberations that surrounded *Caravansérail*'s creative process, William McEvoy notes that the production's textual emphasis on personal testimony, however incongruous with the company's long-standing rejection of realist principles, provided a more direct communication between migrants' *témoignages* and the Théâtre du Soleil's audience members.[51] McEvoy likewise interprets the company's decision to have Hélène Cixous, their long-standing playwright in residence, provide a series of critical "writings about writing"[52] in the program notes (rather than a creative rewriting of the *témoignages* themselves) as an attempt to preserve the three-dimensionality of tape-recorded narratives. A comment from Hélène Cixous on working with ethnographic content fleshes out McEvoy's point:

> It felt like listening in the present and sharing for several hours the bread of exodus offered by these sudden friends. But the tape recorder picked up more than their story. The tremulous music of voices, the chants, the messages of timbres and sighs, the story with its breaths, tears, silences, sudden gusts of wind, its roar of waves, the story with its own actor and poet. The story, live, in a present instantaneously eternal.[53]

Ultimately, the writer's inability to transpose the embodiedness of oral testimony into a form of authorial creativity resulted in the company's decision to retain, as much as possible, their original forms of utterance. In many ways, Cixous's encounter with the recorded residues of individuals' bodily lives resembled Natalie and Anne's own attempts at retaining the three-dimensionality of their interlocutors' existence. What was equally common to all three experiences with oral history and ethnography was the manner in which each context attributed a degree of both in-the-moment liveness and ahistorical truth ("a present instantaneously eternal") to these moments of bodily excess. The ethical deliberations that resulted thus became an integral element of the artwork and the delivery of *témoignage* became fundamental to the deliverable outcome of theater concerned with migration, refuge, and asylum.

From Political Struggles to Ethical Experiences

My rationale in identifying *L'Âge d'or* as one possible precursor for *Caravansérail* is the clear parallel in how both experiences with ethnography involve the search for a particular kind of narrative, one that replaces the language of politics and "great events" with that of emotional life and everyday experience. Indeed, as Bérénice Hamidi-Kim makes clear, *Caravansérail*'s narrative strategies openly stress "the emotional dimension" of audience experience.[54] What is equally interesting about this juxtaposition, however, is the shift in how the Théâtre du Soleil has come to articulate the value and efficacy of such a substitution. In Mnouchkine's 1970s interview, the director's desire to seize a narrative that resides beyond the voices captured by left-wing newspapers is part of a larger political struggle to alter workplace conditions. Conversely, the encounter with personal narrative in *Caravansérail* is articulated as an *ethical* struggle experienced primarily by the company itself. This dynamic was visible to me in my conversations with actors who had been involved with the project's fieldwork phase. One of the actors, who had also worked as a translator during interviews, told me that the greatest challenge had been to "find the correct words, to not betray the etymology of words, their culture, religion, and politics." This search had eventually turned into an "obsession," in this actor's words. Yet when I inquired as to why translation and transmission were such points of tension in their practice, the actor's reply had less to do with the actual "culture, religion, and politics" in question than with the process of representing the pain and suffering associated with migration. My point here is not to identify one approach as more correct than another but merely to point at transformations in the language of political allegiance, as well as in the perceived goal of theater's interest in emotional narrative.[55] Whereas in the 1974 interview, it is the personal dimensions of political struggle that excites interest and merits inquiry, by the early twenty-first century, personal narrative is meaningful insofar as it houses an experience of heightened intensity, often glossed as trauma.

If *L'Âge d'or* is one precursor for *Caravansérail*, Mnouchkine herself identifies another, later production: "*Et soudain . . . des nuits d'éveil* is a transitional show that prefigures *Le Dernier Caravansérail*,"[56] she notes, referencing the 1997 performance that told the story of a fictional troupe of actors from Tibet who arrived in France to perform at the Cartoucherie, decided to apply for political asylum, and were refused by the French state. It is not surprising that Mnouchkine would identify this production as a stepping-stone toward the panoramic look at asylum that characterizes *Caravansérail*, for the performance was a direct result of the company's brief yet very public experience with the intimacies and infrastructures of humanitarian work. The previous year, Ariane Mnouchkine had collaborated with then–Minister of Health Léon Schwartzenberg and Médecins Sans Frontières to move the undocumented immigrants occupying the St. Bernard Church to the Cartoucherie, the company's sizable grounds and buildings in Vincennes. The work of caring for the more than 300 *sans-papiers* fell to the actors, administration, and staff of the Théâtre du Soleil, who struggled to sustain domestic life in this vast space.

The brief references to this episode in my conversations with Soleil members revealed the extent to which the theater practitioners had been caught off guard. "I didn't know what a baby of four months eats," one actor told me, "so I called my mother." Another related that she had been put in charge of cooking, an experience that, in her words, resembled "a tsunami." In an interview with Fabienne Pascaud, Mnouchkine herself remembered the discomforts and surprises that resulted from this episode:

> The experience with the *sans-papiers* had been a very revelatory adventure for us, about us. We saw ourselves, us, during those somewhat crazy weeks. Our territory invaded, our rhythm totally disrupted, our hospitality sometimes severely put to the test. The high idea that we could have of our patience, of our tolerance, of our generosity had been slightly dented. We had known moments when we were neither patient, nor tolerant, nor generous. But, in the end, we held on. We wanted to narrate this. Our ideas being put to the test by the concreteness of life.[57]

This passage is remarkable for the degree of self-reflexivity it brings to bear on humanitarian action, including its imagined origin in "high ideals" and the confusions and disorder that can characterize its everyday practice. Equally visible is the tendency that I had identified earlier, whereby the encounter with those in need of humanitarian aid provides the groundwork for an examination of the ethical principles and limitations of the aid *provider*, encapsulated in Mnouchkine's statement that the St. Bernard experience had revealed something "about us."

On the one hand, these repeated references to the self are part of a broader turn to positionality that has characterized the work of qualitative researchers and artists alike since the 1980s. Where community-based or activist theater is concerned, Mnouchkine's emphasis on the company's experience is one way that we might imagine artists responding to Julie Salverson's call for "a particular kind of self-reflection on the part of the artist," an involvement with fraught material that does not efface artists' own subjectivity.[58] On the other hand, in Mnouchkine's formulation, the emphasis on subjective experience dovetails with a reference to her company's occupation: narrative. Likewise, in my conversation with one of the actors who had been involved with this humanitarian episode, the question of what a humanitarian crisis could reveal about those attending to it resembled Michel's ruminations on what his line of "work" could provide. The actor noted:

> When one finds oneself facing situations like these, that are humanly difficult, one asks oneself: "what can I do, with my work [*avec mon métier*]?" As a witness, it's impressive the work that they [humanitarians] do, to see men and women alongside others, through their work. This is very concrete. With MSF of course, they are doctors and I saw that their know-how is a tool.

Lingering beneath these comments is the familiar designation of humanitarianism as a practice infused with expertise, leading the actor to ask what their theatrical know-how could provide in such a situation. As I have underlined throughout this chapter, it is significant that this individual's participation in humanitarian aid is characterized less by a universal principle of moral obligation (although there is that as well) and more so by a discourse of witnessing and of expertise. Indeed, a closer look at *Le Dernier Caravansérail* is revelatory of how the Théâtre du Soleil's aesthetic choices resonated with those of other artists like Natalie and Michel, particularly when it came to the coupling of amateur narrative sources and expert performer-conduits. At the same time, such choices were absorbed into the fabric of the company's existing philosophy of theatrical proficiency.

Exposed Voices and Disciplinary Facility

Le Dernier Caravansérail was composed of a series of short vignettes which, all together, added up to a two-part performance that lasted approximately seven hours. Each episode was staged on a small platform that actors could roll on and off the stage, a choreographic choice that underlined the relentless mobility depicted in many of the vignettes. Eschewing continuity, the performance skipped between a number of different story lines. A scene in which lovers were torn apart in Taliban-ruled Afghanistan was followed by another set in the Sangatte Refugee Camp, where migrants from various geographic origins were shown experiencing camp politics. Interspersed among these were scenes depicting individuals caught in a state of transit, whether braving the tall waves of an unforgiving sea or climbing over barbed-wire fences. Each of these vignettes was culled from improvisations that actors had based on translations of the company's multinational interviews. Whereas the origins of their interlocutors ranged from Chechnya to Iran, and Kurdistan to Russia, the majority of the stories were told in Persian, Arabic, Dari, and Kurdish, revealing the dominant migratory routes of 2001 and 2002.

If the Théâtre du Soleil actors' skillfully choreographed and staged improvisations threatened to abstract from the personal narratives at their origin, however, a series of shorter (and often difficult to decipher) vignettes were also worked into the fabric of this episodic structure. For example, the filmed version of *Caravansérail* includes several scenes that portray Soleil members recording individuals' narratives.[59] One of the actors who appeared in *Caravansérail* (and later continued to work with the Théâtre du Soleil) was himself residing in Sangatte when he met Ariane Mnouchkine and was invited to work for the company. He appears in several scenes as different characters but is also portrayed as himself, sitting at the Cartoucherie and addressing a letter to his father about his new life in France. In a different Cartoucherie scene, another interlocutor and later Soleil member sits at a table transcribing the words to Paul Éluard's poem "La Liberté." Such scenes are perhaps the subtext to Ariane Mnouchkine's statement that *Et soudain . . . des nuits d'éveil* prefigures *Le Dernier Caravansérail*: both productions look beyond abstract notions of theater as a space of communion to imagine an actual practice of hospitality. In a 2003 *Le Monde* article reporting from the company's rehearsals of *Le Dernier Caravansérail*, Jean-Louis Perrier drives this point home when he notes, "*Le Dernier Caravansérail* could be the other name of the Théâtre du Soleil. How many refugees continue to pass through the Cartoucherie, before finding papers, work, and French language courses? How many among the eighty members of the troupe entered or will enter into this planetary circulation?"[60] This theme is evident in McEvoy's comments as well, who identifies the production's use of actual recordings as a welcoming gesture:

> Likewise in the production, the occasional use of the tapes in voice-over represented another attempt to find a balance between authorial creativity and direct testimony. Mnouchkine and Cixous have constantly rejected realism in the theatre as antithetical to their work, yet here they were prompted to revise their aesthetic practice in line with an ethical imperative to allow other voices to be heard. The wish to inscribe a hospitality-based ethics in their performance by "hosting" these other voices became more important than anti-realistic principles.[61]

McEvoy interprets the production's use of the voices of Soleil's actual interlocutors (the migrants, refugees, and asylum seekers with whom they conducted their interviews) as a "balancing" move that infuses the company's work with an ethical turn toward *realism*, departing from their traditional bias against fidelity to daily life. Whereas subsequent performances such as *Les Ephémères* have focused precisely on the minutiae of the everyday, McEvoy rightly notes that references to the authenticity of the company's field study in *Caravansérail* was a turning point in the Théâtre du Soleil's aesthetic vocabulary. His comments mirror Caroline Wake's broader suggestion that verbatim and documentary theater's blurring of the boundaries between theatrical illusion and refugee reality warrant consideration as a form of realistic mimeticism.[62]

Without disagreeing with these analyses, I would like to suggest that framing genre choices like realism *as* indicative of an ethics of hospitality nonetheless risks disguising the mediated nature of both realism *and* hospitality. Although realism might appear to share certain qualities, like the impression of verisimilitude, with the delivery of direct testimony, modern realism has historically been premised on cultivating audiences' sense of themselves as objective, neutral observers. Audience positioning in refugee theater, as we have seen, privileges different forms of engagement. Where hospitality is concerned, *Caravansérail*'s inclusion of the "direct testimony" of the Théâtre du Soleil's interlocutors nevertheless takes place within a particular ethical frame, and not a particularly novel one. Indeed, when placed against the larger field of humanitarian theater that I have outlined in this chapter, the inclusion of "other voices" accompanied by their actor/interviewers resembles the familiar bundling of narrative sources of "truth" and expert performers of "facts." My goal in identifying this pattern is not to undercut the performance's gesture of hospitality, but merely to take note of how "ethical imperatives" can result in representational strategies that, put simply, come with their own moral universes.

At the same time, it would be equally shortsighted to identify the bundling of sources and conduits (or of realism and anti-realism) as a total break with the Soleil's previous aesthetic tendencies. In fact, this bundling is visible in a great many of the company's long-standing everyday practices: for example, Théâtre du Soleil actors' dressing tables are placed behind a glass panel through which theater audiences can watch their preparation before heading into the auditorium/performance space. This form of Brechtian exposure, however, contrasts with the (equally actor-based) opulence of the company's work. Alan Filewod has referred to this contrast as "the dialectical interface of exposed theatre practice and peak disciplinary facility."[63] I would suggest that the presentation of emotional life and suffering in the untrained "authentic" narratives of Soleil's interlocutors serves as a similar exposure that the peak disciplinary facility of Soleil's ultra-trained actors renders aesthetically rich. Much like Natalie and Michel's staging strategies, the presence of the narrative "source" authorizes the authorial creativity of the artists while the expertise of the performer "conduit" renders that narrative legible for a theatergoing audience. What the Théâtre du Soleil case makes clear is that such humanitarian resonances need not amount to a break from the company's established artistic idioms, replicating existing vocabularies even as they seem to identify changing genre choices.

Conclusion

In concluding these thoughts, it is worth taking a moment to comment on the repeated refrain that characterizes this chapter: "to be clear, my goal here is not to criticize." Indeed, it does not take a great deal of self-reflexivity to notice that this chapter's claims are habitually followed by disclaimers, as I attempt to dissociate myself from a previous criticism. These criticisms and their disclaimers are one way that I have sought to reconcile the (perceived) tensions characterizing my interlocutors' social ideals and the imperfections of their theatrical practices. I find this tension between critique and its repudiation to be productive, for on the one hand, the suggestion underwriting this chapter, if not this book, is that individual artists working on immigration in early twenty-first-century France participate in a regime of representation that is larger than them, and indeed exceeds the boundaries of "political art" proper, placing them in a larger conversation involving transformations in the political management and social life of immigration. Thus, understanding their work requires that the manner in which we attribute relationships, resonances, or even causalities both acknowledges the broader politics of humanitarianism at play in their work and at the same time recognizes the circumstances and limitations within which these artists produce art that rethinks immigration.

On the other hand, this productive tension resonates with a number of voices in theater and performance studies that have underlined the need to depart from a theoretical approach that examines theater practices (particularly those undertaken in activist and cultural humanitarian contexts) with an eye to reporting how closely theater practitioners act on their progressive ideals. Scholars like Laura Edmondson, Sonja Kuftinec, and D. Soyini Madison have noted how such approaches result in analyses that either adopt a moralizing tone or engage in uncritical celebration.[64] My goal therefore has been to heed their call and move beyond this binary to ask: How do people interpret, engage with, and modify certain progressive ideals *in the course of* participating in theatrical practice? What are the aesthetic, political, and moral blueprints that result from these engagements?

Here, I have suggested that humanitarian theater is characterized by a number of overarching qualities. Its portrayal of refugees, asylum seekers, and undocumented immigrants privileges the affective, rather than political, dimensions of these individuals' life experiences. Meanwhile, the representation combines the "source" of the narratives, whose presence on stage endows the project with an authenticity that mere reporting could not generate, with its "conduit," a professional actor whose theatrical expertise is necessary for the narratives' evocative delivery. In other words, emotional experience and affective potential are not only placed at the center of this theatrical world, they create the groundwork for theater's moral authority, an authority that is only further legitimized by the appearance of a body on to which these experiences can be imaginatively inscribed. At the same time, a brief reminder of the opening example of Aminata shows that these representations are not devoid of context, and are instead filtered through gendered and racial tropes. And these dynamics resonate with a series of legislative, medical humanitarian, and representational transformations that have increasingly made immigration, refuge, and asylum into matters with *affective* resolutions, rather than political answers.

If the resonances between these two domains have indeed left us with the possibility of a "theater without borders," a formulation that imbues theater with the dynamics of the original phrase (i.e., certainty in medicine's universal social value), then we might do well to ask: what are the potentials and limitations inherent in positing theater as a universal need, or a universally transparent vehicle of justice?

CONCLUSION

In this book, I have sought to detail the relationship between immigration politics and theatrical practices in Paris during the first decade of the twenty-first century. To offer a conclusion to such a task may therefore generate the impression that the political, cultural, and aesthetic dynamics outlined within are durational and have somehow exhausted their representational lives. Yet a brief glance at the contemporary French "scene" will immediately reveal that the unique dynamics that mark *Aesthetic Citizenship*'s timeline remain more than relevant. Indeed, the trend toward "national republicanism" that Étienne Balibar had identified at the turn of the twenty-first century, a political tendency that congealed around the stigmatization of foreigners and the "development of an abstract communitarianism, centered on the state and its exclusive claim to incarnate the universal,"[1] seems ever significant as the political party led by Nicolas Sarkozy, Union pour un Mouvement Populaire (UMP), renames itself Les Républicains, laying claim to a political identity whose roots, as I hope to have shown, are hardly partisan. That Sarkozy's renewed yet short-lived 2016 campaign for the French presidency (a position which he vacated following the electoral victory of the Socialist François Hollande in 2012) underlined immigration's dangers for "our way of life"[2] is evidence of how deeply the French Right has absorbed the electoral victories of Far Right parties like the Front National, currently led by Marine Le Pen.

At the same time, debates surrounding migratory flows and French identity, and indeed the presentation of these phenomena as inextricably linked, have often united parties across the political spectrum. In 2012, Hollande's newly appointed Minister of the Interior Manuel Valls was widely celebrated for his critique of Sarkozy's immigration policies, with a particular focus on the recent drop in the number of naturalizations. Yet Cimade's comprehensive 2014 report was quick to note that the long-awaited changes signaled by Valls had not yet materialized: accessing residency papers remained difficult, both because of the worsening conditions in prefectures and because of increasingly limited categories for regularization; asylum seekers lacked access to temporary housing as well as employment options as they awaited the results of their asylum applications; the retention centers established under Sarkozy had yet to be closed; forced deportations were common; and the deportation of Roma populations in particular (populations that are often composed of citizens of EU member states like Romania and Bulgaria) revealed the biases of European unification.[3]

If the administrative procedures faced by newly arrived refugees compose one facet of "immigration," however, the experiences of third and fourth-generation nationals for whom immigration is a distant reality is another, for as I hope to have shown throughout this book, the term "immigration" itself has become a reference point of varying stability in contemporary France, including and amalgamating populations ranging from first-, second-, and third-generation citizens of immigrant ancestry to undocumented persons of long-term residence to newly arrived refugees and asylum seekers. As such, references to immigration trigger a series of anxieties regarding history, nationality, and citizenship that are visible in legislative plans as wide-ranging as the 2005 proposal that history textbooks cover the positive role of French colonialism to the 2010 proposal that immigrants naturalized during the previous decade and charged with menacing public security personnel like the police should be stripped of their nationality. Nicolas Bancel notes that migratory flows, and their perceived connections to questions of multiculturalism and communitarianism, have become the reference point for a "widespread sentiment that France is disintegrating, on the verge of collapse, being systematically dismantled and its *grandeur* waning, a *grandeur* which historically has always been inextricably linked to the representation of the history of the nation."[4] In such an environment, Bancel adds, urgent problems like economic and cultural marginalization in the *banlieues*, racial stigmatization and discrimination, and lack of recognition surrounding minority experience are subsumed beneath a broader anxiety regarding French national identity.

Needless to say, performance continues to figure in how these issues are negotiated, represented, and embodied. As an example, let me briefly revisit the Blanc-Mesnil-based women's collective Quelques unes d'entre nous, whose work I had discussed in chapter 4. Their latest project is in direct conversation with the anxieties described by Bancel, anxieties that pertain to issues of national identity and that manifest themselves in relation to colonial and postcolonial history. In *Et puis, nous passions le pantalon Français* (*And Then, We Passed to French Pants*) the collective draws on *La Double Absence,* sociologist Abdelmalek Sayad's encyclopedic study of the experiences of postwar Algerian immigrants to France, to interrogate the relationship between colonialism and immigration.[5] Based on the extended interviews that Sayad conducted with Algerian immigrant workers, the performance moves between these narratives of intimate experience and the delivery of political and historical context. The transition implied by the play's title, from the long, loose-fitting robes of the Maghreb to the French *pantalon*, is an experience that is both individual and collective: shared by the extensive demographic embodied by the *nous*, it is a transition that nonetheless comes into focus in moments when a new garb rubs against one's skin. Yet the "subtle alliance of the intimate with the political," in director Philip Boulay's words,[6] is as much a framework for the career of Quelques unes d'entre nous as it is for the collective history of migrant estrangement depicted by Sayad. As Marina da Silva makes clear, theatrical practice has been key to how Quelques unes d'entre nous members have merged their own experiences of migration with a trajectory of collective political action.[7]

My last visit to Blanc-Mesnil took place during the rehearsal process for *Et puis, nous passions le pantalon Français*; the play would eventually debut at the Cité Nationale de l'Histoire de l'Immigration (the National Museum of Immigration History) in February 2013. As I chatted with actors whom I had met during previous visits, I inquired as to whether they felt anything had changed since their initial work in *Le Bruit du monde m'est rentré dans l'oreille*. Their responses mirrored a trend that was fairly common in my conversations with amateur theater-makers: they felt that their second project was a more professional effort. "We are much more into research and choreography now," one actor told me, adding, "this is a real theatrical work." Indeed, the group had benefited from the dramaturgical assistance of the sociologist Farid Taalba, as well as choreographic help from the Blanc-Mesnil-based hip-hop artist Mehdi Slimani. Several men had joined the troupe, yet quite a few male roles were cast with women, a choice that demanded new sets of actorly skills and added additional layers of meaning to the notion of "passing to French pants." Yet collective members had also made choices that explicitly went against a professional grain. Samia told me that their new emphasis was on *transmission*, their ability to pass this project onto a new generation. Three teenage women (one being a collective member's daughter) had thus been invited to participate in the project, with little to no experience of theater. Whereas "theatrical work" was a source of pride, the collective's sense of lasting results prioritized local inclusion over artistic expertise.

In many ways, *Et puis, nous passions le pantalon Français* embodies the shifting conceptual arrangements that underline the relationship between immigration and theater in France today. Whereas many of the key concepts, categories, and binaries that I have employed throughout this book remain relevant, they are also being rearranged in new ways: personal experience and artistic expertise may no longer be as starkly opposed as they were for previous generations of theater artists thinking about immigration. The immediacy of militancy and longer-term commitments toward professionalism do not exist in a rigid binary. However central it remains to articulations of French national identity, the relationship between individuality and collectivity continues to be negotiated in new and different ways. I do not mean to suggest, of course, that the dilemmas outlined in earlier chapters have been resolved, but merely that the climate of disintegration, collapse, and waning *grandeur* described by Bancel (and experienced in vastly different ways depending on the social context from which one regards such a climate) continues to produce work that reveals performance's unique ability to comment on its surroundings. At times, this ability reveals itself in mimetic overflow, mirroring back to the social that which it experiences. At others, its material practice reveals performance's ability to shape that social, and endow it with new abilities and sensibilities whose consequences remain beyond the scope of performance proper.

To that end, I have argued that theatrical immigration activism in early twenty-first-century Paris provides key insights into the evolution of notions of immigrant rights, integration, and experience in postwar France. Indeed, as early as the 1970s, the theatrical work of Al Assifa and La Kahina revealed how North African immigrant-artists responded to the era's evolving strategies of immigration activism, experiencing the representational dilemmas of identitarian politics while negotiating the complex relationship of labor militancy and professional artistry. These artists sat at the cusp of a transition toward personal narrative that, three decades later, continues to play a significant role in how immigrant self-expression is framed in the public sphere: the perceived urgency of personal speech permeates immigrant women's theater and produces forms of racialization that negotiate French republicanism's central dynamic of universality and particularity. Likewise, the theatrical aid work of nongovernmental organizations interested in migratory flows reveals the ease with which theater can be repurposed to materialize (and in turn, reveal the contradictions of) abstract concepts like social enmeshment and moral autonomy, concepts that have been key to French ideals of integration and republican citizenship. Meanwhile, the connection between theater and immigrant associationalism in a Paris suburb demonstrates the extent to which theater's meanings are dependent on its political circumstances, a contingency that is most visible in the challenges of applying scholarly rubrics like community-based or intercultural theater to a context with a fraught relationship to community *and* culture. Finally, a closer look at theatrical narratives of undocumented immigration, refuge, and exile reveals the multidirectional imbrications of medical humanitarianism, immigrant social movements, and political art in the early twenty-first century.

Whereas this book has sought to examine performance's dual ability to both mirror and engender, I have been hesitant to ascribe transformational potential, either positive or negative, to these abilities. The process of researching this book allowed me to witness precious moments of performance euphoria. It equally exposed me to what Paul Rae has called the "darker purpose" of the imperative that "the show must go on."[8] My approach, therefore, has been to avoid seeking theatrical ideals to celebrate, as well as to stop short of condemning the discrepancies between artistic ideals and their inevitably complex and contradictory realization. Rather, I have sought to understand how aesthetic, political, and ethical ideals are understood, inhabited, and transformed via theater, as well as the consequences of this practice, both intended and unintended. It is my hope that this approach has not dulled the passion of celebration or of critique, but rather confirmed its alliance with the complexity of lived theatrical experience.

NOTES

Introduction

1. *L'Esquive,* DVD, directed by Abdellatif Kechiche (2003; Paris: Noé Productions, 2004).

2. Ari Blatt, "The Play's the Thing: Marivaux and the *Banlieue* in Abdellatif Kechiche's *L'esquive,*" *The French Review* 81, no. 3 (2008): 516.

3. Ibid., 517.

4. For a thorough account of these debates, see Joan W. Scott, *The Politics of the Veil* (Princeton, N.J.: Princeton University Press, 2007).

5. David Looseley, *The Politics of Fun: Cultural Policy and Debate in Contemporary France* (Oxford: Berg, 1995), 36.

6. See Emma Cox, *Theatre and Migration* (Basingstoke, Eng.: Palgrave Macmillan, 2014), 1–32.

7. This is one of the Greek roots of the term "performance" analyzed in Shannon Jackson, *Professing Performance: Theatre in the Academy from Philology to Performativity* (Cambridge: Cambridge University Press, 2004), 13.

8. Tracy Davis, "Introduction: The Pirouette, Detour, Revolution, Deflection, Deviation, Tack, and Yaw of the Performative Turn," in *The Cambridge Companion to Performance Studies*, ed. Tracy Davis (Cambridge: Cambridge University Press, 2008), 6.

9. May Joseph, *Nomadic Identities: The Performance of Citizenship* (Minneapolis: University of Minnesota Press, 1999), 4.

10. See Gérard Noiriel, *The French Melting Pot: Immigration, Citizenship and National Identity,* trans. Geoffroy de Laforcade (Minneapolis: University of Minnesota Press, 1996).

11. Danièle Lochak, "Les Politiques de l'immigration au prisme de la législation sur les étrangers," in *Les Lois de l'inhospitalité: Les Politiques de l'immigration à l'épreuve des sans-papiers*, ed. Didier Fassin, Alain Morice, and Catherine Quiminal (Paris: La Découverte, 1997), 32.

12. See Benjamin Stora, *La Gangrène et l'oubli: La Mémoire de la guerre d'Algérie* (Paris: La Découverte, 1991); and Neil MacMaster, *Colonial Migrants and Racism: Algerians in France 1900–1962* (London: Palgrave Macmillan, 1997).

13. As Driss Maghraoui notes, historical analyses of French government in the North African colonies quickly reveal the contradictory nature of colonial citizenship: "The French settlers were strong supporters of the politics of assimilation, but paradoxically opposed its logical outcome, which would normally grant full citizenship to Algerians." Algerian Muslims, in other words, were considered assimilable yet denied individual rights predicated on citizenship. See Driss Maghraoui, "French Identity, Islam, and North Africans: Colonial Legacies,

Postcolonial Realities," in *French Civilization and Its Discontents: Nationalism, Colonialism, Race*, ed. Tyler Stovall and Georges Van Den Abbeele (Lanham, Md.: Lexington Books, 2003), 217.

14. Lochak, "Les Politiques de l'immigration," 42.

15. Étienne Balibar, *We, the People of Europe? Reflections on Transnational Citizenship*, trans. James Swenson (Princeton, N.J.: Princeton University Press, 2004), 35.

16. *Cette France-là 06/05/2007–30/06/2008,* vol. 1 (Paris: La Découverte, 2009), 95–101.

17. Ibid., 96.

18. Michel Kokoreff and Didier Lapeyronnie, *Refaire la cité: L'Avenir des banlieues* (Paris: Éditions du Seuil, 2013), 29.

19. *Cette France- là*, 98.

20. For perhaps the most famous proponent of the argument that the modernization of the French countryside during the Third Republic was tantamount to its nationalization (and hence linguistic and cultural uniformization), see Eugen Weber, *Peasants into Frenchmen: The Modernization of Rural France 1870–1914* (Palo Alto, Calif.: Stanford University Press, 1976). For the counterargument that the emergence of national identity was in fact the result of local negotiation, see Peter Sahlins, *Boundaries: The Making of France and Spain in the Pyrénées* (Berkeley: University of California Press, 1991).

21. See Jean-Jacques Rousseau, *The Social Contract and the First and Second Discourses,* trans. and ed. Susan Dunn (New Haven, Conn.: Yale University Press, 2002).

22. For a comparison of the French and Anglophone models of citizenship, see Dominique Schnapper (with Christian Bachelier), *Qu'est-ce que la citoyenneté?* (Paris: Éditions Gallimard, 2000), 39–50.

23. Gary Wilder, *The French Imperial Nation-State: Negritude and Colonial Humanism between the Two World Wars* (Chicago: University of Chicago Press, 2005), 16.

24. Ibid.

25. Ibid., 158.

26. For an overview of the journalistic ubiquity of references to *communautarisme* (particularly in relation to Islam) since the 1990s, see the second part of Thomas Deltombe, *L'Islam imaginaire: La Construction médiatique de l'islamophobie en France 1975–2005* (Paris: La Découverte, 2007).

27. Jacques Chirac quoted in Cimade, *Votre voisin n'a pas de papiers: Paroles d'étrangers* (Paris: La Fabrique Éditions, 2006), 12.

28. See Nacira Guénif Souilamas and Eric Macé, *Les Féministes et le garçon arabe* (Tour d'Aigues: Éditions de l'Aube, 2004).

29. Nacira Guénif Souilamas, "La Réduction à son corps de l'indigène de la république," in *La Fracture coloniale: La Société française au prisme de l'héritage colonial,* ed. Pascal Blanchard, Nicolas Bancel and Sandrine Lemaire (Paris: La Découverte, 2006), 207–8.

30. For a detailed account, see Joan W. Scott, *Only Paradoxes to Offer: French Feminists and the Rights of Man* (Cambridge, Mass.: Harvard University Press, 1997).

31. Scott, *The Politics of the Veil,* 27.

32. Dounia Bouzar and Saïda Kada, *L'Une voilée, l'autre pas* (Paris: Albin Michel, 2003), 76.

33. Ibid., 83.

34. Ibid., 84–85.

35. Ibid., 85.

36. Paul Silverstein, *Algeria in France: Transpolitics, Race and Nation* (Bloomington: Indiana University Press, 2004), 136.

37. Ibid., 123.

38. Olivier Neveux, *Théâtres en lutte: Le Théâtre militant en France des années 1960 à aujourd'hui* (Paris: La Découverte, 2007), 236.

39. Emile Durkheim, *The Elementary Forms of the Religious Life,* trans. Joseph Ward Swain (New York: Free, 1965).

40. Nobert Elias, *The Civilizing Process: Sociogenetic and Psychogenetic Investigations*, trans. Edmund Jephcott (Oxford: Blackwell, 2003).

41. Looseley, *The Politics of Fun*, 13.

42. Loren Kruger, *The National Stage: Theatre and Cultural Legitimation in England, France and America* (Chicago: University of Chicago Press, 1992), 32.

43. Pascale Goetschel, *Renouveau et décentralisation du théâtre 1945–1981* (Paris: Presses Universitaires de France, 2004), 48.

44. Ibid., 68.

45. Ibid., 37.

46. David Bradby, *Modern French Drama 1940–1990* (Cambridge: Cambridge University Press, 1991), 90–94.

47. Laurent quoted in Looseley, *The Politics of Fun*, 28.

48. See Mona Ozouf, *Festivals and the French Revolution*, trans. Alan Sheridan (Cambridge, Mass.: Harvard University Press, 1991).

49. Jeremy Ahearne, "Introduction," in *French Cultural Policy Debates: A Reader,* ed. Jeremy Ahearne (New York: Routledge, 2002), 8.

50. Dominique Darzacq, "1945–1970 les premières utopies du théâtre populaire à la popularité de théâtre," in *Missions d'artistes: Les Centres dramatiques de 1946 à nos jours*, ed. Jean-Claude Penchenat (Paris: Éditions Théâtrales, 2006), 16.

51. André Malraux, "Text 216: La Culture, un projet de civilisation," in *Les Politiques de la culture en France*, ed. Philippe Poirrier (Paris: La Documentation Française, 2016), 326–34.

52. From the "Discours prononcé à Dakar par M. André Malraux, Ministre d'Etat chargé des Affaires Culturelle à la séance d'ouverture du colloque organisé à l'occasion du premier Festival Mondial des Arts Nègres le 30 mars 1966," http://www.culture.gouv.fr/culture/actualites/dossiers/malraux2006/discours/a.m-dakar.htm.

53. Herman Lebovics, *Mona Lisa's Escort: André Malraux and the Reinvention of French Culture* (Ithaca, N.Y.: Cornell University Press, 1999), 5.

54. Quoted in Vincent Dubois, *La Politique Culturelle: Genèse d'une catégorie d'intervention publique* (Paris: Éditions Belin, 1999), 226.

55. Lebovics, *Mona Lisa's Escort,* 99.

56. Ibid., 5–6.

57. Silverstein, *Algeria in France*, 136.

58. Marilyn Ivy, *Discourses of the Vanishing: Modernity, Phantasm, Japan* (Chicago: University of Chicago Press, 1995), 10.

59. Pierre Bourdieu, *The Field of Cultural Production: Essays on Art and Literature* (Cambridge, Eng.: Polity, 1993), 215.
60. Ibid., 231.
61. Ibid., 230.
62. Francis Jeanson, "La Réunion de Villeurbanne," in *La Décentralisation théâtrale*, vol. 3: *1968, le tournant*, ed. Robert Airached (Arles: Actes Sud-Papiers, 2005), 87.
63. "La Déclaration de Villeurbanne," in *La Décentralisation théâtrale*, vol. 3: *1968, le tournant*, ed. Robert Airached (Arles: Actes Sud-Papiers, 2005), 195–96.
64. For more on Brecht's influence on French theater of the late 1960s and 1970s, see Judith Miller, *Theater and Revolution in France since 1968* (Lexington, Ky.: French Forum, 1977).
65. Neveux, *Théâtres en lutte*, 236.
66. Catherine Bell, *Ritual Theory Ritual Practice* (New York: Oxford University Press, 1992), 6.
67. Ibid., 19.
68. Clifford Geertz, *The Interpretation of Cultures* (New York: Basic Books, 1973), 448.
69. Ibid.
70. Victor Turner, *From Ritual to Theatre: The Human Seriousness of Play* (New York: PAJ, 1982), 68.
71. See Victor Turner, *The Anthropology of Performance* (New York: PAJ, 1988).
72. Bell, *Ritual Theory*, 43.
73. Willmar Sauter, *The Theatrical Event: Dynamics of Performance and Perception* (Iowa City: University of Iowa Press, 2000), 12.
74. Marvin Carlson, "Semiotics and Its Heritage," in *Critical Theory and Performance*, ed. Janelle G. Reinelt and Joseph R. Roach (Ann Arbor: University of Michigan Press, 2010), 20.
75. Stanton B. Garner, *Bodied Spaces: Phenomenology and Performance in Contemporary Drama* (Ithaca, N.Y.: Cornell University Press, 1994), 50.
76. Paul Connerton, *How Societies Remember* (Cambridge: Cambridge University Press, 2004), 95.
77. For a thorough analysis of the problems associated with the corporeality vs. meaning binary, see Ruth Leys, "The Turn to Affect: A Critique," *Critical Inquiry* 37 (2011): 434–72.
78. Saba Mahmood, *Politics of Piety: The Islamic Revival and the Feminist Subject* (Princeton, N.J.: Princeton University Press, 2005), 131.
79. Talal Asad, *Genealogies of Religion: Discipline and Reasons of Power in Christianity and Islam* (Baltimore: Johns Hopkins University Press, 1993), 62.
80. See Joseph Roach, *Cities of the Dead: Circum-Atlantic Performance* (New York: Columbia University Press, 1996); Shannon Jackson, *Lines of Activity: Performance, Historiography, Hull-House Domesticity* (Ann Arbor: University of Michigan Press, 2001); and Diana Taylor, *The Archive and the Repertoire: Performing Cultural Memory in the Americas* (Durham, N.C.: Duke University Press, 2003).
81. Jackson, *Lines of Activity*, 238.
82. Roach, *Cities of the Dead*, 26.

83. May Joseph, *Nomadic Identities,* 4.
84. Ibid., 3.
85. Ibid., 5.
86. J. L. Austin, *How to Do Things with Words* (Cambridge, Mass.: Harvard University Press, 1975), 9.
87. See Judith Butler, *Excitable Speech: A Politics of the Performative* (New York: Routledge, 1997).
88. Judith Butler, *Bodies That Matter: On the Discursive Limits of "Sex"* (New York: Routledge, 1993), 2.
89. See Amy Hollywood, "Performativity, Citationality, Ritualization," *History of Religions* 42, no. 2 (2002): 93–115. See also Mahmood, *Politics of Piety,* 161–67.
90. Butler, *Excitable Speech,* 140.
91. Richard Bauman, *Verbal Art as Performance* (Long Grove, Ill.: Waveland, 1984), 28.
92. See Emma Cox, *Performing Noncitizenship: Asylum Seekers in Australian Theatre, Film, and Activism* (London: Anthem, 2015); Charlotte McIvor, *Migration and Performance in Contemporary Ireland: Towards a New Interculturalism* (Basingstoke, Eng.: Palgrave Macmillan, 2016); and Alison Jeffers, *Refugees, Theatre and Crisis: Performing Global Identities* (Basingstoke, Eng.: Palgrave Macmillan, 2012).
93. Engin F. Isin, "Citizenship in Flux: The Figure of the Activist Citizen," *Subjectivity* 29 (2009): 379.
94. Micaela di Leonardo, "Oral History as Ethnographic Encounter," *Oral History Review* 15 (1987): 5.
95. Arjun Appadurai, *Modernity at Large: Cultural Dimensions of Globalization* (Minneapolis: University of Minnesota Press, 1996), 4.
96. Bell, *Ritual Theory,* 32.

Chapter One

1. Al Assifa, "Bilan de la réunion des 'anciens' d'Al Assifa," Fonds Saïd Bouziri, F Delta rés 705, carton 1/no.1, Bibliothèque de Documentation Internationale Contemporaine, Nanterre. All of the following archival references on Al Assifa are from this institution.
2. Al Assifa, "L'Ordre du jour a été défini comme suit," Fonds Saïd Bouziri, F Delta rés 705, carton 1/no.2.
3. Ibid.
4. See Nancy Fraser, *Justice Interruptus: Critical Reflections on the "Postsocialist" Condition* (New York: Routledge, 1997), especially chapter 1. See also Nancy Fraser and Axel Honneth, *Redistribution or Recognition? A Political-Philosophical Exchange* (London: Verso Books, 2003).
5. See Axel Honneth, *The Struggle for Recognition: The Moral Grammar of Social Conflicts,* trans. Joel Anderson (Cambridge, Eng.: Polity, 1995); and Butler, *Excitable Speech.*
6. Furthermore, the binary categories of recognition and redistribution have themselves come under critique; see Iris Marion Young, "Unruly Categories: A Critique of Nancy Fraser's Dual Systems Theory," *New Left Review* 222 (1997): 147–60.

7. Jean-Marc Lachaud, "Théâtre et rue en France des années soixante-dix à aujourd'hui," in *Une histoire du spectacle militant: Théâtre et cinéma militants 1966–1981,* ed. Olivier Neveux and Christian Biet (Paris: L'Entretemps, 2007), 95.

8. Robert Eric Livingston, "Decolonizing the Theatre: Césaire, Serreau and the Drama of Negritude," in *Imperialism and Theatre: Essays on World Theatre, Drama and Performance*, ed. J. Ellen Gainor (London: Routledge, 1995), 195.

9. Jeanne Le Gallic, "Le Théâtre de l'immigration algérienne en France dans les années 1970s: Un espace de représentation et de témoignage," *Synergies Algérie,* no. 10 (2010): 155.

10. See, for example, Angeline Escafré-Dublet's detailed account of the political contexts in which *Mohamed prends ta valise* circulated: "L'Aventure de *Mohamed prends ta valise* de Kateb Yacine: Histoire d'un théâtre de la contestation en milieu immigré (France-Algérie, 1972)," in *Théâtre des minorités: Mises en scène de la marge à l'époque contemporaine*, ed. Patrice Brasseur and Madelena Gonzalez (Paris: L'Harmattan, 2008), 92.

11. Alec G. Hargreaves, *Multi-Ethnic France: Immigration, Politics, Culture and Society* (New York: Routledge, 2007), 166.

12. Abdelmalek Sayad, *The Suffering of the Immigrant*, trans. David Macey (Cambridge, Eng.: Polity, 2004), 67.

13. For a detailed account of this process, see Beth Epstein, *Collective Terms: Race, Culture and Community in a State-Planned City in France* (New York: Berghahn Books, 2011).

14. Sayad, *The Suffering of the Immigrant*, 72.

15. Kokoreff and Lapeyronnie, *Refaire la cité*, 11–41.

16. Eric Bleich, *Race Politics in Britain and France: Ideas and Policymaking since the 1960s* (Cambridge: Cambridge University Press, 2003), 115.

17. Stora, *La Gangrène et l'oubli*, 288.

18. Kristin Ross, *May '68 and Its Afterlives* (Chicago: University of Chicago Press, 2002), 25.

19. Ibid., 167.

20. Ibid., 12.

21. Stora, *La Gangrène et l'oubli*, 224.

22. Ross, *May '68 and Its Afterlives*, 57.

23. Jacques Rancière, "The Cause of the Other," trans. David Macey, *Parallax* 4, no. 2 (1998): 25.

24. Ibid., 32.

25. From the "Déclaration sur le droit à l'insoumission dans la Guerre d'Algérie," quoted in Eric Levine, "The French Intellectual and the Algerian War" (Ph.D. dissertation, Columbia College, 1962), 125.

26. Ibid., 85.

27. Jean Genet, "Pour Blin: Des réflexions à mesure qu'elles me viennent," in *La Bataille des paravents: Théâtre de l'Odéon, 1966*, ed. Linda Bellity Peskine and Albert Dichy (Paris: IMEC Éditions, 1991), 20.

28. Tom McDonough, *"The Beautiful Language of My Century": Reinventing the Language of Contestation in Postwar France, 1945–1968* (Cambridge, Mass.: MIT Press, 2007), 97.

29. Al Assifa, "La Troupe Al Assifa présente: *Ça travaille, ça travaille et ça ferme sa gueule*," Fonds Saïd Bouziri, F Delta rés 705, carton 1/no.1.

30. Michelle Zancarini-Fournel, "Racisme et antiracisme dans les 'années 68,' " in *Histoire politique des immigrations (post)coloniales: France, 1920–2008*, ed. Ahmed Boubeker and Abdellali Hajjat (Paris: Éditions Amsterdam, 2008), 116.

31. Hélène Trappo, "De la clandestinité à la reconnaissance: Propos recueillis par Hélène Trappo," *Plein Droit* 11 (1990), http://www.gisti.org/doc/plein-droit/11/clandestinite.html.

32. Ibid.

33. Mouvement des Travailleurs Arabes (MTA), "Unnamed Pamphlet," Fonds Saïd Bouziri, F Delta rés 705, carton 1/no. 1.

34. Rabah Aissaoui, "Political Mobilization of North African Migrants in 1970s France: The Case of the Mouvement des Travailleurs Arabes (MTA)," *Journal of Muslim Minority Affairs* 26, no. 2 (2006): 172–75.

35. Johanna Siméant, *La Cause des sans-papiers* (Paris: Presses de Sciences Po, 1998), 186.

36. Trappo, "De la clandestinité."

37. Olivier Neveux, "Apparition d'une scène politique: Le Théâtre révolutionnaire de l'immigration," in *Une histoire du spectacle militant: Théâtre et cinéma militants 1966–1981,* ed. Olivier Neveux and Christian Biet (Paris: L'Entretemps, 2007), 331.

38. See David Bradby, *Modern French Drama 1940–1990* (Cambridge: Cambridge University Press, 1991), especially chapters 8 and 9.

39. Siméant, *La Cause des sans-papiers*, 188–89.

40. Philippe Tancelin, personal interview with author, March 20, 2008. All of the following quotes from Tancelin were recorded during this interview.

41. Al Assifa, "La Troupe Al Assifa présente: *Ça travaille, ça travaille et ça ferme sa gueule*," Fonds Saïd Bouziri, F Delta rés 705, carton 1/no.1.

42. Frédéric Maatouk, "Le Théâtre des travailleurs immigrés en France" (Ph.D. dissertation, Université François-Rabelais de Tours, 1979), 133.

43. Ibid., 135.

44. Ibid., 211.

45. Geneviève Clancy and Philippe Tancelin, *Les Tiers Idées* (Paris: Hachette, 1977), 35.

46. Lachaud, "Théâtre et rue," 95.

47. Clancy and Tancelin, *Les Tiers Idées*, 85.

48. Ibid.

49. Nick Kaye, *Site-Specific Art: Performance, Place and Documentation* (London: Routledge, 2000), 111.

50. Augusto Boal, *The Theatre of the Oppressed*, trans. Charles A. McBride and Maria-Odilia Leal McBride (New York: Theatre Communications Group, 1985), 141.

51. Clancy and Tancelin, *Les Tiers Idées*, 86.

52. Boal, *The Theatre of the Oppressed*, 141.

53. Clancy and Tancelin, *Les Tiers Idées,* 59.

54. Théâtre du Soleil, *L'Âge d'or* (video recording of the September 23, 1975, performance at the Venice Biennial), Fonds Théâtre du Soleil, Département des Arts du Spectacle, Bibliothèque Nationale de France, Paris.

55. Denis Bablet, "Towards a New Form: From an Interview with Ariane Mnouchkine," in *Collaborative Theater: The Théâtre du Soleil Sourcebook*, ed. David Williams (London: Routledge, 1999), 54.

56. Al Assifa, "Bilan de la réunion des 'anciens' d'Al Assifa."

57. Quoted in Le Gallic, "Le théâtre de l'immigration," 160.

58. Jeanson, "La Réunion de Villeurbanne," 87.

59. Looseley, *The Politics of Fun*, 53.

60. Maurice Druon quoted in Jeremy Ahearne, "Introduction," in *French Cultural Policy Debates: A Reader*, ed. Jeremy Ahearne (London: Routledge, 2002), 15.

61. Bourdieu, *The Field of Cultural Production*, 129.

62. Clancy and Tancelin, *Les Tiers Idées*, 33.

63. Ibid., 26.

64. Al Assifa, "El Assifa," Fonds Saïd Bouziri, F Delta rés 705, carton 1/no.1.

65. Neveux, "Apparition d'une scène politique," 329.

66. Clancy and Tancelin, *Les Tiers Idées*, 224.

67. Al Assifa, "Bilan de la réunion des 'anciens' d'Al Assifa."

68. Salikha Amara, personal interview with author, June 18, 2009. All of the following quotes from Amara were recorded during this interview.

69. Jane Freedman, "Women and Immigration: Nationality and Citizenship," in *Women, Immigration and Identities in France*, ed. Jane Freedman and Carrie Tarr (Oxford: Berg, 2000), 14.

70. Claudie Lesselier, "Mouvements et initiatives des femmes des années 1970 au milieu des années 1980," in Boubeker and Hajjat, eds., *Histoire politique des immigrations (post)coloniales: France, 1920–2008*, 157–58.

71. Wendy Brown, *States of Injury: Power and Freedom in Late Modernity* (Princeton, N.J.: Princeton University Press, 1995), 61.

72. Lesselier, "Mouvements et initiatives," 159.

73. *Larmes de Sang*, documentary directed by Anne-Marie Autissier and Ali Akika (1979). Available for viewing at the Forum des Images, Paris.

74. Adil Jazouli, *L'Action collective des jeunes maghrébins de France* (Paris: C.I.E.M.I and L'Harmattan, 1986), 103.

75. Ibid., 95.

76. Ibid., 101.

77. Ibid., 92.

78. Ibid., 94.

79. Ibid.

80. Le Gallic, "Le Théâtre de l'immigration," 162.

81. K. Anthony Appiah, "Identity, Authenticity, Survival: Multicultural Societies and Social Reproduction," in *Multiculturalism: Examining the Politics of Recognition*, ed. Amy Gutmann (Princeton, N.J.: Princeton University Press, 1994), 151.

82. Joan W. Scott, "Experience," in *Feminists Theorize the Political*, ed. Judith Butler and Joan W. Scott (London: Routledge, 1992), 24.

83. Zancarini-Fournel, "Racisme et antiracisme," 116.

84. Clancy and Tancelin, *Les Tiers Idées*, 209.

85. Ibid., 208.

86. Ibid.

87. Ibid.
88. Ross, *May '68 and Its Afterlives*, 110.
89. Clancy and Tancelin, *Les Tiers Idées*, 208.
90. Ibid., 207.
91. Pierre Gaudibert, *Action culturelle: Intégration et/ou subversion* (Paris: Castermann, 1977), 167.
92. Youcef Boussaa, "Femmes maghrébines en fugue: Histoire d'une structure d'accueil et d'hébergement originale" (Ph.D. dissertation, Université Paris 12 Val-de-Marne-Faculté de Médecine de Créteil, 1985), 5–6.
93. Ibid., 25.
94. Ibid., 118.
95. Ibid., 157.
96. Ibid., 155.
97. Ibid., 154.
98. Vincent Dubois, *La Politique culturelle: Genèse d'une catégorie d'intervention publique* (Paris: Belin, 1999), 280.
99. Alec G. Hargreaves, "The *Beurgeoisie*: Mediation or Mirage?" *Journal of European Studies* 28 (1998): 89.
100. Ibid., 93.
101. Angeline Escafré-Dublet, "L'État et la culture des immigrés, 1974–1984," *Histoire@Politique: Politique, Culture, Societe* 4 (2008): 8.
102. Guy Jacquet, "Preface," in Chérif Chikh and Ahsène Zehraoui, *Le Théâtre Beur* (Paris: Arcantère, 1984), 11.
103. Chérif Chikh and Ahsène Zehraoui, *Le Théâtre Beur* (Paris: Arcantère, 1984), 17.

Chapter Two

1. *La Vie rêvée de Fatna*, DVD, directed by Selim Isker (2005; La Compagnie des Indes, Warner Vision France, 2006). This DVD is the filmed version of an October 2005 performance at the Théâtre de Suresnes Jean Vilar, directed by Hélène Darche and written by Rachida Khalil and Guy Bedos.
2. Della Pollock, "Introduction: Remembering," in *Remembering: Oral History Performance*, ed. Della Pollock (New York: Palgrave Macmillan, 2005), 3. Della Pollock's comment pertains to the dynamics of spectatorship in the oral historical interview, a setting with a far more precise political and ethical imaginary than the unruly feedback loops of a widely circulated one-woman show. Yet *La Vie rêvée de Fatna*'s subtle and semi-fictionalized inclusion of Khalil's own life trajectory allows us to treat it within the sphere of personal narrative performance.
3. Susan E. Chase, "Narrative Inquiry: Still a Field in the Making," in *The Sage Handbook of Qualitative Research*, ed. Norman K. Denzin and Yvonna S. Lincoln (Thousand Oaks, Calif.: Sage, 2011), 427.
4. See José Esteban Muñoz, *Disidentifications: Queers of Color and the Performance of Politics* (Minneapolis: University of Minnesota Press, 1999); Jon McKenzie, *Perform or Else: From Discipline to Performance* (New York: Routledge, 2001).
5. Accueil Goutte d'Or, *Rapport d'Activités 2008* (Paris: Accueil Goutte d'Or, 2008), 9.

6. At the time of my research, Paroles de Femmes received financial, administrative, or logistical support from Goutte d'Or institutions such as the city's Institut des Cultures d'Islam, the arts center Lavoir Moderne Parisien, and the social center Accueil Goutte d'Or. As this manuscript went to press, however, the specific framework of Paroles de Femmes appeared to have been discontinued.

7. See Scott, *The Politics of the Veil*; Tevanian, *La République du mépris*; D. Fassin and E. Fassin, eds., *De la question sociale à la question raciale?*

8. Kristin M. Langellier, "Personal Narrative, Performance, Performativity: Two or Three Things I Know for Sure," *Text and Performance Quarterly* 19 (1999): 128.

9. Chandra Talpade Mohanty, "Under Western Eyes: Feminist Scholarship and Colonial Discourses," in *Third World Women and the Politics of Feminism*, ed. Chandra Talpade Mohanty, Ann Russo, and Lourdes Torres (Bloomington: Indiana University Press, 1991), 55.

10. Ibid., 66.

11. See Lionel Trilling, *Sincerity and Authenticity* (Cambridge, Mass.: Harvard University Press, 1972).

12. Aesthetic choices like Angela's were common in my conversations with artists working on personal narrative and immigration. Many writers, directors, and actors commented on the relative ease of working with professional actors, whose everyday sensibilities not only accommodated the highly specific human practice that is theatrical rehearsal but also generated a product that was aesthetically rich. Yet they used different political, ethical, and theatrical principles to arrive at this conclusion. For example, one of my interlocutors was Fabienne, an accomplished actor and playwright who had also worked extensively with personal narrative performances. In a 2006 piece, she drew on three personal narratives from among the many that she had collected from Goutte d'Or inhabitants, in an effort to bear witness to the diversity of lives and political sensibilities that structured the neighborhood. Whereas Angela worked with professional actors for their expertise, Fabienne's reasoning referenced moral principles, arguing against the often unquestioned assumption that the ritual nature of theatrical delivery can serve a therapeutic function. During our conversation, she noted: "Actors begin, they begin again, again, again, raise your hand here, take it from the top, again, again, again . . . I would never ask this of anybody." For Fabienne, to ask a non-actor to undertake the emotionally numbing work of rehearsal constituted too large an ethical compromise. Nevertheless, what united Angela and Fabienne was their sense that the staged narratives of women, in Fabienne's words, "no longer showed a single person but a collective, and became a character," able to function as a vehicle for a larger collective.

13. The first and perhaps best-known reference to the idea of a late twentieth-century *théâtre de parole* is playwright Valère Novarina's collection of essays, *Le Théâtre des paroles* (Paris: Éditions P.O.L, 1989). Jean-Pierre Ryngaert and Julie Sermon have used the phrase occasionally, and authored the encyclopedia entry on "théâtres de la parole" in the *Dictionnaire encyclopédique du théâtre a travers le monde*, ed. Michel Corvin (Paris: Bordas, 2008), 1036–37.

14. Donia Mounsef and Josette Féral, "Editors' Preface," *Yale French Studies* 112 (2007): 1.

15. See Hans-Thies Lehmann, *Postdramatic Theatre*, trans. Karen Jürs-Munby (New York: Routledge, 2006).

16. Jean-Pierre Ryngaert, "Speech in Tatters: The Interplay of Voices in Recent Dramatic Writing," *Yale French Studies* 112 (2007): 25.

17. Clare Finburgh, "*Voix/Voie/Vie:* The Voice in Contemporary French Theater," *Yale French Studies* 112 (2007): 105–6.

18. Butler, *Bodies That Matter*, 16.

19. Ric Knowles, *Theatre & Interculturalism* (London: Palgrave Macmillan, 2010), 11.

20. Antonin Artaud, *Selected Writings*, ed. Susan Sontag, trans. Helen Weaver (Berkeley: University of California Press, 1988), 216.

21. Ibid., 215.

22. Ibid., 216.

23. Ibid., 217.

24. Ibid., 221.

25. Kimberly Jannarone, *Artaud and His Doubles* (Ann Arbor: University of Michigan Press, 2010), 15.

26. Rebecca Schneider, *The Explicit Body in Performance* (London: Routledge, 1997), 130.

27. Julie Stone Peters, "Intercultural Performance, Theatre Anthropology, and the Imperialist Critique: Identities, Inheritances, and Neo-Orthodoxies," in *Imperialism and Theatre: Essays on World Theatre, Drama and Performance*, ed. J. Ellen Gainor (London: Routledge, 1995), 205.

28. Victor Li, *The Neo-Primitivist Turn: Critical Reflections on Alterity, Culture and Modernity* (Toronto: University of Toronto Press, 2006), 17.

29. Thomas Yadan, "Interview de Khalid Tamer: Un Festival en Or," *Evene.fr* (February 2008), http://www.evene.fr/theatre/actualite/interview-khalid-tamer-festival-au-feminin-1195.php.

30. Nancy L. Green, "Le *Melting-Pot*: Made in America, Produced in France," *The Journal of American History* 86, no. 3 (1999): 1196. Not surprisingly, recent scholarship on French national membership in the early part of the twentieth century has increasingly underlined the racial dimensions of this belonging, arguing that racial hierarchies were central to the administrative management and social life of immigration. See Elisa Camiscioli, *Reproducing the French Race: Immigration, Intimacy and Embodiment in the Early Twentieth Century* (Durham, N.C.: Duke University Press, 2009).

31. Green, "Le *Melting-Pot*," 1195.

32. Peter Fysh and Jim Wolfreys, *The Politics of Racism in France* (New York: Palgrave Macmillan, 1998), 171.

33. Pierre Tevanian, *La Mécanique raciste* (Paris: Éditions Dilecta, 2008), 53.

34. See ibid.

35. Eric Fassin, "Aveugles à la race ou au racisme? Une approche stratégique," in D. Fassin and E. Fassin, eds., *De la question sociale à la question raciale?* 106.

36. Alain Finkielkraut quoted in Didier Fassin, "Du déni à la dénégation: Psychologie politique de la représentation des discriminations," in D. Fassin and E. Fassin, eds., *De la question sociale à la question raciale?* 150.

37. For an interesting discussion of the use of the term "république" in late century racial discourses, see Tevanian, *La République du mépris*.

38. Vincent Geisser, *La Nouvelle Islamophobie* (Paris: La Découverte, 2003).

39. Tevanian, *La Mécanique raciste*, 5.

40. Miriam Ticktin, "Sexual Violence as the Language of Border Control: Where French Feminist and Anti-Immigrant Rhetoric Meet," *Signs: Journal of Women in Culture and Society* 33, no. 4 (2008): 866.

41. Ibid.

42. Yadan, "Interview de Khalid Tamer."

43. Ibid.

44. Ibid.

45. Graines de Soleil, "Festival au Féminin Brochure" (Paris: Compagnie Graines de Soleil, 2008).

46. Michel Foucault, *This Is Not a Pipe*, ed. and trans. James Harkness (Berkeley: University of California Press, 1983), 44.

47. See Sylvie Chalaye, "Théâtre et cabarets: Le 'Nègre' Spectacle," in *Zoos humains: XIXème et XXème siècles*, ed. Nicolas Bancel et al. (Paris: La Découverte, 2002).

48. Of course, it is critical to note that many theatrical aid projects do in fact use preexisting texts and mount productions in which actors assume theatrical roles. For example, in *La Vie plus douce* (Paris: aaa production, 2009), Laurent Cibien's documentary of the Secours Populaire Français Morsang/Orge chapter's staging of Federico Garcia Lorca's *The House of Bernarda Alba*, director Natascha Rudolf notes that it is precisely "the pride of entering into a text" rather than being asked to speak of their own lives that allows the women who participate to express not only a range of emotions but to discover new physical actions. The Secours Populaire Français is a nonprofit association that works on poverty.

49. Accueil Goutte d'Or, *Rapport d'Activités, Rapport Moral 2007* (Paris: Accueil Goutte d'Or, 2007), 75.

50. See Miranda Joseph, *Against the Romance of Community* (Minneapolis: University of Minnesota Press, 2002). See in particular the chapter on voluntary associations.

51. Mark Ingram, *Rites of the Republic: Citizens' Theatre and the Politics of Culture in Southern France* (Toronto: University of Toronto Press, 2011), 161.

52. Accueil Goutte d'Or, *Rapport d'Activités, Rapport Moral 2007*, 75.

53. Kristin M. Langellier, "Personal Narratives: Perspectives on Theory and Research," *Text and Performance Quarterly* 9, no. 4 (1989): 251.

54. Della Pollock, "Memory, Remembering, and Histories of Change: A Performance Praxis," in *The Sage Handbook of Performance Studies*, ed. D. Soyini Madison and Judith Hamera (Thousand Oaks, Calif.: Sage, 2006), 91.

55. For more on the experiences of North African women immigrants of the postwar era, see *Mémoires d'immigrés: L'Héritage Maghrébin*, DVD, directed by Yamina Benguigui (Paris: Canal Plus and Bandits, 2004).

56. Jane Freedman, "Women and Immigration: Nationality and Citizenship," in *Women, Immigration and Identities in France*, ed. Jane Freedman and Carrie Tarr (Oxford: Berg, 2000), 15.

57. Ticktin, "Sexual Violence," 865.

58. Bellil's book was translated into English as Samira Bellil, *To Hell and Back: The Life of Samira Bellil*, trans. Lucy R. McNair (Lincoln, Neb.: Bison Books, 2008).

59. Souilamas and Macé, *Les Féministes et le garçon arabe*, 83–84.

60. Fadela Amara and Sylvia Zappi, *Breaking the Silence: French Women's Voices from the Ghetto*, trans. Helen Harden Chenut (Berkeley: University of California Press, 2006), 100.

61. While the history of the struggle for gender equality in France is too complicated to parse here, it is important to note that republican universality has in fact played a problematic role in the development of discourses of sexual difference. See Joan W. Scott, *Only Paradoxes to Offer: French Feminists and the Rights of Man* (Cambridge, Mass.: Harvard University Press, 1997).

62. For a different reading of the relationship between personal agency and religious authority in the context of both French Muslim subjectivities and the Islamic revival more broadly, see Mayanthi Fernando, "Reconfiguring Freedom: Muslim Piety and the Limits of Secular Law and Public Discourse in France," *American Ethnologist* 37, no. 1 (2010): 19–35; and Mahmood, *Politics of Piety*.

63. These contrasting models of bodily practice and the formative powers of ritual action have been analyzed in both historical and anthropological studies, from Caroline Bynum's *Fragmentation and Redemption: Essays on Gender and the Human Body in Medieval Religion* (New York: Zone Books, 1991) to Saba Mahmood's *Politics of Piety* and Talal Asad's *Formations of the Secular: Christianity, Islam, Modernity* (Stanford, Calif.: Stanford University Press, 2003). And there are certainly resonances with post-structuralist accounts of the relationship between the body, authority, and agency. See, for example, Butler, *Bodies That Matter*.

64. Epstein, *Collective Terms*, 73.

65. McKenzie, *Perform or Else*, 29.

66. Ibid., 50.

67. Muñoz, *Disidentifications*, 189.

68. Ibid., 182.

Chapter Three

1. Catherine Coroller, "Des jeunes sans papiers mettent leurs maux en pièce," *Libération*, May 4, 2007.

2. See Emine Fişek, "Framing Témoignage: Personal Narrative, Theatrical Aid and the Politics of Immigration Activism in France," *Text and Performance Quarterly* 36, no. 2–3 (2016): 77–94.

3. See Theodor Adorno, "Commitment," in *Aesthetics and Politics* (London: Verso Books, 2007), 177–96.

4. See Shannon Jackson, *Social Works: Performing Arts, Supporting Publics* (New York: Routledge, 2011).

5. Ibid., 39.

6. The publication of *Votre voisin n'a pas de papiers* (Paris: La Fabrique Éditions, 2006) has been followed by a variety of *témoignage*-based accounts of both *sans-papiers* experience and activist engagement. These include the comic book *Paroles sans papiers* (Paris: Éditions Délcourt, 2007), based on nine *témoignages* collected by Cimade and Migreurop; *La Chasse aux enfants: L'Effet miroir de l'éxpulsion des sans-papiers* (Paris: La Découverte, 2008), Miguel Benasayag, Angélique del Rey, and RESF members' chronicle of the varied motivations underlining RESF activism as well as of the broader social and psychic

aftereffects of the deportation of youth on French society; *Feu au centre de rétention: Des sans-papiers témoignent* (Paris: Éditions Libertalia, 2008), an account of the six months of activism and resistance that took place in the Retention Center of Vincennes (where undocumented immigrants are locked away prior to their deportation) prior to the center's being set on fire in June 2008; and *La Geste des irréguliers: Sans-papiers sur les routes de France* (Paris: Rue des Cascades, 2011), Métie Navajo's account of *sans-papiers*' solidarity and struggle.

7. Director Peter Tournier, personal interview with author, February 14, 2008.

8. *La Chasse aux enfants* similarly rejects ideological motivations. Reminding readers that original members were people whose *sans-papiers* students and neighbors were being deported, the authors underline the larger social implications of broken families: "One does not engage in RESF because of ideology," they write, "but because of the 'mirror effect' of the rupturing of bonds" (12).

9. The full text of the Circulaire is available at http://www.interieur.gouv.fr/sections/a_votre_service/publications/circulaires/2006/intk0600058c/view. The quotations are my own translations and are borrowed from Part Three: "Réexamen de la situation en vue d'une admission au séjour à titre exceptionnel et humanitaire."

10. For a detailed analysis of the Circulaire's application, see Cimade, *De la loterie à la tromperie: Enquête citoyen sur la Circulaire du 13 juin 2006 relative à la régularisation des familles étrangères d'enfants scolarisés* (Paris: Expressions II, 2007).

11. Trica Danielle Keaton, *Muslim Girls and the Other France: Race, Identity Politics and Social Exclusion* (Bloomington: Indiana University Press, 2006), 97.

12. Réseau Education Sans Frontières de l'Essonne, *La Plume sans papier* (Massy: RESF de l'Essonne, 2007), 68.

13. Marine Legrand, "Rachida Brakni met en scène de jeunes sans-papiers," *Le Parisien: Essonne Matin*, August 8, 2007.

14. Ibid.

15. Ibid.

16. Ibid.

17. Lise Hourdel, "Sans-papiers et comédiens," *Le Républicain*, August 16, 2007.

18. Chloé Leprince, "La Galère des majeurs sans-papiers pour être scolarisés," *Rue89*, August 9, 2007, http://www.rue89.com/2007/09/09/la-galere-des-majeurs-sans-papiers-pour-etre-scolarises.

19. Garner, *Bodied Spaces*, 50.

20. Jacques Derrida, "Signature Event Context," in *A Derrida Reader: Between the Blinds*, ed. Peggy Kamuf (New York: Columbia University Press, 1991), 107.

21. Silverstein, *Algeria in France*, 113.

22. Réseau Education Sans Frontières de l'Essonne, *La Plume sans papier*, 47–48.

23. Frantz Fanon, *Black Skin, White Masks* (New York: Grove, 1967), 138.

24. Richard Schechner, *Between Theater and Anthropology* (Philadelphia: University of Pennsylvania Press, 1985), 36.

25. Réseau Education Sans Frontières de l'Essonne, *La Plume sans papier*, 16.

26. Ibid., 24.

27. Ibid., 49.

28. Ibid., 30.
29. Ibid., 28.
30. Wilder, *The French Imperial Nation-State*, 159.
31. Ibid.
32. Ibid., 159–60.
33. Bertolt Brecht, "Short Description of a New Technique of Acting which Produces an Alienation Effect," in *Brecht on Theatre: The Development of an Aesthetic*, ed. John Willett (New York: Hill and Wang, 1992), 138.
34. Ibid., 136.
35. See Adrian Favell, *Philosophies of Integration: Immigration and the Idea of Citizenship in France and Britain* (New York: St. Martin's, 1998).
36. See Henri Giordan, *Démocratie culturelle et droit à la différence: Rapport présenté à Jack Lang, Ministre de la Culture par Henri Giordan, Maitre de Recherche au CNRS* (Paris: La Documentation Française, 1982).
37. Favell, *Philosophies of Integration*, 51.
38. Ibid., 52.
39. Ibid., 64.
40. Ibid., 44.
41. Dominique Schnapper, Pascale Krief, and Emmanuel Peignard, "French Immigration and Integration Policy: A Complex Combination," in *The Integration of Immigrants in European Societies: National Differences and Trends of Convergence*, ed. Friedrich Heckmann and Dominique Schnapper (Stuttgart: Lucius and Lucius, 2003), 15.
42. For a comparison of the French and German models, see Rogers Brubaker, *Citizenship and Nationhood in France and Germany* (Cambridge, Mass.: Harvard University Press, 1998).
43. Rousseau, *The Social Contract*, 164.
44. Dominique Schnapper, *Qu'est-ce que l'intégration?* (Paris: Éditions Gallimard, 2007), 90.
45. Ibid., 92.
46. Ibid., 93.
47. Favell, *Philosophies of Integration,* 76.
48. Ibid., 82.
49. For a fuller history of Cimade, see http://www.lacimade.org/la_cimade/cimade/rubriques/4-histoire. The language quoted here is from the final paragraph of the first section: "Les années 30 et la seconde guerre mondiale."
50. Exchanges was funded by the EQUAL program of the European Social Fund, a community initiative program which funds several "themes," including asylum. From 2003 to 2005, the French theater workshops were funded by the Euraccueil Development Partnership (Accueil et Formation des Demandeurs d'Asile) and from 2005 to 2007 by the FAAR Development Partnership (Formation, Accueil des Demandeurs d'Asile et Réfugiés).
51. Cimade/FAAR DP, *Empowering Asylum Seekers to Integrate in Europe: A Transnational Report Based on Experiences in Hungary, France and England* (Paris: Expressions II, 2007), 8.
52. Cimade, *Bilan 2007 Deuxième Période: Juin-Décembre* (Paris: Cimade, 2007), 4.
53. Cimade/FAAR DP, *Empowering Asylum Seekers*, 56.

54. Ibid., 20.

55. A brief overview of France's asylum policies (especially in the aftermath of the legal changes of the early 2000s) is available at the end of Cimade's *Votre voisin n'a pas de papiers*.

56. Cimade, *Main basse sur l'asile: Le Droit d'asile (mal)traité par les préfets* (Paris: Expressions II, 2007), 32.

57. For an extensive commentary on "the wait," see *Visages de l'attente: Droit d'asile*, DVD, directed by Nadège Bonnet-Chelhi (Cimade, 2007).

58. Sonia Dayan-Herzbrun, "The Issue of the Islamic Headscarf," in *Women, Immigration and Identities in France*, ed. Jane Freedman and Carrie Tarr (Oxford: Berg, 2000), 71.

59. See specifically the first chapter of Alison Jeffers, *Refugees, Theatre and Crisis: Performing Global Identities* (Basingstoke, Eng.: Palgrave Macmillan, 2012).

60. Aihwa Ong, *Neoliberalism as Exception: Mutations in Citizenship and Sovereignty* (Durham, N.C.: Duke University Press, 2006), 198.

61. A good overview of these developments is the recent issue of *Vacarme* on nongovernmental politics edited by Michel Feher. See *Vacarme* 34 (2006).

62. Cimade/Véronique Laurens, *Théâtre et apprentissage du français: Expériences de formations avec des adultes primo-arrivants en France* (Paris: Cimade, 2005), 54.

63. Ibid., 14.

64. Paul Connerton, *How Societies Remember*, 72.

65. Ibid., 74.

66. Cimade/Véronique Laurens, *Théâtre et apprentissage du français*, 15.

67. Indeed, the first two months of the theater workshops comprised weekly language lessons, accompanied by Cinque's articulation exercises. Over the following four months, the group met four to five consecutive and full days each month, beginning their theater work with warm-up and vocalization exercises. These were followed by improvisation projects that evolved from both imaginary circumstances and the participants' personal memories and experiences, of which the latter eventually served as the fabric of the final performance. Throughout, oral improvisations were set in writing and vice versa, creating the text that then served as the basis for more articulation and memorization exercises. And in the final months, the workshops resembled a more traditional theatrical rehearsal process, coordinating the choreography of onstage and backstage labor.

68. Cimade/Véronique Laurens, *Théâtre et apprentissage du français*, 46.

69. Connerton, *How Societies Remember*, 83.

70. In differentiating cultivation from inculcation, I found Saba Mahmood's brief but instructive distinction between the two terms helpful. See Mahmood, *Politics of Piety*, 151–52.

71. Mireille Rosello, *Postcolonial Hospitality: The Immigrant as Guest* (Stanford, Calif.: Stanford University Press, 2001), 2.

72. Ibid., 23–24.

73. Alain Montandon, *Le Livre de l'hospitalité: Accueil de l'étranger dans l'histoire et les cultures* (Paris: Éditions Bayard, 2004), 6.

74. Rosello, *Postcolonial Hospitality*, 39.

75. Cimade/Véronique Laurens, *Théâtre et apprentissage du français*, 58.
76. Ibid., 75.
77. Cimade, *Je serai où demain?* (Paris: Cimade, 2006), 3.
78. Cimade, *Bilan 2007.*
79. Cimade, "Errances . . . d'un hotel à l'autre," in *Théâtre et apprentissage du français.*
80. Ibid., 68.
81. Cimade/Véronique Laurens, *Theatre et apprentissage du français*, 70.
82. Sauter, *The Theatrical Event*, 12.

Chapter Four

1. Ric Knowles, *Theatre & Interculturalism* (New York: Palgrave Macmillan, 2010), 1.
2. Jacqueline Lo and Helen Gilbert, "Toward a Topography of Cross-Cultural Theatre Praxis," *TDR: The Drama Review* 46, no. 3 (2002): 34.
3. See Herman Lebovics, *True France: The Wars over Cultural Identity 1900–1945* (Ithaca, N.Y.: Cornell University Press, 1994); and Herman Lebovics, *Bringing the Empire Back Home: France in the Global Age* (Durham, N.C.: Duke University Press, 2004).
4. Mark Ingram, *Rites of the Republic: Citizens' Theatre and the Politics of Culture in Southern France* (Toronto: University of Toronto Press, 2011), xxi.
5. Kokoreff and Lapeyronnie, *Refaire la cité*, 17.
6. Jan Cohen-Cruz, *Local Acts: Community-Based Performance in the United States* (New Brunswick, N.J.: Rutgers University Press, 2005), 2.
7. Ibid.
8. Sonja Kuftinec, *Staging America: Cornerstone and Community-Based Theater* (Carbondale: Southern Illinois University Press, 2005), 6–7.
9. Susan C. Haedicke and Tobin Nellhaus, "Introduction," in *Performing Democracy: International Perspectives on Urban Community Based Performance*, ed. Susan C. Haedicke and Tobin Nellhaus (Ann Arbor: University of Michigan Press, 2001), 4–5.
10. Miranda Joseph, *Against the Romance of Community* (Minneapolis: University of Minnesota Press, 2002), 1.
11. Ibid.
12. Jean-Luc Nancy, *The Inoperative Community*, ed. Peter Connor, trans. Peter Connor et al. (Minneapolis: University of Minnesota Press, 1991), 9.
13. Alan Filewod, "Coalitions of Resistance: Ground Zero's Community Mobilization," in *Performing Democracy: International Perspectives on Urban Community-Based Performance*, ed. Susan C. Haedicke and Tobin Nellhaus (Ann Arbor: University of Michigan Press, 2001), 89.
14. Miranda Joseph, *Against the Romance,* 111.
15. Ibid., 113.
16. Jacques Rancière, *The Emancipated Spectator*, trans. Gregory Elliott (London: Verso, 2009), 16.
17. Ibid., 17.
18. Ibid., 16.
19. Ibid., 6.

20. Judith Hamera, "Performance, Performativity, and Cultural Poiesis in Practices of Everyday Life," in Madison and Hamera, eds., *The Sage Handbook of Performance Studies*, 47.

21. Rancière, *The Emancipated Spectator*, 56.

22. Knowles, *Theatre & Interculturalism*, 1.

23. Ibid., 4.

24. Raymond Williams, *Keywords: A Vocabulary of Culture and Society* (New York: Oxford University Press, 1985), 87.

25. Ibid., 90.

26. Daphne Lei, "Interruption, Intervention, Interculturalism: Robert Wilson's HIT Productions in Taiwan," *Theatre Journal* 63, no. 4 (2011): 575.

27. James Clifford, *The Predicament of Culture: Twentieth-Century Ethnography, Literature, and Art* (Cambridge, Mass.: Harvard University Press, 1988), 10.

28. Lo and Gilbert, "Toward a Topography of Cross-Cultural Theatre Praxis," 37.

29. Yasemin Nuhoğlu Soysal, *Limits of Citizenship: Migrants and Postnational Membership in Europe* (Chicago: University of Chicago Press, 1994), 106.

30. Catherine Wihtol de Wenden and Rémy Leveau, *La Beurgeoisie* (Paris: CNRS Éditions, 2007), 11.

31. Dominique Schnapper (with Christian Bachelier), *Qu'est-ce que la Citoyenneté?* (Paris: Éditions Gallimard, 2000), 44.

32. Ibid.

33. Scott, *The Politics of the Veil*, 11.

34. Jocelyne Cesari, *Être musulman en France: Associations, militants et mosquées* (Paris: Éditions Karthala and Iremam, 1994), 227.

35. For some groups the 1981 law merely provided new institutional partners and new avenues of subsidy for existing frameworks of social action. See Adil Jazouli, *L'Action collective des jeunes maghrébins de France* (Paris: C.I.E.M.I. and L'Harmattan, 1986).

36. Wihtol de Wenden and Leveau, *La Beurgeoisie,* 13.

37. Silverstein, *Algeria in France*, 164.

38. Soysal, *Limits of Citizenship,* 3.

39. Cesari, *Être musulman,* 192.

40. Ibid.

41. Wihtol de Wenden and Leveau, *La Beurgeoisie,*14.

42. Epstein, *Collective Terms*, 33.

43. Silverstein, *Algeria in France*, 92–98.

44. Ahmed Boubeker, "La 'Petite Histoire' d'une génération d'expérience: Du mouvement Beur aux banlieues de l'islam," in Boubeker and Hajjat, eds., *Histoire politique des immigrations (post)coloniales: France, 1920–2008*, 187.

45. For an excellent discussion of the role of Beur elites, see Alec Hargreaves, "The Beurgeoisie: Meditation or Mirage?" *Journal of European Studies* 28 (1998): 89–102.

46. Silverstein, *Algeria in France*, 172.

47. Kokoreff and Lapeyronnie, *Refaire la cité*, 24.

48. See Bérénice Hamidi-Kim, *Les Cités du théâtre politique en France depuis 1989* (Montpellier: Éditions L'Entretemps, 2013), 332–48.

49. Patrice Pavis, *Theatre at the Crossroads of Culture,* trans. Loren Kruger (New York: Routledge, 2005), 7.

50. Ibid., 203.

51. David Bradby and Maria M. Delgado, "Introduction: Piecing Together the Paris Jigsaw," in *The Paris Jigsaw: Internationalism and the City's Stages*, ed. David Bradby and Maria M. Delgado (Manchester: Manchester University Press, 2002), 4.

52. For a detailed overview of this transition, see Richard Derderian, *North Africans in Contemporary France: Becoming Visible* (New York: Palgrave Macmillan, 2004).

53. "L'Environnement social du centre," http://www.maisondestilleuls.org/maisondestilleuls.html.

54. Abdellali Hajjat, "Révolte des quartiers populaires, crise du militantisme et postcolonialisme," in Boubeker and Hajjat, eds., *Histoire politique des immigrations (post)coloniales: France, 1920–2008*, 256.

55. "Une maison au service d'un projet humain et citoyen," http://www.maisondestilleuls.org/maisondestilleuls.html.

56. Elsa Solal, *Le Bruit du monde m'est rentré dans l'oreille* (Paris: L'Harmattan, 2008).

57. In its various stages, *Le Bruit du monde m'est rentré dans l'oreille* was supported by the Forum Social des Quartiers Populaires, the Fondation Abbé Pierre, the Conseil Régional de l'Île-de-France, the Maison des Tilleuls, and the Agence Nationale pour la Cohésion Sociale et l'Egalité des Chances.

58. Christopher Dickey, "The Fire This Time," *Newsweek*, November 14, 2005.

59. These are chronicled in detail in Thomas Deltombe, *L'Islam imaginaire: La Construction médiatique de l'islamophobie en France 1975–2005* (Paris: La Découverte, 2005).

60. Christopher Dickey, "Europe's Time Bomb," *Newsweek*, November 21, 2005.

61. Stéphane Beaud and Michel Pialoux, "La 'Racaille' et les 'vrais jeunes': Critique d'une vision binaire du monde des cités," in *Banlieue, lendemains de révolte*, ed. Clémentine Autain (Paris: La Dispute, 2006), 19.

62. Patrick Braouezze, "Un autre monde est nécessaire," in *Banlieue, lendemains de révolte*, 47.

63. Mehdi Charef, *Le Thé au harem d'Archi Ahmed* (Paris: Gallimard, 1988).

64. Laurent Mucchielli, "Il faut changer la façon de 'faire la police' dans les 'quartiers sensibles,'" in *Banlieue, lendemains de révolte*, 94–95.

65. Stéphane Beaud and Sabrina Hamache, "Retour sur les émeutes de novembre 2005: Quand les femmes de quartiers prennent la parole," *Vu d'Ici* 8 (2008): 2.

66. Ibid., 3.

67. Ibid., 4.

68. Ibid., 2.

69. Paul Silverstein and Chantal Tetreault, "Urban Violence in France," *MERIP: Middle East Report Online*, November, 2005, http://www.merip.org/mero/interventions/urban-violence-france.

70. Beaud and Hamache, "Retour sur les émeutes de novembre 2005," 4.

71. Ibid.

72. Azouz Begag, *Le Gone du Chaâba* (Paris: Éditions du Seuil, 2005).

73. Epstein, *Collective Terms,* 38.

74. Kristin Langellier and Eric E. Peterson, "Shifting Contexts in Personal Narrative Performance," in Madison and Hamera, eds., *The Sage Handbook of Performance Studies*, 157.

75. This and the following comments are all chronicled in "Une aventure formidable" in *Le Bruit du monde*, 45.

76. Ibid., 47.

77. Ibid.

78. Ibid., 48.

79. Nicholas Ridout, *Passionate Amateurs: Theatre, Communism, and Love* (Ann Arbor: University of Michigan Press, 2015), 15.

80. Ibid., 21.

81. Solal, *Le Bruit du monde*, 8.

82. Ibid., 11–12.

83. Ibid., 18.

84. Ibid., 21.

85. My thanks to Mark Ingram for helping me clarify this point, as well as for his generosity as a reader.

86. Solal, *Le Bruit du monde*, 21.

87. Ibid., 22.

88. Ibid., 34.

89. Emile Chabal, *A Divided Republic: Nation, State and Citizenship in Contemporary France* (Cambridge: Cambridge University Press, 2015), 26.

90. Solal, *Le Bruit du mond*, 31.

91. Ibid., 33.

92. Richard Bauman, *Verbal Art as Performance* (Long Grove, Ill.: Waveland, 1984), 9.

Chapter Five

1. See Julie Salverson, "Change on Whose Terms? Testimony and an Erotics of Injury," *Theater* 31, no. 3 (2001): 119–25; and James Thompson, *Performance Affects: Applied Theatre and the End of Effect* (Houndmills, Eng.: Palgrave Macmillan, 2009).

2. Caroline Wake, "To Witness Mimesis: The Politics, Ethics, and Aesthetics of Testimonial Theatre in *Through the Wire*," *Modern Drama* 56, no. 1 (2013): 103.

3. Azadeh Sharifi and S. E. Wilmer, "Reflections on Theatre and Statelessness," special topic: "Theatre and Statelessness in Europe," edited by Sharifi and Wilmer, *Critical Stages/Scènes Critiques* 14 (2016), http://www.critical-stages.org/14/special-topic/.

4. For more on the impact of the Pasqua laws, see Didier Fassin, Alan Morice, and Catherine Quiminal, eds., *Les Lois de l'inhospitalité: Les politiques de l'immigration à l'épreuve des sans-papiers* (Paris: Éditions La Découverte, 1997).

5. For more on these media labels and their larger political and philosophical implications, see Mireille Rosello, *Postcolonial Hospitality: The Immigrant as Guest* (Palo Alto, Calif.: Stanford University Press, 2002); and Jacques Derrida (with Anne Dufourmantelle), *Of Hospitality*, trans. Rachel Bowlby (Palo Alto, Calif.: Stanford University Press, 2002).

6. Paul Ricoeur, *Memory, History, Forgetting*, trans. Kathleen Blamey and David Pellauer (Chicago: University of Chicago Press, 2004), 165.

7. Ibid., 163.

8. Liisa Malkki, "Speechless Emissaries: Refugees, Humanitarianism and Dehistoricization," *Cultural Anthropology* 11, no. 3 (1996): 378.

9. Ibid., 390.

10. Thompson, *Performance Affects*, 163.

11. Ibid., 164.

12. Didier Fassin and Richard Rechtman, *The Empire of Trauma: An Inquiry into the Condition of Victimhood*, trans. Rachel Gomme (Princeton, N.J.: Princeton University Press, 2009), 247.

13. Ibid., 242.

14. Emma Cox, "Victimhood, Hope and the Refugee Narrative: Affective Dialectics in Magnet Theatre's *Every Year, Every Day, I Am Walking*," *Theatre Research International* 37, no. 2 (2012): 128.

15. Didier Fassin, "Compassion and Repression: The Moral Economy of Immigration Policies in France," *Cultural Anthropology* 20, no. 3 (2005): 368.

16. For an excellent discussion of the theme of compassion in Nicolas Sarkozy's early statements as president, see Eric Fassin, *Démocratie précaire: Chroniques de la déraison d'état* (Paris: La Découverte, 2012), 68–72.

17. Miriam Ticktin, *Casualties of Care: Immigration and the Politics of Humanitarianism in France* (Berkeley: University of California Press, 2011), 2.

18. For Ticktin, a significant dimension of this trend was its emphasis on biological suffering, as exemplified by "the illness clause" of 1998, which granted legal permits to *sans-papiers* individuals already living in France if they could prove that they suffered from a life-threatening illness that could not be treated in their country of origin. The fact that these exceptional residency permits were not accompanied by work permits is revelatory of the dual dynamics that Ticktin has traced: whereas the illness clause is premised on the imagined universality of bodily pain (one which applicants then have to learn to perform in efficacious ways), it cannot recognize the political and social needs of the particular human experiencing it.

19. Didier Fassin, *Humanitarian Reason: A Moral History of the Present* (Berkeley: University of California Press, 2012), 24.

20. For an overview, see Erica Bornstein and Peter Redfield, "An Introduction to the Anthropology of Humanitarianism," in *Forces of Compassion: Humanitarianism between Ethics and Politics*, ed. Erica Bornstein and Peter Redfield (Santa Fe, N.M.: School for Advanced Research Press, 2010), 3–31.

21. Christiane Vollaire, *Humanitaire: Le Coeur de la guerre* (Paris: L'Insulaire, 2007), 13.

22. Bornstein and Redfield, "An Introduction," 6.

23. D. Fassin, *Humanitarian Reason*, 206.

24. Renée C. Fox, "Medical Humanitarianism and Human Rights: Reflections on Doctors Without Borders and Doctors of the World," *Social Science and Medicine* 41, no. 12 (1995): 1608.

25. Peter Redfield, "The Impossible Problem of Neutrality," in *Forces of Compassion: Humanitarianism between Ethics and Politics*, ed. Erica Bornstein and

Peter Redfield (Santa Fe, N.M.: School for Advanced Research Press, 2010), 60–61.

26. Esther D'Halluin, "Entre expertise et témoignage: L'Éthique humanitaire à l'épreuve des politiques migratoires," *Vacarme* 34 (2006): 113.

27. Peter Redfield, "A Less Modest Witness: Collective Advocacy and Motivated Truth in a Medical Humanitarian Environment," *American Ethnologist* 33, no. 1 (2006): 5.

28. See Michel Feher, "Constancy in Context," *Wisconsin International Law Journal* 24, no. 3 (2006): 775–84.

29. Bernard Kouchner, *Le Malheur des autres* (Paris: Éditions Odile Jacob, 1991), 10.

30. Fox, "Medical Humanitarianism and Human Rights," 1609.

31. Malkki, "Speechless Emissaries," 388.

32. Hannah Arendt, *On Revolution* (New York: Penguin Books, 2006), 75.

33. Lauren Berlant, "Introduction: Compassion and Withholding," in *Compassion: The Culture and Politics of an Emotion*, ed. Lauren Berlant (New York: Routledge, 2004), 1–15.

34. For more on the concept of bare life, see Giorgio Agamben, *Homo Sacer: Sovereign Power and Bare Life* (Palo Alto, Calif.: Stanford University Press, 1998).

35. For a discussion of this statement, please see chapter 1.

36. Peter Nyers, *Rethinking Refugees: Beyond States of Emergency* (New York: Routledge, 2006), 99.

37. Ricoeur, *Memory, History, Forgetting*, 164.

38. Michael Balfour, ed., *Refugee Performance: Practical Encounters* (Bristol, Eng.: Intellect Books, 2013).

39. Alison Jeffers, "Hospitable Stages and Civil Listening: Being an Audience for Participatory Refugee Theatre," in *Refugee Performance: Practical Encounters*, ed. Michael Balfour (Bristol, Eng.: Intellect Books, 2013), 301.

40. Malkki, "Speechless Emissaries," 384.

41. See Silvija Jestrovic, "Performing like an Asylum Seeker: Paradoxes of Hyper Authenticity," *Research in Drama Education* 13, no. 2 (2008): 159–70.

42. Ibid., 160.

43. I have elaborated on the relationship between aesthetics and politics with regard to personal narrative and immigration activism elsewhere. See Emine Fişek, "Framing Témoignage: Personal Narrative, Theatrical Aid and the Politics of Immigration Activism in France," *Text and Performance Quarterly* 36, no. 2–3 (2016): 77–94.

44. Judith Miller, *Ariane Mnouchkine* (London: Routledge, 2007), 13.

45. Ibid., 11.

46. Ibid., 48.

47. Catherine Bédarida, "Le Théâtre du Soleil porte la voix des réfugiés," *Le Monde*, April 1, 2003.

48. Malkki, "Speechless Emissaries," 388.

49. Bablet, "Towards a New Form," 54.

50. Ross, *May '68 and Its Afterlives*, 112.

51. See William McEvoy, "Finding the Balance: Writing and Performing Ethics in Théâtre du Soleil's *Le Dernier Caravansérail* (2003)," *New Theatre Quarterly* 22, no. 3 (2006): 211–26.

52. Ibid., 211. In his phrasing, McEvoy is echoing a quotation from David Williams.

53. Ibid., 216

54. Bérénice Hamidi-Kim, *Les Cités du théâtre politique en France depuis 1989* (Montpellier: Éditions l'Entretemps, 2013), 263.

55. For a related argument on changing perceptions of the Théâtre du Soleil as an activist entity, especially with regard to notions of people's vs. citizen theater, see Bérénice Hamidi-Kim, "The Théâtre du Soleil's Trajectory from 'People's Theatre' to 'Citizen Theatre': Involvement or Renunciation?" in *Political Performances: Theory and Practice*, ed. Susan C. Hedicke, Deirdre Haddon, Avraham Oz, and E. J. Westlake (Amsterdam: Rodopi, 2009), 71–95.

56. Ariane Mnouchkine, *L'Art du présent: Entretiens avec Fabienne Pascaud* (Paris: Plon, 2005), 104.

57. Ibid., 102–3.

58. Salverson, "Change on Whose Terms?" 121.

59. *Le Dernier Caravansérail: Odyssées*, DVD, directed by Ariane Mnouchkine (Paris: Bel Air Classiques, ARTE France Développement, CNDP, 2006).

60. Jean-Louis Perrier, "A la Cartoucherie, les flux et les reflux de la misère des hommes," *Le Monde*, January 16, 2003.

61. McEvoy, "Finding the Balance," 216–17.

62. Wake, "To Witness Mimesis," 107.

63. Alan Filewod, "Theatrical Migrations and Digital Bodies: The Migrant Voices Project," unpublished paper presentation, conference on "Performance and Asylum: Ethics, Embodiment and Community" at Royal Holloway, University of London, November 3–5, 2007. Used with the permission of the author.

64. See Laura Edmondson, "TDR Comment: Of Sugarcoating and Hope," *The Drama Review* 51, no. 2 (2007): 7–10; Sonja Kuftinec, *Theatre, Facilitation, and Nation Formation in the Balkans and Middle East* (New York: Palgrave Macmillan, 2009); D. Soyini Madison, *Acts of Activism: Human Rights as Radical Performance* (Cambridge: Cambridge University Press, 2010).

Conclusion

1. Balibar, *We, the People of Europe?*, 37.

2. Alexandre Lemarié, "L'Immigration, thème de campagne à l'UMP," *Le Monde*, November 3, 2014.

3. Cimade, *Migrations: État des lieux 2014* (Paris: Cimade, 2014), http://www.lacimade.org/publications/88.

4. Nicolas Bancel, "France, 2005: A Postcolonial Turning Point," *French Cultural Studies* 24, no. 2 (2013): 212.

5. Abdelmalek Sayad's *La Double Absence: Des illusions de l'émigré aux souffrances de l'immigré* (Paris: Éditions du Seuil, 1999) has been translated into English as *The Suffering of the Immigrant*. (The full citation is available in the bibliography.)

6. Marina da Silva, with Philip Boulay, Albertine M. Itela, and Zouina Meddour, "Et puis, nous passions le pantalon français: Une création artistique et politique," *Tumultes* 42 (2014): 117.

7. Ibid., 115.

8. Paul Rae, *Theatre & Human Rights* (New York: Palgrave Macmillan, 2009), 65.

BIBLIOGRAPHY

Accueil Goutte d'Or. *Rapport d'activités 2008*. Paris: Accueil Goutte d'Or, 2008.

———. *Rapport d'activités, rapport moral 2007*. Paris: Accueil Goutte d'Or, 2007.

Agamben, Giorgio. *Homo Sacer: Sovereign Power and Bare Life*. Palo Alto, Calif.: Stanford University Press, 1998.

Ahearne, Jeremy. "Introduction." In *French Cultural Policy Debates: A Reader*, edited by Jeremy Ahearne, 1–35. New York: Routledge, 2002.

Aissaoui, Rabah. "Political Mobilization of North African Migrants in 1970s France: The Case of the Mouvement des Travailleurs Arabes (MTA)." *Journal of Muslim Minority Affairs* 26, no. 2 (2006): 171–86.

Al Assifa Papers. Fonds Saïd Bouziri. Bibliothèque de Documentation Internationale Contemporaine, Nanterre.

Amara, Fadela, and Sylvia Zappi. *Breaking the Silence: French Women's Voices from the Ghetto*. Translated by Helen Harden Chenut. Berkeley: University of California Press, 2006.

Appadurai, Arjun. *Modernity at Large: Cultural Dimensions of Globalization*. Minneapolis: University of Minnesota Press, 1996.

Arendt, Hannah. *On Revolution*. New York: Penguin Books, 2006.

Artaud, Antonin. *Selected Writings*. Edited by Susan Sontag, translated by Helen Weaver. Berkeley: University of California Press, 1988.

Asad, Talal. *Formations of the Secular: Christianity, Islam, Modernity*. Stanford, Calif.: Stanford University Press, 2003.

———. *Genealogies of Religion: Discipline and Reasons of Power in Christianity and Islam*. Baltimore: Johns Hopkins University Press, 1993.

Austin, J. L. *How to Do Things with Words*. Cambridge, Mass.: Harvard University Press, 1975.

Autain, Clémentine, ed. *Banlieue, lendemains de révolte*. Paris: La Dispute, 2006.

Autissier, Anne-Marie, and Ali Akika. *Larmes de Sang*. DVD. 1979. Available for viewing at the Forum des Images, Paris.

Bablet, Denis. "Towards a New Form: From an Interview with Ariane Mnouchkine." In *Collaborative Theater: The Théâtre du Soleil Sourcebook*, edited by David Williams, 51–59. London: Routledge, 1999.

Balfour, Michael, ed. *Refugee Performance: Practical Encounters*. Bristol, Eng.: Intellect Books, 2013.

Balibar, Étienne. *We, the People of Europe? Reflections on Transnational Citizenship*. Trans. James Swenson. Princeton, N.J.: Princeton University Press, 2004.

Bancel, Nicolas. "France, 2005: A Postcolonial Turning Point." *French Cultural Studies* 24, no. 2 (2013): 208–18.

Bauman, Richard. *Verbal Art as Performance*. Long Grove, Ill.: Waveland, 1984.

Beaud, Stéphane, and Sabrina Hamache. "Retour sur les émeutes de novembre 2005: Quand les femmes de quartiers prennent la parole." *Vu d'Ici* 8 (2008).

Beaud, Stéphane, and Michel Pialoux. "La 'Racaille' et les 'vrais jeunes': Critique d'une vision binaire du monde des cités." In Autain, ed., *Banlieue, lendemains de révolte*, 17–29.

Bédarida, Catherine. "Le Théâtre du Soleil porte la voix des réfugiés." *Le Monde*, April 1, 2003.

Begag, Azouz. *Le Gone du Chaâba*. Paris: Éditions du Seuil, 2005.

Bell, Catherine. *Ritual Theory Ritual Practice*. New York: Oxford University Press, 1992.

Bellil, Samira. *To Hell and Back: The Life of Samira Bellil*. Translated by Lucy R. McNair. Lincoln, Neb.: Bison Books, 2008.

Benasayag, Miguel, Angélique del Rey, and RESF. *La Chasse aux enfants: L'Effet miroir de l'éxpulsion des sans-papiers*. Paris: La Découverte, 2008.

Benguigui, Yamina. *Mémoires d'immigrés: L'Héritage Maghrébin*. DVD. Paris: Canal Plus and Bandits, 2004.

Berlant, Lauren. "Introduction: Compassion and Withholding." In *Compassion: The Culture and Politics of an Emotion*, edited by Lauren Berlant, 1–15. New York: Routledge, 2004.

Blatt, Ari. "The Play's the Thing: Marivaux and the *Banlieue* in Abdellatif Kechiche's *L'esquive*." *The French Review* 81, no. 3 (2008): 516–27.

Bleich, Eric. *Race Politics in Britain and France: Ideas and Policymaking since the 1960s*. Cambridge: Cambridge University Press, 2003.

Boal, Augusto. *The Theatre of the Oppressed*. Translated by Charles A. McBride and Maria-Odilia Leal McBride. New York: Theatre Communications Group, 1985.

Bonnet-Chelhi, Nadège. *Visages de l'attente: Droit d'asile*. DVD. Paris: Cimade, 2007.

Bornstein, Erica, and Peter Redfield. "An Introduction to the Anthropology of Humanitarianism." In *Forces of Compassion: Humanitarianism between Ethics and Politics*, edited by Erica Bornstein and Peter Redfield, 3–31. Santa Fe, N.M.: School for Advanced Research Press, 2010.

Boubeker, Ahmed. "La 'Petite Histoire' d'une génération d'expérience: Du mouvement Beur aux banlieues de l'islam." In Boubeker and Hajjat, eds., *Histoire politique des immigrations (post)coloniales: France, 1920–2008*, 179–93.

Boubeker, Ahmed, and Abdellali Hajjat, eds. *Histoire politique des immigrations (post)coloniales: France, 1920–2008*. Paris: Éditions Amsterdam, 2008.

Bourdieu, Pierre. *The Field of Cultural Production: Essays on Art and Literature*. Cambridge, Eng.: Polity, 1993.

Bourdieu, Pierre, Alain Darbel, and Dominique Schnapper. *The Love of Art: European Art Museums and Their Public*. Translated by Caroline Beattie and Nick Merriman. Cambridge, Eng.: Polity, 1997.

Boussaa, Youcef. "Femmes maghrébines en fugue: Histoire d'une structure d'accueil et d'hébergement originale." Ph.D. dissertation. Université Paris 12 Val-de-Marne-Faculté de Médecine de Créteil, 1985.

Bouzar, Dounia, and Saïda Kada. *L'Une voilée, l'autre pas*. Paris: Albin Michel, 2003.

Bradby, David. *Modern French Drama 1940–1990*. Cambridge: Cambridge University Press, 1991.

Bradby, David, and Maria M. Delgado. "Introduction: Piecing Together the Paris Jigsaw." In *The Paris Jigsaw: Internationalism and the City's Stages*, edited by David Bradby and Maria M. Delgado, 1–33. Manchester: Manchester University Press, 2002.

Braouezze, Patrick. "Un autre monde est nécessaire." In Autain, ed., *Banlieue, lendemains de révolte*, 43–51.

Brecht, Bertolt. *Brecht on Theatre: The Development of an Aesthetic*. Edited by John Willett. New York: Hill and Wang, 1992.

Brown, Wendy. *States of Injury: Power and Freedom in Late Modernity*. Princeton, N.J.: Princeton University Press, 1995.

Brubaker, Rogers. *Citizenship and Nationhood in France and Germany*. Cambridge, Mass.: Harvard University Press, 1998.

Butler, Judith. *Bodies That Matter: On the Discursive Limits of "Sex."* New York: Routledge, 1993.

———. *Excitable Speech: A Politics of the Performative*. New York: Routledge, 1997.

Bynum, Caroline. *Fragmentation and Redemption: Essays on Gender and the Human Body in Medieval Religion*. New York: Zone Books, 1991.

Camiscioli, Elisa. *Reproducing the French Race: Immigration, Intimacy and Embodiment in the Early Twentieth Century*. Durham, N.C.: Duke University Press, 2009.

Carlson, Marvin. "Semiotics and Its Heritage." In *Critical Theory and Performance*, edited by Janelle G. Reinelt and Joseph R. Roach, 13–25. Ann Arbor: University of Michigan Press, 2010.

Cesari, Jocelyne. *Être musulman en France: Associations, militants et mosquées*. Paris: Éditions Karthala and Iremam, 1994.

Cette France-là 06/05/2007–30/06/2008. Volume 1. Paris: La Découverte, 2009.

Chabal, Emile. *A Divided Republic: Nation, State and Citizenship in Contemporary France*. Cambridge: Cambridge University Press, 2015.

Chalaye, Sylvie. "Théâtre et cabarets: Le 'Nègre' Spectacle." In *Zoos humains: XIXème et XXème siècles*, edited by Nicolas Bancel et al., 296–305. Paris: La Découverte, 2002.

Charef, Mehdi. *Le Thé au harem d'Archi Ahmed*. Paris: Gallimard, 1988.

Chase, Susan E. "Narrative Inquiry: Still a Field in the Making." In *The Sage Handbook of Qualitative Research*, edited by Norman K. Denzin and Yvonna S. Lincoln, 421–35. Thousand Oaks, Calif.: Sage, 2011.

Chikh, Chérif, and Ahsène Zehraoui. *Le Théâtre Beur*. Paris: Arcantère, 1984.

Cibien, Laurent. *La Vie plus douce*. DVD. Paris: aaa production, 2009.

Cimade. *Bilan 2007 deuxième période: Juin-Décembre*. Paris: Cimade, 2007.

———. *De la loterie à la tromperie: Enquête citoyen sur la Circulaire du 13 juin 2006 relative à la régularisation des familles étrangères d'enfants scolarisés*. Paris: Expressions II, 2007.

———. *Je serai où demain?* Paris: Cimade, 2006.

———. *Main basse sur l'asile: Le Droit d'asile (mal)traité par les préfets*. Paris: Expressions II, 2007.

———. *Migrations: Etat des lieux 2014*. Paris: Cimade, 2014.

———. *Votre voisin n'a pas de papiers: Paroles d'étrangers*. Paris: La Fabrique Éditions, 2006.

Cimade and Migreurop. *Paroles sans papiers*. Paris: Éditions Délcourt, 2007.
Cimade/FAAR DP. *Empowering Asylum Seekers to Integrate in Europe: A Transnational Report Based on Experiences in Hungary, France and England*. Paris: Expressions II, 2007.
Cimade/Véronique Laurens. *Théâtre et apprentissage du français: Expériences de formations avec des adultes primo-arrivants en France*. Paris: Cimade, 2005.
Clancy, Geneviève, and Philippe Tancelin. *Les Tiers Idées*. Paris: Hachette, 1977.
Clifford, James. *The Predicament of Culture: Twentieth-Century Ethnography, Literature, and Art*. Cambridge, Mass.: Harvard University Press, 1988.
Cohen-Cruz, Jan. *Local Acts: Community-Based Performance in the United States*. New Brunswick, N.J.: Rutgers University Press, 2005.
Connerton, Paul. *How Societies Remember*. Cambridge: Cambridge University Press, 2004.
Coroller, Catherine. "Des jeunes sans papiers mettent leurs maux en pièce." *Libération*, May 4, 2007.
Cox, Emma. *Performing Noncitizenship: Asylum Seekers in Australian Theatre, Film, and Activism*. London: Anthem, 2015.
———. *Theatre & Migration*. Basingstoke, Eng.: Palgrave Macmillan, 2014.
———. "Victimhood, Hope and the Refugee Narrative: Affective Dialectics in Magnet Theatre's *Every Year, Every Day, I Am Walking*." *Theatre Research International* 37, no. 2 (2012): 118–33.
Da Silva, Marina, with Philip Boulay, Albertine M. Itela, and Zouina Meddour. "Et puis, nous passions le pantalon français: Une création artistique et politique." *Tumultes* 42 (2014): 113–22.
Darzacq, Dominique. "1945–1970 les premières utopies du théâtre populaire à la popularité de théâtre." In *Missions d'artistes: Les Centres dramatiques de 1946 à nos jours*, edited by Jean-Claude Penchenat. Paris: Éditions Théâtrales, 2006.
Davis, Tracy. "Introduction: The Pirouette, Detour, Revolution, Deflection, Deviation, Tack, and Yaw of the Performative Turn." In *The Cambridge Companion to Performance Studies*, edited by Tracy Davis, 1–11. Cambridge: Cambridge University Press, 2008.
Dayan-Herzbrun, Sonia. "The Issue of the Islamic Headscarf." In *Women, Immigration and Identities in France*, edited by Jane Freedman and Carrie Tarr, 69–85. Oxford: Berg, 2000.
Deltombe, Thomas. *L'Islam imaginaire: La Construction médiatique de l'islamophobie en France 1975–2005*. Paris: La Découverte, 2007.
Derderian, Richard. *North Africans in Contemporary France: Becoming Visible*. New York: Palgrave Macmillan, 2004.
Derrida, Jacques, in collaboration with Anne Dufourmantelle. *Of Hospitality*. Translated by Rachel Bowlby. Palo Alto, Calif.: Stanford University Press, 2002.
D'Halluin, Esther. "Entre expertise et témoignage: L'Éthique humanitaire à l'épreuve des politiques migratoires." *Vacarme* 34 (2006): 112–18.
Di Leonardo, Micaela. "Oral History as Ethnographic Encounter." *Oral History Review* 15 (1987): 1–20.
Dickey, Christopher. "Europe's Time Bomb." *Newsweek*, November 21, 2005.
———. "The Fire This Time." *Newsweek*, November 14, 2005.

Dubois, Vincent. *La Politique culturelle: Genèse d'une catégorie d'intervention publique*. Paris: Éditions Belin, 1999.
Durkheim, Emile. *The Elementary Forms of the Religious Life*. Translated by Joseph Ward Swain. New York: Free, 1965.
Edmondson, Laura. "TDR Comment: Of Sugarcoating and Hope." *The Drama Review* 51, no. 2 (2007): 7–10.
Elias, Norbert. *The Civilizing Process: Sociogenetic and Psychogenetic Investigations*. Translated by Edmund Jephcott. Oxford: Blackwell, 2003.
Epstein, Beth S. *Collective Terms: Race, Culture and Community in a State-Planned City in France*. New York: Berghahn Books, 2011.
Escafré-Dublet, Angeline. "L'Aventure de *Mohamed prends ta valise* de Kateb Yacine: Histoire d'un théâtre de la contestation en milieu immigré (France-Algérie, 1972)." In *Théâtre des minorités: Mises en scène de la marge à l'époque contemporaine*, edited by Patrice Brasseur and Madelena Gonzalez, 87–101. Paris: L'Harmattan, 2008.
———. "L'État et la culture des immigrés, 1974–1984." *Histoire@Politique: Politique, Culture, Société* 4 (2008).
Fanon, Frantz. *Black Skin, White Masks*. New York: Grove, 1967.
Fassin, Didier. "Compassion and Repression: The Moral Economy of Immigration Policies in France." *Cultural Anthropology* 20, no. 3 (2005): 362–87.
———. "Du déni à la dénégation: Psychologie politique de la représentation des discriminations." In D. Fassin and E. Fassin, *De la question sociale à la question raciale? Représenter la société française*, 133–58.
———. *Humanitarian Reason: A Moral History of the Present*. Berkeley: University of California Press, 2012.
Fassin, Didier, and Eric Fassin, eds. *De la question sociale à la question raciale? Représenter la société française*. Paris: La Découverte, 2006.
Fassin, Didier, Alan Morice, and Catherine Quiminal, eds. *Les Lois de l'inhospitalité: Les Politiques de l'immigration à l'épreuve des sans-papiers*. Paris: Éditions La Découverte, 1997.
Fassin, Didier, and Richard Rechtman. *The Empire of Trauma: An Inquiry into the Condition of Victimhood*. Translated by Rachel Gomme. Princeton, N.J.: Princeton University Press, 2009.
Fassin, Eric. "Aveugles à la race ou au racisme? Une approche stratégique." In Fassin and Fassin, *De la question sociale à la question raciale? Représenter la société française*, 106–33.
———. *Démocratie précaire: Chroniques de la déraison d'état*. Paris: La Découverte, 2012.
Favell, Adrian. *Philosophies of Integration: Immigration and the Idea of Citizenship in France and Britain*. New York: St. Martin's, 1998.
Feher, Michel. "Constancy in Context." *Wisconsin International Law Journal* 24, no. 3 (2006): 775–84.
———. ed. "Politique non-gouvernementale." Special issue, *Vacarme* 34 (2006).
Fernando, Mayanthi. "Reconfiguring Freedom: Muslim Piety and the Limits of Secular Law and Public Discourse in France." *American Ethnologist* 37, no. 1 (2010): 19–35.
Feu au centre de retention: Des sans-papiers témoignent. Paris: Éditions Libertalia, 2008.

Filewod, Alan. "Coalitions of Resistance: Ground Zero's Community Mobilization." In *Performing Democracy: International Perspectives on Urban Community-Based Performance*, edited by Susan C. Haedicke and Tobin Nellhaus, 89–103. Ann Arbor: University of Michigan Press, 2001.

———. "Theatrical Migrations and Digital Bodies: The Migrant Voices Project." Paper presented at "Performance and Asylum: Ethics, Embodiment and Community," Royal Holloway, University of London, November 3–5, 2007.

Finburgh, Clare. "*Voix/Voie/Vie:* The Voice in Contemporary French Theater." *Yale French Studies* 112 (2007): 99–115.

Fişek, Emine. "Framing Témoignage: Personal Narrative, Theatrical Aid and the Politics of Immigration Activism in France." *Text and Performance Quarterly* 36, no. 2–3 (2016): 77–94.

Foucault, Michel. *This Is Not a Pipe*. Edited and translated by James Harkness. Berkeley: University of California Press, 1983.

Fox, Renée C. "Medical Humanitarianism and Human Rights: Reflections on Doctors Without Borders and Doctors of the World." *Social Science and Medicine* 41, no. 12 (1995): 1607–26.

Fraser, Nancy. *Justice Interruptus: Critical Reflections on the "Postsocialist" Condition*. New York: Routledge, 1997.

Fraser, Nancy, and Axel Honneth. *Redistribution or Recognition? A Political-Philosophical Exchange*. London: Verso Books, 2003.

Freedman, Jane. "Women and Immigration: Nationality and Citizenship." In *Women, Immigration and Identities in France*, edited by Jane Freedman and Carrie Tarr, 13–28. Oxford: Berg, 2000.

Fysh, Peter, and Jim Wolfreys. *The Politics of Racism in France*. New York: Palgrave Macmillan, 1998.

Garner, Stanton B. *Bodied Spaces: Phenomenology and Performance in Contemporary Drama*. Ithaca, N.Y.: Cornell University Press, 1994.

Gaudibert, Pierre. *Action culturelle: Intégration et/ou subversion*. Paris: Castermann, 1977.

Geertz, Clifford. *The Interpretation of Cultures*. New York: Basic Books, 1973.

Geisser, Vincent. *La Nouvelle Islamophobie*. Paris: La Découverte, 2003.

Genet, Jean. "Pour Blin: Des réflexions à mesure qu'elles me viennent." In *La Bataille des Paravents: Théâtre de l'Odéon, 1966*, edited by Linda Bellity Peskine and Albert Dichy, 18–22. Paris: IMEC Éditions, 1991.

Giordan, Henri. *Démocratie culturelle et droit à la différence: Rapport présenté à Jack Lang, Ministre de la Culture par Henri Giordan, Maitre de Recherche au CNRS*. Paris: La Documentation Française, 1982.

Goetschel, Pascale. *Renouveau et décentralisation du théâtre 1945–1981*. Paris: Presses Universitaires de France, 2004.

Graines de Soleil. "Festival au Feminin Brochure." Paris: Compagnie Graines de Soleil, 2008.

Green, Nancy L. "Le *Melting-Pot*: Made in America, Produced in France." *The Journal of American History* 86, no. 3 (1999): 1188–1208.

Haedicke, Susan C., and Tobin Nellhaus. "Introduction." In *Performing Democracy: International Perspectives on Urban Community-Based Performance*, edited by Susan C. Haedicke and Tobin Nellhaus, 1–23. Ann Arbor: University of Michigan Press, 2001.

Hajjat, Abdellali. "Révolte des quartiers populaires, crise du militantisme et postcolonialisme." In Boubeker and Hajjat, eds., *Histoire politique des immigrations (post)coloniales: France, 1920–2008*, 249–65.

Hamera, Judith. "Performance, Performativity, and Cultural Poiesis in Practices of Everyday Life." In Madison and Hamera, eds., *The Sage Handbook of Performance Studies*, 46–64.

Hamidi-Kim, Bérénice. *Les Cités du théâtre politique en France depuis 1989.* Montpellier: Éditions L'Entretemps, 2013.

———. "The Théâtre du Soleil's Trajectory from 'People's Theatre' to 'Citizen Theatre': Involvement or Renunciation?" In *Political Performances: Theory and Practice*, edited by Susan C. Hedicke, Deirdre Haddon, Avraham Oz, and E. J. Westlake, 71–95. Amsterdam: Rodopi, 2009.

Hargreaves, Alec G. "The *Beurgeoisie*: Mediation or Mirage?" *Journal of European Studies* 28 (1998): 89–102.

———. *Multi-Ethnic France: Immigration, Politics, Culture and Society.* New York: Routledge, 2007.

Hollywood, Amy. "Performativity, Citationality, Ritualization." *History of Religions* 42, no. 2 (2002): 93–115.

Honneth, Axel. *The Struggle for Recognition: The Moral Grammar of Social Conflicts.* Translated by Joel Anderson. Cambridge: Polity, 1995.

Hourdel, Lise. "Sans-papiers et comédiens." *Le Républicain*, August 16, 2007.

Ingram, Mark. *Rites of the Republic: Citizens' Theatre and the Politics of Culture in Southern France.* Toronto: University of Toronto Press, 2011.

Isin, Engin F. "Citizenship in Flux: The Figure of the Activist Citizen." *Subjectivity* 29 (2009): 367–88.

Isker, Selim. *La Vie rêvée de Fatna.* DVD. La Compagnie des Indes, Warner Vision France, 2006.

Ivy, Marilyn. *Discourses of the Vanishing: Modernity, Phantasm, Japan.* Chicago: University of Chicago Press, 1995.

Jackson, Shannon. *Lines of Activity: Performance, Historiography, Hull-House Domesticity.* Ann Arbor: University of Michigan Press, 2001.

———. *Professing Performance: Theatre in the Academy from Philology to Performativity.* Cambridge: Cambridge University Press, 2004.

———. *Social Works: Performing Arts, Supporting Publics.* New York: Routledge, 2011.

Jacquet, Guy. "Preface." In *Le Théâtre Beur*, edited by Chérif Chikh and Ahsène Zehraoui, 11–14. Paris: Arcantère, 1984.

Jannarone, Kimberly. *Artaud and His Doubles.* Ann Arbor: University of Michigan Press, 2010.

Jazouli, Adil. *L'Action collective des jeunes maghrébins de France.* Paris: C.I.E.M.I and L'Harmattan, 1986.

Jeanson, Francis. "La Réunion de Villeurbanne." In *La Décentralisation théâtrale.* Vol. 3, *1968, le tournant*, edited by Robert Abirached, 85–93. Arles: Actes Sud-Papiers, 2005.

Jeffers, Alison. "Hospitable Stages and Civil Listening: Being an Audience for Participatory Refugee Theatre." In *Refugee Performance: Practical Encounters*, edited by Michael Balfour, 297–311. Bristol, Eng.: Intellect Books, 2013.

———. *Refugees, Theatre and Crisis: Performing Global Identities*. Basingstoke, Eng.: Palgrave Macmillan, 2012.

Jestrovic, Silvija. "Performing Like an Asylum Seeker: Paradoxes of Hyper Authenticity." *Research in Drama Education* 13, no. 2 (2008): 159–70.

Joseph, May. *Nomadic Identities: The Performance of Citizenship*. Minneapolis: University of Minnesota Press, 1999.

Joseph, Miranda. *Against the Romance of Community*. Minneapolis: University of Minnesota Press, 2002.

Kaye, Nick. *Site-Specific Art: Performance, Place and Documentation*. London: Routledge, 2000.

Keaton, Trica Danielle. *Muslim Girls and the Other France: Race, Identity Politics and Social Exclusion*. Bloomington: Indiana University Press, 2006.

Kechiche, Abdellatif. *L'Esquive*. DVD. Paris: Noé Productions, 2004.

Knowles, Ric. *Theatre & Interculturalism*. London: Palgrave Macmillan, 2010.

Kokoreff, Michel, and Didier Lapeyronnie. *Refaire la cité: L'Avenir des banlieues*. Paris: Éditions du Seuil, 2013.

Kouchner, Bernard. *Le Malheur des autres*. Paris: Éditions Odile Jacob, 1991.

Kruger, Loren. *The National Stage: Theatre and Cultural Legitimation in England, France and America*. Chicago: University of Chicago Press, 1992.

Kuftinec, Sonja. *Staging America: Cornerstone and Community-Based Theater*. Carbondale: Southern Illinois University Press, 2005.

———. *Theatre, Facilitation, and Nation Formation in the Balkans and Middle East*. New York: Palgrave Macmillan, 2009.

"La Déclaration de Villeurbanne." In *La Décentralisation théâtrale*. Vol. 3, *1968, le tournant*, edited by Robert Airached, 193–99. Arles: Actes Sud-Papiers, 2005.

Lachaud, Jean-Marc. "Théâtre et rue en France des années soixante-dix à aujourd'hui." In *Une histoire du spectacle militant: Théâtre et cinéma militants 1966–1981*, edited by Olivier Neveux and Christian Biet, 91–103. Paris: L'Entretemps, 2007.

Langellier, Kristin M. "Personal Narrative, Performance, Performativity: Two or Three Things I Know for Sure." *Text and Performance Quarterly* 19, no. 2 (1999): 125–44.

———. "Personal Narratives: Perspectives on Theory and Research." *Text and Performance Quarterly* 9, no. 4 (1989): 243–76.

Langellier, Kristin, and Eric E. Peterson. "Shifting Contexts in Personal Narrative Performance." In Madison and Hamera, eds., *The Sage Handbook of Performance Studies*, 151–68.

Lebovics, Herman. *Bringing the Empire Back Home: France in the Global Age*. Durham, N.C.: Duke University Press, 2004.

———. *Mona Lisa's Escort: André Malraux and the Reinvention of French Culture*. Ithaca, N.Y.: Cornell University Press, 1999.

———. *True France: The Wars over Cultural Identity 1900–1945*. Ithaca, N.Y.: Cornell University Press, 1994.

Le Gallic, Jeanne. "Le Théâtre de l'immigration algérienne en France dans les années 1970s: Un espace de représentation et de témoignage." *Synergies Algérie* no. 10 (2010): 153–64.

Legrand, Marine. "Rachida Brakni met en scène de jeunes sans-papiers." *Le Parisien: Essonne Matin*, August 8, 2007.
Lehmann, Hans-Thies. *Postdramatic Theatre*. Translated by Karen Jürs-Munby. New York: Routledge, 2006.
Lei, Daphne. "Interruption, Intervention, Interculturalism: Robert Wilson's HIT Productions in Taiwan." *Theatre Journal* 63, no. 4 (2011): 571–86.
Lemarié, Alexandre. "L'Immigration, thème de campagne à l'UMP." *Le Monde*, November 3, 2014.
Leprince, Chloé. "La Galère des majeurs sans-papiers pour être scolarisés." *Rue89*, August 9, 2007. http://www.rue89.com/2007/09/09/la-galere-des-majeurs-sans-papiers-pour-etre-scolarises.
Lesselier, Claudie. "Mouvements et initiatives des femmes des années 1970 au milieu des années 1980." In Boubeker and Hajjat, eds., *Histoire politique des immigrations (post)coloniales: France, 1920–2008*, 157–67.
Levine, Eric. "The French Intellectual and the Algerian War." Ph.D. dissertation, Columbia College, 1962.
Leys, Ruth. "The Turn to Affect: A Critique." *Critical Inquiry* 37 (2011): 434–72.
Li, Victor. *The Neo-Primitivist Turn: Critical Reflections on Alterity, Culture and Modernity*. Toronto: University of Toronto Press, 2006.
Livingston, Robert Eric. "Decolonizing the Theatre: Césaire, Serreau and the Drama of Negritude." In *Imperialism and Theatre: Essays on World Theatre, Drama and Performance*, edited by J. Ellen Gainor, 182–99. London: Routledge, 1995.
Lo, Jacqueline, and Helen Gilbert. "Toward a Topography of Cross-Cultural Theatre Praxis." *TDR: The Drama Review* 46, no. 3 (2002): 31–53.
Lochak, Danièle. "Les Politiques de l'immigration au prisme de la législation sur les étrangers." In *Les Lois de l'inhospitalité: Les Politiques de l'immigration à l'épreuve des sans-papiers*, edited by Didier Fassin, Alain Morice, and Catherine Quiminal, 29–45. Paris: La Découverte, 1997.
Looseley, David. *The Politics of Fun: Cultural Policy and Debate in Contemporary France*. Oxford: Berg, 1995.
Maatouk, Frédéric. "Le Théâtre des travailleurs immigrés en France." Ph.D. dissertation, Université François-Rabelais de Tours, 1979.
MacMaster, Neil. *Colonial Migrants and Racism: Algerians in France 1900–1962*. London: Palgrave Macmillan, 1997.
Madison, D. Soyini. *Acts of Activism: Human Rights as Radical Performance*. Cambridge: Cambridge University Press, 2010.
Madison, D. Soyini, and Judith Hamera. *The Sage Handbook of Performance Studies*. Thousand Oaks, Calif.: Sage, 2006.
Maghraoui, Driss. "French Identity, Islam, and North Africans: Colonial Legacies, Postcolonial Realities." In *French Civilization and Its Discontents: Nationalism, Colonialism, Race*, edited by Tyler Stovall and Georges Van Den Abbeele, 213–35. Lanham, Md.: Lexington Books, 2003.
Mahmood, Saba. *Politics of Piety: The Islamic Revival and the Feminist Subject*. Princeton, N.J.: Princeton University Press, 2005.
Maison des Tilleuls. "L'Environnement social du centre." http://www.maisondestilleuls.org/maisondestilleuls.html.

———. "Une maison au service d'un projet humain et citoyen." http://www.maisondestilleuls.org/maisondestilleuls.html.

Malkki, Liisa, "Speechless Emissaries: Refugees, Humanitarianism and Dehistoricization." *Cultural Anthropology* 11, no. 3 (1996): 377–404.

Malraux, André. "Discours prononcé à Dakar par M. André Malraux, Ministre d'Etat chargé des Affaires Culturelle à la séance d'ouverture du colloque organisé à l'occasion du premier Festival Mondial des Arts Nègres le 30 mars 1966." http://www.culture.gouv.fr/culture/actualites/dossiers/malraux2006/discours/a.m-dakar.htm.

———. "Text 216: La Culture, un projet de civilisation." In *Les Politiques de la culture en France*, edited by Philippe Poirrier, 326–34. Paris: La Documentation Française, 2016.

McDonough, Tom. *"The Beautiful Language of My Century": Reinventing the Language of Contestation in Postwar France, 1945–1968*. Cambridge, Mass.: MIT Press, 2007.

McEvoy, William. "Finding the Balance: Writing and Performing Ethics in Théâtre du Soleil's *Le Dernier Caravansérail* (2003)." *New Theatre Quarterly* 22, no. 3 (2006): 211–26.

McIvor, Charlotte. *Migration and Performance in Contemporary Ireland: Towards a New Interculturalism*. Basingstoke, Eng.: Palgrave Macmillan, 2016.

McKenzie, Jon. *Perform or Else: From Discipline to Performance*. New York: Routledge, 2001.

Miller, Judith. *Ariane Mnouchkine*. London: Routledge, 2007.

———. *Theater and Revolution in France since 1968*. Lexington, Ky.: French Forum, 1977.

Mnouchkine, Ariane. *L'Art du présent: Entretiens avec Fabienne Pascaud*. Paris: Plon, 2005.

———. *Le Dernier Caravansérail: Odyssées*. DVD. Paris: Bel Air Classiques, ARTE France Développement, CNDP, 2006.

Mohanty, Chandra Talpade. "Under Western Eyes: Feminist Scholarship and Colonial Discourses." In *Third World Women and the Politics of Feminism*, edited by Chandra Talpade Mohanty, Ann Russo, and Lourdes Torres, 51–81. Bloomington: Indiana University Press, 1991.

Montandon, Alain. *Le Livre de l'hospitalité: Accueil de l'étranger dans l'histoire et les cultures*. Paris: Éditions Bayard, 2004.

Mounsef, Donia, and Josette Féral. "Editors' Preface." *Yale French Studies* 112 (2007): 1–4.

Mouvement des Travailleurs Arabes (MTA) Papers. Fonds Saïd Bouziri. Bibliothèque de Documentation Internationale Contemporaine, Nanterre.

Mucchielli, Laurent. "Il faut changer la façon de 'faire la police' dans les 'quartiers sensibles.' " In Autain, ed., *Banlieue, lendemains de révolte*, 93–107.

Muñoz, José Esteban. *Disidentifications: Queers of Color and the Performance of Politics*. Minneapolis: University of Minnesota Press, 1999.

Nancy, Jean-Luc. *The Inoperative Community*. Edited by Peter Connor, translated by Peter Connor et al. Minneapolis: University of Minnesota Press, 1991.

Navajo, Métie. *La Geste des irréguliers: Sans-papiers sur les routes de France*. Paris: Rue des Cascades, 2011.

Neveux, Olivier. "Apparition d'une scène politique: Le Théâtre révolutionnaire de l'immigration." In *Une histoire du spectacle militant: Théâtre et cinéma militants 1966–1981,* edited by Olivier Neveux and Christian Biet, 324–44. Paris: L'Entretemps, 2007.

———. *Théâtres en lutte: Le Théâtre militant en France des années 1960 à aujourd'hui.* Paris: La Découverte, 2007.

Noiriel, Gérard. *The French Melting Pot: Immigration, Citizenship and National Identity.* Translated by Geoffroy de Laforcade. Minneapolis: University of Minnesota Press, 1996.

Novarina, Valère. *Le Théâtre des paroles.* Paris: Éditions P.O.L, 1989.

Nyers, Peter. *Rethinking Refugees: Beyond States of Emergency.* New York: Routledge, 2006.

Ong, Aihwa. *Neoliberalism as Exception: Mutations in Citizenship and Sovereignty.* Durham, N.C.: Duke University Press, 2006.

Ozouf, Mona. *Festivals and the French Revolution.* Translated by Alan Sheridan. Cambridge, Mass.: Harvard University Press, 1991.

Pavis, Patrice. *Theatre at the Crossroads of Culture.* Translated by Loren Kruger. New York: Routledge, 2005.

Perrier, Jean-Louis. "A la Cartoucherie, les flux et les reflux de la misère des hommes." *Le Monde,* January 16, 2003.

Peters, Julie Stone. "Intercultural Performance, Theatre Anthropology, and the Imperialist Critique: Identities, Inheritances, and Neo-Orthodoxies." In *Imperialism and Theatre: Essays on World Theatre, Drama and Performance,* edited by J. Ellen Gainor, 199–214. London: Routledge, 1995.

Pollock, Della. "Introduction: Remembering." In *Remembering: Oral History Performance,* edited by Della Pollock, 1–19. New York: Palgrave Macmillan, 2005.

———. "Memory, Remembering, and Histories of Change: A Performance Praxis." In Madison and Hamera, eds., *The Sage Handbook of Performance Studies,* 87–105.

Rae, Paul. *Theatre & Human Rights.* New York: Palgrave Macmillan, 2009.

Rancière, Jacques. "The Cause of the Other." Translated by David Macey. *Parallax* 4, no. 2 (1998): 25–33.

———. *The Emancipated Spectator.* Translated by Gregory Elliott. London: Verso, 2009.

Redfield, Peter. "The Impossible Problem of Neutrality." In *Forces of Compassion: Humanitarianism between Ethics and Politics,* edited by Erica Bornstein and Peter Redfield, 53–71. Santa Fe, N.M.: School for Advanced Research Press, 2010.

———. "A Less Modest Witness: Collective Advocacy and Motivated Truth in a Medical Humanitarian Environment." *American Ethnologist* 33, no. 1 (2006): 3–26.

Réseau Education Sans Frontières de l'Essonne. *La Plume sans papier.* Massy: RESF de l'Essonne, 2007.

Ricoeur, Paul. *Memory, History, Forgetting.* Translated by Kathleen Blamey and David Pellauer. Chicago: University of Chicago Press, 2004.

Ridout, Nicholas. *Passionate Amateurs: Theatre, Communism, and Love.* Ann Arbor: University of Michigan Press, 2015.

Roach, Joseph. *Cities of the Dead: Circum-Atlantic Performance*. New York: Columbia University Press, 1996.

Rosello, Mireille. *Postcolonial Hospitality: The Immigrant as Guest*. Palo Alto, Calif.: Stanford University Press, 2002.

Ross, Kristin. *May '68 and Its Afterlives*. Chicago: University of Chicago Press, 2002.

Rousseau, Jean-Jacques. *The Social Contract and the First and Second Discourses*. Translated and edited by Susan Dunn. New Haven, Conn.: Yale University Press, 2002.

Ryngaert, Jean-Pierre. "Speech in Tatters: The Interplay of Voices in Recent Dramatic Writing." *Yale French Studies* 112 (2007): 14–28.

Ryngaert, Jean-Pierre, and Julie Sermon. "Théâtres de la parole." In *Dictionnaire encyclopédique du théâtre à travers le monde*, edited by Michel Corvin, 1036–37. Paris: Bordas, 2008.

Sahlins, Peter. *Boundaries: The Making of France and Spain in the Pyrénées*. Berkeley: University of California Press, 1991.

Salverson, Julie. "Change on Whose Terms? Testimony and an Erotics of Injury." *Theater* 31, no. 3 (2001): 119–25.

Sauter, Willmar. *The Theatrical Event: Dynamics of Performance and Perception*. Iowa City: University of Iowa Press, 2000.

Sayad, Abdelmalek. *The Suffering of the Immigrant*. Translated by David Macey. Cambridge, Eng.: Polity, 2004.

Schechner, Richard. *Between Theater and Anthropology*. Philadelphia: University of Pennsylvania Press, 1985.

Schnapper, Dominique. *Qu'est-ce que l'intégration?* Paris: Éditions Gallimard, 2007.

Schnapper, Dominique, in collaboration with Christian Bachelier. *Qu'est-ce que la citoyenneté?* Paris: Éditions Gallimard, 2000.

Schnapper, Dominique, Pascale Krief, and Emmanuel Peignard. "French Immigration and Integration Policy: A Complex Combination." In *The Integration of Immigrants in European Societies: National Differences and Trends of Convergence*, edited by Friedrich Heckmann and Dominique Schnapper, 15–45. Stuttgart: Lucius and Lucius, 2003.

Schneider, Rebecca. *The Explicit Body in Performance*. London: Routledge, 1997.

Scott, Joan W. "Experience." In *Feminists Theorize the Political*, edited by Judith Butler and Joan W. Scott, 22–41. London: Routledge, 1992.

———. *Only Paradoxes to Offer: French Feminists and the Rights of Man*. Cambridge, Mass.: Harvard University Press, 1997.

———. *The Politics of the Veil*. Princeton, N.J.: Princeton University Press, 2007.

Sharifi, Azadeh, and S. E. Wilmer. "Reflections on Theatre and Statelessness." Special Topic: "Theatre and Statelessness in Europe," edited by Azadeh Sharifi and S. E. Wilmer. *Critical Stages/Scènes Critiques* 14 (2016). http://www.critical-stages.org/14/special-topic/.

Silverstein, Paul. *Algeria in France: Transpolitics, Race and Nation*. Bloomington: Indiana University Press, 2004.

Silverstein, Paul, and Chantal Tetreault. "Urban Violence in France." *MERIP: Middle East Report Online*, November, 2005. http://www.merip.org/mero/interventions/urban-violence-france.

Siméant, Johanna. *La Cause des sans-papiers*. Paris: Presses de Sciences Po, 1998.

Solal, Elsa. *Le Bruit du monde m'est rentré dans l'oreille*. Paris: L'Harmattan, 2008.

Souilamas, Nacira Guénif. "La Réduction a son corps de l'indigène de la république." In *La Fracture coloniale: La Société française au prisme de l'héritage colonial,* edited by Pascal Blanchard, Nicolas Bancel, and Sandrine Lemaire, 205–13. Paris: La Découverte, 2006.

Souilamas, Nacira Guénif, and Eric Macé. *Les Féministes et le garçon arabe*. Tour d'Aigues: Éditions de l'Aube, 2004.

Soysal, Yasemin Nuhoğlu. *Limits of Citizenship: Migrants and Postnational Membership in Europe*. Chicago: University of Chicago Press, 1994.

Stora, Benjamin. *La Gangrène et l'oubli: La Mémoire de la guerre d'Algérie*. Paris: La Découverte, 1991.

Taylor, Diana. *The Archive and the Repertoire: Performing Cultural Memory in the Americas*. Durham, N.C.: Duke University Press, 2003.

Tevanian, Pierre. *La Mécanique raciste*. Paris: Éditions Dilecta, 2008.

———. *La République du mépris: Les Métamorphoses du racisme dans la France des années Sarkozy*. Paris: La Découverte, 2007.

Théâtre du Soleil Papers. Département des Arts du Spectacle, Bibliothèque Nationale de France, Paris.

Thompson, James. *Performance Affects: Applied Theatre and the End of Effect*. Houndmills, Eng.: Palgrave Macmillan, 2009.

Ticktin, Miriam. *Casualties of Care: Immigration and the Politics of Humanitarianism in France*. Berkeley: University of California Press, 2011.

———. "Sexual Violence as the Language of Border Control: Where French Feminist and Anti-Immigrant Rhetoric Meet." *Signs: Journal of Women in Culture and Society* 33, no. 4 (2008): 863–89.

Tissot, Sylvie. *L'État et les quartiers: Genèse d'une catégorie de l'action publique*. Paris: Éditions du Seuil, 2007.

Trappo, Hélène. "De la clandestinité à la reconnaissance: Propos recueillis par Hélène Trappo." *Plein Droit* 11 (1990). http://www.gisti.org/doc/plein-droit/11/clandestinite.html.

Trilling, Lionel. *Sincerity and Authenticity*. Cambridge, Mass.: Harvard University Press, 1972.

Turner, Victor. *The Anthropology of Performance*. New York: PAJ, 1988.

———. *From Ritual to Theatre: The Human Seriousness of Play*. New York: PAJ, 1982.

Vollaire, Christiane. *Humanitaire: Le Coeur de la guerre*. Paris: L'Insulaire, 2007.

Wake, Caroline. "To Witness Mimesis: The Politics, Ethics, and Aesthetics of Testimonial Theatre in *Through the Wire*." *Modern Drama* 56, no. 1 (2013): 102–25.

Weber, Eugen. *Peasants into Frenchmen: The Modernization of Rural France 1870–1914*. Palo Alto, Calif.: Stanford University Press, 1976.

Wihtol de Wenden, Catherine, and Rémy Leveau. *La Beurgeoisie*. Paris: CNRS Éditions, 2007.

Wilder, Gary. *The French Imperial Nation-State: Negritude and Colonial Humanism between the Two World Wars*. Chicago: University of Chicago Press, 2005.

Williams, Raymond. *Keywords: A Vocabulary of Culture and Society*. New York: Oxford University Press, 1985.

Yadan, Thomas. "Interview de Khalid Tamer: Un Festival en Or." *Evene.fr*, February 2008. http://www.evene.fr/theatre/actualite/interview-khalid-tamer-festival-au-feminin-1195.php.

Young, Iris Marion. "Unruly Categories: A Critique of Nancy Fraser's Dual Systems Theory." *New Left Review* 222 (1997): 147–60.

Zancarini-Fournel, Michelle. "Racisme et antiracisme dans les 'années '68.' " In Boubeker and Hajjat, eds., *Histoire politique des immigrations (post)coloniales: France, 1920–2008*, 113–25.

INDEX